# How the Weak Win Wars

How do the weak win wars? The likelihood of victory and defeat in asymmetric conflicts depends on the interaction of the strategies weak and strong actors use. Using statistical and in-depth historical analyses of conflicts spanning two hundred years, Ivan Arreguín-Toft shows that, independent of regime type and weapons technology, the interaction of similar strategic approaches favors strong actors, while opposite strategic approaches favor the weak. This new approach to understanding asymmetric conflicts allows us to makes sense of how the United States was able to win its war in Afghanistan (2002) in a few months, while the Soviet Union lost after a decade of brutal war (1979–1989). Arreguín-Toft's strategic interaction theory has implications not only for international relations theory, but for policymakers grappling with interstate and civil wars, as well as terrorism.

IVAN ARREGUÍN-TOFT is Fellow in the International Security Program, at the John F. Kennedy School of Government, Harvard University. He has authored numerous conference papers and his articles have appeared in *International Security* and *the Cambridge Review of International Affairs*. He is a veteran of the US Army where he served in Augsburg, Germany as a military intelligence analyst from 1985 to 1987.

CAMBRIDGE STUDIES IN INTERNATIONAL RELATIONS: 99

# How the Weak Win Wars
A Theory of Asymmetric Conflict

*Cambridge Studies in International Relations* is a joint initiative of Cambridge University Press and the British International Studies Association (BISA). The series will include a wide range of material, from undergraduate textbooks and surveys to research-based monographs and collaborative volumes. The aim of the series is to publish the best new scholarship in International Studies from Europe, North America and the rest of the world.

CAMBRIDGE STUDIES IN INTERNATIONAL RELATIONS

100  *Michael C. Williams*
     **The Realist Tradition and the Limits of International Relations**

 99  *Ivan Arreguín-Toft*
     **How the Weak Win Wars**
     A theory of asymmetric conflict

 98  *Michael Barnett and Raymond Duvall (eds.)*
     **Power in Global Governance**

 97  *Yale H. Ferguson and Richard W. Mansbach*
     **Remapping Global Politics**
     History's revenge and future shock

 96  *Christian Reus-Smit (ed.)*
     **The Politics of International Law**

 95  *Barry Buzan*
     **From International to World Society?**
     English School theory and the social structure of globalisation

 94  *K. J. Holsti*
     **Taming the Sovereigns**
     Institutional change in international politics

 93  *Bruce Cronin*
     **Institutions for the Common Good**
     International protection regimes in international society

 92  *Paul Keal*
     **European Conquest and the Rights of Indigenous Peoples**
     The moral backwardness of international society

 91  *Barry Buzan and Ole Wæver*
     **Regions and Powers**
     The structure of international security

 90  *A. Claire Cutler*
     **Private Power and Global Authority**
     Transnational merchant law in the global political economy

     *Series list continued after index*

# How the Weak Win Wars:

## A Theory of Asymmetric Conflict

Ivan Arreguín-Toft

CAMBRIDGE
UNIVERSITY PRESS

CAMBRIDGE UNIVERSITY PRESS
Cambridge, New York, Melbourne, Madrid, Cape Town, Singapore, São Paulo

CAMBRIDGE UNIVERSITY PRESS
The Edinburgh Building, Cambridge CB2 2RU, UK

Published in the United States of America by Cambridge University Press,
New York

www.cambridge.org
Information on this title: www.cambridge.org/9780521548694

First published 2005

Printed in the United Kingdom at the University Press, Cambridge

*A catalogue record for this book is available from the British Library*

*Library of Congress Cataloging-in-Publication Data*

Arreguín-Toft, Ivan.
How the weak win wars: a theory of asymmetric conflict / Ivan Arreguín-Toft.
    p.   cm. – (Cambridge studies in international relations; 99)
Includes bibliographical references and index.
ISBN 0 521-83976-9 – ISBN 0-521-54869-1 (pbk.)
1. Asymmetric warfare – Case studies.   2. Military history, Modern – Case
studies.   I. Title.   II. Series.

U163.A776 2005
355.4′2 – dc 22      2004058131

ISBN-13 978-0-521-83976-1 hardback
ISBN-10 0-521-83976-9 hardback
ISBN-13 978-0-521-54869-4 paperback
ISBN-10 0-521-54869-1 paperback

*To Monica*

# Epigraph

*Do not press a desperate enemy*

*Sun Tzu*

# Contents

List of figures                                                  *page* x
Preface                                                             xi
Acknowledgments                                                   xiii
List of abbreviations                                              xv

1   Introduction                                                     1
2   Explaining asymmetric conflict outcomes                        23
3   Russia in the Caucasus: the Murid War, 1830–1859              48
4   Britain in Orange Free State and Transvaal: the
    South African War, 1899–1902                                   72
5   Italy in Ethiopia: the Italo-Ethiopian War, 1935–1940         109
6   The United States in Vietnam: the Vietnam War,
    1965–1973                                                      144
7   The USSR in Afghanistan: the Afghan Civil War,
    1979–1989                                                      169
8   Conclusion                                                     200

    Appendix                                                       228
    References                                                     235
    Index                                                          243

# Figures

1 Percentage of asymmetric conflict victories by
  type of actor, 1800–2003                                      *page* 3
2 Percentage of conflict victories by type of actor
  over time                                                            4
3 Expected effects of strategic interaction on
  conflict outcomes                                                   39
4 Strategic interaction and asymmetric conflict outcomes,
  1800–2003                                                           45
5 Strategic interaction and conflict outcomes when weak
  actor received no external support                                  46

# Preface

This is a book about power, and how common understandings about power can lead to disaster.

The term "asymmetric conflict" is meant to bracket the broad topic of inquiry in the fewest words and syllables – yet it suffers from a whiff of academic conceit and ivory tower detachment.

The real topic at hand is naked brutality.

In war the primary recipients of this brutality should be soldiers. They are trained to supply it, within limits; and they expect to be injured or killed by other soldiers in the course of their duties. But nowadays war's brutality is less and less often restricted to soldiers (some would say it is a myth that it ever was). It is perhaps an unintended consequence of the attempt to use the Geneva Conventions (and subsequent instruments of international humanitarian law) to protect infants, the injured, the sick, the mentally ill, the crippled, small children, women who do not bear arms, and the elderly, that it is precisely *these* human beings, and not soldiers, who have increasingly become targets of knives, rifle butts, flame, and flying metal. They are targets because desperate men find it useful to shelter behind and among them, while their enemies lack either the will or the ability to strike them without also striking say, the nine-year-old girl huddled nearby.

In asymmetric conflicts – those in which one side is possessed of overwhelming power with respect to its adversary – this is especially true. It is true because the weak *are* desperate. It is true also because the strong cannot abide the offense of resistance: if power demands obedience then resistance to overwhelming power supplies proof of evil or madness; and neither the evil nor the mad need be treated as fellow human beings.

The real brutality of war is missing from most social science analyses of war. It is missing because we are *ignorant*: most of us have never directly experienced the horror whose analysis has become our life's work. It is missing because it is *necessary*: to get close to the reality of our subject would be intolerable, unbearable. And some cruelties cannot be described. There are simply no words in any language capable of bearing the weight of their experience. Finally, the brutality of war is missing from most social science analyses because it is *useful*: it allows us to detect patterns and make generalizations that may someday persuade others to alter how conflicts are resolved – to end those ongoing and to prevent them from escalating to violence alltogether.

It is in this spirit I offer this analysis, flaws and all.

# Acknowledgments

I have read many of these acknowledgments sections over the years. They almost always strike me as alternately maudlin and boring. Mine will be no different.

I was trained at the University of Chicago in the last decade of the twentieth century. It was a challenging process. One might call it benign neglect; intended – designed even – to enable me to recognize, frame, and answer good questions with little help beyond my own resources. To two of my mentors then, John Mearsheimer and Stephen Walt, I owe thanks for my intellectual self-sufficiency. Like an Army Ranger I can now be dropped solo into an academic wilderness and I will always find my way, survive, and fulfill my mission.

But the ability to work alone has not altered my inclination to work with others, nor in any way dulled my love of teaching. I owe thanks to more colleagues at the University of Chicago than I can list here. But for good conversations, penetrating criticism, and unstinting support I especially want to thank Ann Davies, Sharon Morris, Jordan Seng, David Michel, Kim Germain, Brett Klopp, Andy Kydd, Susan Liebell, John McCormick, Jen Mitzen, David Edelstein, and Paul Kapur.

Thanks to Daniel Verdier, Charles Lipson, and especially Charles Glaser, for insightful criticism on early versions of this work, for their help in training me by example, and for their support.

I also owe thanks to three men who in my view count as towering intellectuals: Peter Digeser, Bernard Manin, and Lloyd Rudolph. Without their patient efforts and generosity I'd never have learned to be circumspect about what it is I think I know.

For friendship and support vital to this intellectual enterprise I owe a special debt of gratitude to Tom Reisz, Ty (and Lynn) Aponte, Queta (and Ron) Bauer, and Marvin Zonis. Each in his or her own way helped to make me a better man.

Here at Harvard's Kennedy School of Government I have been blessed also with outstanding criticism and support. I'd especially like to thank Steve Miller, Sean Lynn-Jones, John Garofano, Arman Grigorian, and Rose McDermott.

I also owe thanks to Andrew Mack, without whose originality, keen criticism, advice, and support this book would never have been possible.

Thanks also to the Institute for the Study of World Politics and Smith Richardson Foundation for generous support.

Finally, I owe a debt to my families. My father Alfredo I thank for reminding me that I do what I do because it's who I am, rather than because I have expectations of social science as a career. My mother JoAnne I thank for her absolute love of ideas, as well as, of course, her faith in me come what may. My stepmom Susie, and my sisters, Kristine and Lesley, I thank for the inspiring passion with which they live their lives. My uncle Paul I thank for his patience, and unflagging support over these many years. My in-laws I thank for putting up with me; and for forgiving me (now and then) for not having chosen to become a lawyer.

Above all else and always I thank the three dearest to me in this world, without whom even a life as rich as mine has been would not have been much worth living: my wife Monica, my son Samuel, and my daughter Ingrid Anne.

# Abbreviations

ARVN   Army of Vietnam
COIN   Counterinsurgency
DMZ   demilitarized zone
DRA   Democratic Republic of Afghanistan
DRV   Democratic Republic of Vietnam
FLN   Front de Libération Nationale
GVN   Government of Vietnam
GWS   guerrilla warfare strategy
KLA   Kosovo Liberation Army
NATO   North Atlantic Treaty Organization
NVA   North Vietnamese Army
SAM   surface-to-air missile
VC   Viet Cong

# 1    Introduction

And there went out a champion out of the camp of the Philistines, named Goliath . . .

And all the men of Israel, when they saw the man, fled from him, and were sore afraid . . .

And David said to Saul, Let no man's heart fail because of him; thy servant will go and fight with this Philistine . . .

And Saul armed David with his armour, and he put an helmet of brass upon his head; also he armed him with a coat of mail. And David girded his sword upon his armour . . . And David said unto Saul, I cannot go with these; for I have not proved them. And David put them off him. And he took his staff in his hand, and chose him five smooth stones out of the brook, and put them in a shepherd's bag . . . and his sling was in his hand: and he drew near to the Philistine.

. . . And the Philistine said to David, Come to me, and I will give thy flesh unto the fowls of the air, and to the beasts of the field.

And David put his hand in his bag, and took thence a stone, and slang it, and smote the Philistine in his forehead . . . and he fell upon his face to the earth. So David prevailed over the Philistine with a sling and with a stone . . .                                         I. Samuel 17

Why do the strong lose to the weak?

Because we expect strong actors[1] to defeat weak actors in contests ranging from wars and fist fights to business competitions

---

[1] "Actors" in this context mean states or coalitions of states, although the same dynamics would apply to governments fighting against rebels or rival national or ethnic groups in civil wars. "Conflicts" in this analysis mean wars (1000 battle deaths per year), although again, similar dynamics may apply in conflicts which are not wars, such as terrorism, trade wars, and labor disputes. Because this analysis focuses on explaining asymmetric conflicts I exclude those few wars in which the ratio of forces changed dramatically (toward symmetry) between the start and end of a conflict.

and sports contests, the fact that the strong sometimes lose is puzzling.[2]

## Relative power and realist international relations theory: the strong do as they will . . .

As far back as Thucydides' description of the wars between Athens and Sparta, the link between power and conflict outcomes has been *the* root principle of realist international relations theory.[3] More power means winning wars, and less power means losing them. And defeat in war means death or slavery. This is not the same thing as saying that either international relations scholars, or political and military elites, imagine that raw material power is the only thing that explains who wins or loses a battle, campaign, or war. Many things – ranging from resolve, technology, strategy, luck, leadership, and even heroism or cowardice – can lead to unexpected outcomes. But power is useful. It is useful both because in the real world enough of it can overwhelm deficiencies in the other categories, and because in the theoretical world it is quantifiable, measurable, and comparable in a way that luck or leadership, for example, are not.

If it is true that power matters most, then in very asymmetric conflicts – conflicts between actors with wide disparities in power – the strong

---

[2] Power is one of the trickier concepts in international relations theory. Here I follow a long tradition by introducing a quantifiable proxy for power which is an admittedly imperfect one. By "strong," for instance, I mean an actor whose relative material power exceeds that of its adversary or adversaries by large ratio (see below). "Weak" and "strong" then only have meaning in a particular dyadic context: Italy in 1935 is weak compared to the Soviet Union, but strong compared to Ethiopia. By "material power," I mean the product of a given state's population and armed forces. Other quantifiable proxies for state power have been proposed and used over the years; including iron and steel production, gross national product (GNP), and so on. However, no single measure appears to be sufficient on its own; and GNP, perhaps on balance the most useful, suffers because these data were not kept prior to the 1920s. For a review and analysis of the literature on empirical and quantifiable measures of relative power, see Nutter, (1994: 29–49). On the empirical measurement of power in asymmetric conflicts in particular, see Paul (1994: 22).

[3] My use of the term "realist IR theory" throughout this essay refers to a simple version of realist theory that has two key tenets: (1) there is no authority above states capable of regulating state interactions, and (2) all states have some capacity to harm other states. As a result, states seek to increase their relative power by various means, including buying or manufacturing armaments, and forming alliances. Power in this view is expected to have a number of positive consequences for states that acquire it: it can deter other states from attack, cow them into concessions, or defeat them in wars. For a cogent summary of realist IR theory, see Mearsheimer (2001: chapters 1–3). On the limits of power in relation to objectives, see Waltz (1979: 188–192).

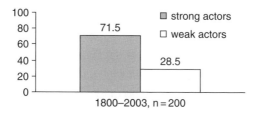

Figure 1. Percentage of asymmetric conflict victories by type of actor, 1800–2003

should always win.[4] Indeed, a review of all asymmetric wars fought since 1800 supports this claim, as seen in Figure 1.

Again, "strong" and "weak" only have meaning in particular conflict dyads; though as noted above these may include individual actors or coalitions of actors. Moreover, in this analysis I've sharpened the puzzle by making the strong *much* stronger than the weak. A literally asymmetric conflict, for example, only requires a slight disparity – say, 1.1:1. But in this analysis the aim is to test competing explanations against the assertion that relative *power* matters most. For this reason the disparity in power is raised to 10:1, and then adjusted to account for the fact that strong actors – great powers and superpowers in particular – often have other security commitments that constrain the application of all their resources to a single conflict.[5]

That said, since 1816 strong actors have won more than twice as many asymmetric conflicts as weak actors. On the other hand, since in this analysis strong actors outpower weak actors by a large margin, it remains puzzling that strong actors have lost such fights as often as they have. What explains these unexpected outcomes?

A number of answers seem plausible besides bad luck. Perhaps the strong actors lost because they were squeamish in some way. Perhaps

---

[4] As Mearsheimer puts it, "There are definite limits to the utility of measuring force levels. After all, even a cursory study of military history would show that it is impossible to explain the outcome of many important military campaigns by simply comparing the number of forces on each side. Nevertheless, it is clear that if one side has an overwhelming advantage in forces, the glaring asymmetry is very likely to portend a decisive victory" (Mearsheimer, 1983: 168). See also Mack (1975: 107).

[5] "Power" in this analysis is represented as the halved product of a strong actor's armed forces and population at the start of a conflict versus the simple product of the weak actor's armed forces and population. Data for this survey come primarily from Small and Singer (1983), and from the 1992 revision of that data set. Additional data are from Laqueur (1976); and from Ellis (1995). For a comprehensive list of the cases used in the statistical analysis, see Appendix.

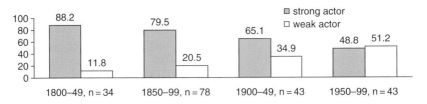

Figure 2. Percentage of conflict victories by type of actor over time

authoritarian strong actors win asymmetric conflicts but democratic strong actors lose them. Perhaps they were irresolute, or poorly led. Perhaps weak actors had come into possession of sophisticated military technology of some sort,[6] and this tilted the balance *enough* that strong actors lost interest in victory when the costs of conflict and occupation suddenly exceeded the expected benefits. Thinking more about it, and since these explanations seem to resonate more or less with different historical periods, it would be useful to know whether the distribution of outcomes is consistent over time.

It isn't. If the total record of asymmetric conflicts since 1816 is divided into discrete time periods, a striking trend emerges: strong actors have been losing asymmetric conflicts *more and more over time* (see Figure 2).

From 1800 until 1849, strong actors won 88.2 percent of all asymmetric conflicts. That proportion dropped slightly to 79.5 percent in the next fifty-year period. But starting in 1900, the number of asymmetric conflicts won by strong actors began to fall off significantly, down to 65.1 percent through 1949. By the last fifty-year period – 1950 to 1999– strong actors won only 48.8 percent of all asymmetric conflicts.[7]

Here then are two puzzles represented graphically. On the one hand, realist international relations theory leads us to expect that in a two-actor conflict, the larger the ratio of forces favors one actor the more quickly and decisively that actor will win; and this is supported in

[6] In this analysis, *technology* is presented as a power multiplier or divider, not an increment of power itself. Power is captured – crudely but sufficiently – by the multiplication of population and armed forces. This leads to some distortions – e.g., nuclear weapons and maritime *vs.* continental power distinctions do matter – but the impact of these distortions is marginal on the overall analysis.

[7] The colonial wars that distinguish this period are arguably a special case. But, if so, they must be special in a way that overcomes the expected effects of relative power (i.e. they still challenge realist IR theory's primacy of power pillar). The overall trend is the same whether the data are divided into fifty-, ten-, or five-year periods. The four-fold division represented here is valuable analytically because it represents more data per period, and because it presents the trend more clearly. Cases from the period 2000–2010 (Afghanistan 2002, and Iraq 2003) were not included because the period has not yet lasted five years.

4

Figure 1. On the other hand, strong states have *lost* nearly 30 percent of all conflicts in which they out-powered their adversaries by a factor of at least 5:1. In addition, as shown in Figure 2, strong states have been losing such fights more and more often over time. What explains this trend?

A good way to begin is to think about what was different in the early nineteenth century that may have favored strong actors so dramatically as compared to strong actors at the end of the twentieth century. Again, a number of plausible explanations come to mind. Perhaps early strong actors won because of their *technological* advantages: artillery, firearms, and blue-water navies must have been tremendous force multipliers. Perhaps the strong actor defeats concentrated in the last period were due to the rise of *national* self-determination as a norm of interstate politics? Nationalist resistance to European rule might have made conquest and occupation too costly. We might also observe that after World War I and especially World War II, the number of authoritarian strong actors declined. And, after 1991, the Soviet Union collapsed and ceased to be an authoritarian actor in interstate politics. If authoritarian strong actors fight asymmetric conflicts better than democratic strong actors, perhaps the *nature of the actor* explains the trend.

This speculation points to an important utility of the trend observation independent of the fact that until recently it remained unidentified: an ideal theory of asymmetric conflict outcomes should be able to account for both the *fact* of strong actor failure and the *trend* toward increasing strong actor failure over time. Explanations of the trend which don't plausibly explain strong actor failure will be less persuasive than those which can. Also, accounts of strong actor failure inconsistent with the trend will be less persuasive than those which can explain both.

In sum, the problem with our international relations-theory-informed expectations is that they appear to be only partly right, and only in aggregate. When the aggregate data are divided into discrete time periods, the expected correlation between power and victory becomes significantly less useful as a guide to policy.

## Competing explanations of asymmetric conflict outcomes

As observed by Andrew J. R. Mack more than a quarter century ago (Mack, 1975: 176), few international relations scholars have advanced explanations focused specifically on the subject of asymmetric conflict,[8] and with the exception of my own work and Mack's, none has advanced a general explanation of asymmetric conflict outcomes (Arreguín-Toft, 2001).

In this book I argue that although relative power matters, the interaction of the strategies actors use matters more than how much power they have at the start of their conflict. This strategic interaction thesis may seem intuitively plausible to readers, but before its explanatory power can be evaluated competing explanations must be introduced and explored. As noted above, a good way to think about these explanations is in terms of how well they explain both the outcome and the trend puzzles.

This section offers four competing explanations of strong actor failure in asymmetric conflicts and the trend toward increasing strong actor failure. Some, such as the arms diffusion explanation or democratic social squeamishness argument, are strongest when explaining the trend, but offer equivocal explanations of why strong actors lose. Others, such as Mack's interest asymmetry argument, are good at explaining strong actor failure, but cannot account for the trend. A sound general theory of asymmetric conflict outcomes should be able to explain the fact of strong actor failure in a way consistent with the observed trend, and vice versa. What follows is an introduction to these competing explanations.[9] In Chapter 2, the logic of each explanation

---

[8] Chief among those Mack cites are Katzenbach (1962: 11–21); and Taber (1965). More recently, T. V. Paul devoted a book to the question of why the weak *start* wars against the strong. Paul's threshold of analysis for asymmetry was a power ratio of 1:2, where power was measured in traditional – that is to say, material – terms. On Paul's definition of asymmetry, see Paul (1994: 20).

[9] These three hardly exhaust the possibilities, but they offer the strongest general explanations of both unexpected outcomes and the trend. Three additional explanations worthy of note are (1) social structure; (2) the rise of nationalism; and (3) Cold War bipolarity. The social structure argument links key aspects of a given society's social structure to the military effectiveness of the forces it is capable of fielding. In this view, the reason states such as the United States and USSR lost their respective fights against the North Vietnamese and mujahideen is because their societies were not as efficient at producing effective militaries as were the North Vietnamese and mujahideen. On the importance of social structure, see Rosen (1995: 5–31). The rise of nationalism argument is that the post-World War II period in particular was an era in which nations came to see self-determination as a necessity which could not be put off because the structural changes forced on them by colonial powers had begun to irreparably destroy their social fabric. The logic of this argument is that nationalists are more stubborn and more willing to risk death in pursuit of autonomy than people motivated by other concerns. See, e.g., Wolf (1973); and Anderson (1991: 9–10, 36). The Cold War bipolarity argument is that the USSR and United States intervened more often in order to counter the perceived interests of the other superpower. Each justified these interventions by means of domino logic,

will be reduced to testable propositions which will later be compared in the historical case studies – some formally and some informally – against those derived from my own explanation.

## The nature of the actor

One way to explain how a strong actor loses a war against a weak actor is to argue that authoritarian actors fight wars better than democratic actors.[10] If true, then isolating the key differences between how each type of actor fights could explain why strong actors sometimes win asymmetric wars quickly, while other times they lose, or "win" at a cost far out of proportion to their initial estimates. If authoritarian regimes fight better than democratic regimes, and if fewer strong actors over time have been authoritarian, then this explanation could explain both the fact of strong actor failure (democratic strong actors lose asymmetric conflicts) and the trend (fewer tough authoritarian actors mean fewer strong actor victories).

Consider that authoritarian regimes are defined by several key characteristics.[11] First, authority for making domestic and foreign policy is restricted to a single person or a small group of people. Second, authoritarian regimes maintain strict control over the public's access to information about the consequences of domestic and foreign policies. Finally, public attempts to criticize or change domestic or foreign policy are often punishable by severe sanctions, such as death, torture, or indefinite imprisonment.

In theory, these characteristics have four important implications for warfighting effectiveness. First, authoritarian regimes should be able to mobilize resources more effectively than democratic regimes because they control the public's perception of a war's legitimacy, how it is being fought by both sides, and the outcomes of specific battles. Second, on the battlefield authoritarian regimes can coerce their soldiers to fight

---

which inflated even minor skirmishes into conflicts of vital importance in the struggle between the West and the Socialist world. In other words, bipolarity implies the reduction of all extra-core fights to mere proxy wars between the United States and USSR. This is another way of saying that due to constant US and Soviet support and interference there effectively *were* no asymmetric conflicts during the Cold War.

[10] For a comprehensive introduction to the question of regime type and military effectiveness, see Desch (2002: 5–47). For a pessimistic view of the military effectiveness of democratic regime types at war, see, e.g., Waltz (1967); LeMay and Smith (1968: vii–viii); Blaufarb and Tanham (1989); and especially Iklé (1991: xiv).

[11] Mack discounts the argument that regime type matters in asymmetric conflicts. See Mack (1975: 188–189).

by threatening to execute them for "cowardice," where cowardice is defined as any hesitation to engage the enemy regardless of objective circumstances. Third, authoritarian soldiers may not be constrained by the laws of war regarding noncombatants such as prisoners of war and civilians in combat zones. Instead of having to provide captured enemy soldiers with food and medical services, for example, an authoritarian regime's soldiers may be ordered to murder them, thus conserving resources. Finally, lack of responsibility to a cost-bearing public may allow authoritarian regimes to sustain higher combat casualties in pursuit of military objectives than can democratic regimes.

If an axiomatically just cause, just conduct, fearless soldiers, disregard for the laws of war, and casualty insensitivity make authoritarian regimes more effective in battle than democratic regimes, then the trend toward increasing strong actor failure would have to be explained by the fact of decreasing participation in asymmetric conflicts by authoritarian strong actors. This seems intuitively persuasive: the progressive dissolution of authoritarian states after 1918 (Austria-Hungary, the Russian Empire, the Ottoman Empire), 1945 (the Third Reich, fascist Italy, and imperial Japan) and 1991 (the Soviet Union) implies fewer authoritarian strong actors involved in asymmetric conflicts.

### Problems with the argument

But there are a number of problems with both the logic of the nature-of-actor argument and the evidence used to support that logic. First, even assuming that there are real differences in the capabilities of authoritarian and democratic actors in war, why assume that regime types stay constant in war? Most democratic actors become more conservative in war, restricting many of the civil liberties that define them *as* democracies (one thinks most famously of the fate of Japanese Americans in the United States after December 1941). Authoritarian regimes may also become more liberal under stress: Stalin's rehabilitation of the Orthodox church during World War II is a classic example. And the threat need not be existential to have this effect: the United States passed the USA Patriot act – which allowed the state greater freedom to pry into the private affairs of its citizens – in the wake of the terrorist attacks of September 11, 2001.

Second, an authoritarian regime's control over information about the justness of a war only benefits a regime that wishes to fight a war its own public would otherwise think unjust. The argument therefore *generally* assumes that publics in authoritarian regimes would consider their government's wars unjust, when there's no way to know, *a priori*, whether this is likely. Moreover, even assuming total resource mobilization, the tight control of information necessary to achieve that efficiency may impose severe limitations on the total amount of resources available to mobilize in the first place: the command economies typical of authoritarian regimes are notorious for being inefficient. This is the unifying theme of a number of recent comparisons of authoritarian and democratic regimes at war. According to this very sound logic, democratic states will, all other things being equal, be relatively more effective at fighting and winning wars than authoritarian states.[12] The use of extreme coercive measures to motivate soldiers is also logically suspect. Regimes resorting to these methods may achieve a tactical advantage in rare circumstances, but such a system can only motivate soldiers to take actions they know to be excessively costly or futile. To soldiers as yet uncommitted, this would signal that their leaders care nothing for their lives, and thus ultimately decrease their combat effectiveness. Such soldiers may desert at any opportunity, and cease to function without the threat of harsh reprisals. They may even resort to murdering their commanders. The systematic harm of noncombatants – a strategy referred to here as barbarism – also has drawbacks. For one thing, it is technically quite difficult to murder prisoners or noncombatants without one's opponents finding out about it. Once they do, they fight harder, avoiding surrender at all costs (they also often start reprisals in kind). Another problem is that sustained resort to barbarism ruins soldiers for conventional missions:[13] Here Richard Rhodes records the complaint by Eastern Territories Commander Johannes Blaskowitz of "excesses" by Heinrich Himmler's *Einsatzgruppen* in Poland in a memo to the German High Command:

> It is wholly misguided to slaughter a few ten thousand Jews and Poles as is happening at the moment; for this will neither destroy the idea of

[12] See Lake (1992); Reiter and Stam (1998: 259); and Reiter and Stam (2002). On the contrary argument that regime type doesn't matter much, see Desch (2002).

[13] See, e.g., Stanislas Andreski, who argues that Latin America has had few interstate wars because its states have soldiers who specialize in domestic oppression (torture, murder, rape, and so on) (Andreski, 1968). The logic is the same: soldiers used for barbarism will become ineffective as regular combat soldiers, putting states who face threats from other states' regular soldiers at increased risk. This logic is supported by a study of military disintegration by Bruce Watson. Watson argues that when, for example, a platoon of the US Army 20th Infantry Division under the command of Lieutenant William Calley murdered civilians in the village of My Lai in 1968, they were not acting as soldiers, but as a mob. See Watson (1997: 151).

a Polish state in the eyes of the mass of the population, nor do away with the Jews...

The worst damage affecting Germans which has developed as a result of the present conditions, however, is the tremendous brutalization and moral depravity which is spreading rapidly among precious German manpower like an epidemic. (Rhodes, 2002: 9–10)

This is why authoritarian regimes who resort to this strategy almost invariably develop "special forces" or "para" militaries to do the work. Even *within* the Einsatzgruppen, Himmler worried that certain practices (e.g., the unauthorized murder of Jews by SS units tasked with other functions) would damage discipline and hence, mission effectiveness (Rhodes, 2002: 187). Finally, the ratio of acceptable combat casualties to the value of military objectives should logically depend on the relative populations of the combatants, not their regime types: a small authoritarian regime could not win by selling its soldiers lives cheaply for objectives that in any other regime type would matter little.

On the evidence side, the nature-of-actor argument is difficult to support in its general form, because authoritarian regimes don't win wars more often than democratic regimes. This would appear to limit the power of this explanation to account for unexpected asymmetric conflict outcomes.

On balance then, although the nature-of-actor argument may offer important insights into key causes of strong actor failure, by itself it is unlikely to stand as a sound general explanation of why strong actors lose asymmetric conflicts.

## Arms diffusion

A second explanation for strong actor failure begins by observing the trend that accelerated after World War II. During the war, Allied and Axis powers struggled to defeat each other in the developing world. Throughout Asia and Africa, in particular, both sides shipped, stored, and distributed relatively sophisticated small arms and ammunition, including semi-automatic rifles, portable mortars, hand grenades, and machine guns. After the war, these arms remained in the developing world, along with a considerable number of indigenous soldiers expert in their effective use.[14] When colonial powers returned to their former

---

[14] Examples include the Hukbalahap in the Philippines and the Malayan communists in Malaya. For an account of the Hukbalahap insurgency in the Philippines from the insurgent perspective, see Pomeroy (1964). For an account of the Malayan Emergency and British responses to it, see Thompson (1966); Stubbs (1989); and Ramakrishna (2002).

colonies after the war, they were often violently opposed by these better-trained and armed soldiers. The net effect was to increase the costs of conquest and occupation as compared to the expected benefits; and strong actors lost wars against weak actors because they failed to anticipate these higher costs.

Thus, the logic of the arms diffusion argument is that weapons technology equals power, and as a result of this fact, "weak" actors were not as weak as anticipated. As Eliot Cohen puts it:

> The enormous increase in the quality and quantity of arms in the hands of Third World nations, coupled with increased organizational competence in the handling of such weapons, renders many local conventional balances far more even than before. (Cohen, 1984: 162)

The empirical evidence appears to support this logic, because the sharp rise in strong actor failures in asymmetric conflicts correlates with the increase in small arms availability to developing countries following World War II.

### Problems with the argument

There are three problems with the logic of the arms diffusion explanation. First, the argument assumes that the costs of conquest or occupation rose *relative* to the benefits, or that the benefits remained constant. Second, the acquisition of a weapons technology in no way assures an increase in combat effectiveness.[15] Third, even assuming an increase in combat effectiveness attributable solely to arms diffusion, any absolute increase in effectiveness may be far outweighed by the relative technology capabilities of strong actors.

The Cold War that began soon after the conclusion of World War II in Europe altered states' perceptions of the value or benefits of occupation in the developing world. Especially following the invasion of South Korea by the North in 1950, a new understanding of the linkage of values came to dominate state calculations of power and interest. In the context of a new US strategy of communist containment, domino logic could transform an intrinsically low-value country – such as the then

---

[15] For a recent and comprehensive treatment of the relationship between arms, arms transfers, and conflict outcomes, see Craft (1999: 92–93), and especially p. 121. Craft briskly summarizes hypotheses on the proposed relationships between arms and outcomes, and undertakes a sophisticated statistical analysis of them. Craft concludes that "Arms transfers that take place during a war do not predict war outcomes (winners, duration, or casualties) to commonly accepted statistical significance" (Craft, 1999: 121).

South Korea – into a vital US security interest. The logic was the same for the Soviet Union. Thus, even if the absolute costs of conquest, occupation, or stabilization of distant countries in the developing world were rising, so were the perceived benefits.

There is no doubt that weapons technology can increase a military's combat effectiveness. But logically, it could also decrease it. Many key military-technical innovations – ranging from the machine gun to the tank – decreased combat effectiveness until the proper mix of strategy and tactics for their effective use was established.[16] This is why, in his remarks above, Cohen is careful to specify "that organizational competence in the handling of such weapons" is a key component of any expectation of increased military effectiveness. Moreover, there is no reason to assume that weapons systems that are highly integrated into the doctrine, training, tactics, and strategy of an industrial power can be assimilated into militaries working within different historical, geographical, or social contexts.[17] One risk in particular is that the acquisition of unassimilated military technology may tempt a premature or inappropriate shift in strategy, with disastrous results.[18] Finally, in "Command of the Commons," Barry Posen shows that even the most efficient integration of doctrine, technology, and tactics may produce counterproductive specialization: the United States – and the United States is not alone among advanced industrial powers in this regard – is particularly good at leveraging firepower and maneuver

---

[16] This may explain the striking empirical finding that increased availability of weapons to an actor increases its likelihood of defeat in war (Craft, 1999: 73).

[17] Mearsheimer, for example, notes that his theory only applies to large-scale armored warfare, and hence only to states whose geography favors such warfare (there is no attempt to assess the distribution of such territory as a percentage of a total) (see Mearsheimer, 1983: 15). Thus, the same technology (and associated doctrine) which allows states to achieve decisive results in one geographical setting, may prove useless in another (on this point, see also Posen, 2003). Cultural factors may also constrain the adoption of non-indigenous technologies. Rosen notes that after World War II, Japanese businessmen attempted to duplicate the success of US industry by adopting a host of US business practices, only to abandon them due to cultural incompatibilities (see Rosen, 1995: 16). Finally, Chris Parker argues that not all weak states are equally successful at assimilating nonindigenous military technology. Insofar as assimilation and military effectiveness are the same thing (or at least covary), then anything which hampers assimilation should hinder effectiveness (Parker, 1999).

[18] Usually, actors seek the technology to facilitate their adopted strategy. When the reverse occurs, disaster can result (see, e.g. Johnson, 1973: 50; and Karnow, 1983: 182, 610). Perhaps this century's most famous philosopher of guerrilla warfare, Mao Tse-tung, warned against both premature escalation to conventional confrontation, and its opposite, something he came to call "guerrillaism" (staying on the strategic defensive too long) (see Hamilton, 1998: 28; and Paret and Shy, 1962: 35).

advantages in *open* terrain, but less effective in closed, and, in particular, *urban* terrain (Posen, 2003).

But even assuming that arms diffusion increased the absolute capabilities of armed forces in the developing world, it is hard to argue a relative increase over the advances maintained by industrial powers. Weak actors, for example, may have gained reliable compact automatic weapons, but strong actors gained combat helicopters, night vision, and better communications capability.

In sum, arms diffusion offers an at best equivocal explanation of the trend toward increasing strong actor failures after World War II. It is particularly weak when relied upon to explain unexpected outcomes. By itself, then, arms diffusion will probably not constitute a sound general explanation of asymmetric conflict outcomes.

## Interest asymmetry

A third explanation for strong actor failure in asymmetric conflicts is Andrew J. R. Mack's. Mack's explanation for how weak states win wars has three key elements: (1) relative power explains relative interests; (2) relative interests explain relative political vulnerability; and (3) relative vulnerability explains why strong actors lose. According to the logic of this argument, strong actors have a lower interest in a fight's outcome because their survival is not at stake, whereas weak actors have a high interest in a fight's outcome because their survival is at stake (Snyder and Diesing, 1977: 190; Mack, 1975: 181). Mack introduces the important concept of *political vulnerability* to describe the likelihood that an actor's people (in democratic regimes) or competing elites (in authoritarian regimes) will force an actor's leaders to halt the war short of achieving its initial objectives (Mack, 1975: 180–182). A strong actor's low interests imply high political vulnerability, and a weak actor's high interests imply low political vulnerability. Mack argues that this political vulnerability explains why the strong lose to the weak (Mack, 1975: 194–195): delays and reverses on the battlefield will eventually encourage war weary publics or greedy elites to force the strong actor's leaders to abandon the fight. Mack's argument therefore reduces to the claim that relative power explains strong actor defeat in asymmetric wars: power asymmetry determines interest asymmetry (high power equals low interest), which varies inversely with political vulnerability (low interest equals high vulnerability), which varies inversely with outcomes (high vulnerability equals low probability of victory). Interest

13

asymmetry is the key causal mechanism and Mack's argument is in this sense an interest asymmetry thesis.

Mack applies this logic to the case of US intervention in Vietnam, where it appears to provide a strong explanation of that war's unexpected outcome. According to Mack, the United States lost the war because it had less to lose than North Vietnam. Over time, the United States failed to coerce North Vietnam and was eventually forced by an angry and frustrated American public to withdraw short of achieving its main political objective: a viable, independent, noncommunist South Vietnam.

### Problems with the argument

Mack's interest asymmetry thesis has at least three weaknesses. First, relative power is a poor predictor of relative interest or resolve in peace or war. In peacetime, a strong state may act as if its survival is at stake when it is not. A state whose leaders and citizens imagine it to be "leader of the free world," for example, might rationally calculate that although the defeat of an ally in a distant civil war would be materially insignificant, its own survival as free world leader depended on a favorable outcome. These calculations are often intensified by domino logic, in which a series of individually insignificant interests are linked so that their cumulative loss constitutes a material threat to survival. Both identity survival and domino rationales, for example, affected the US decision to intervene in the civil war in Vietnam.[19] In war, once strong actors get involved in a fight – even one acknowledged to have been initially peripheral to their interests – their resolve to win may increase dramatically. This was as true of Soviet calculations in Afghanistan as of US calculations in Vietnam.[20]

Second, the operation of political vulnerability, which Mack uses to explain weak actor success, presupposes a span of time. Mack's argument assumes rather than explains a weak actor's capacity to avoid defeat and impose costs on its stronger adversary. This leaves us wondering why some asymmetric conflicts are over quickly yet others drag on.[21]

---

[19] See, for example, Herring (1986: 70); and Karnow (1983: 169–170, 377–378, 399, 423).
[20] On Soviet calculations in Afghanistan, see Magnus and Naby (1998: 68, 122). For apt examples from the US intervention in Vietnam, see Herring (1986: 222).
[21] Mack recognizes this weakness and suggests that guerrilla warfare strategy explains the longer duration of asymmetric conflicts (Mack, 1975: 195). But this argument suffers

Third, if the interest asymmetry thesis is right there should be little or no variation over time in the distribution of asymmetric conflict outcomes when relative power is held constant. But, as shown in Figure 2, in which relative power is held constant, weak actors are increasingly winning asymmetric conflicts.

In sum, Mack's interest asymmetry thesis is not so much wrong as incomplete. It is weakest when explaining actor interests as a function of their relative power and strongest when explaining strong actor failure as a consequence of political vulnerability.

## Democratic social squeamishness

A variant of the nature-of-actor argument worthy of brief discussion on its own is that in one particular kind of asymmetric conflict, small wars, regime type matters so much as to constitute a strong general explanation of both the trend and a strong actor's defeat. In *How Democracies Lose Small Wars*, Gil Merom argues that essentially, democratic strong actors can't win small wars because the state is constrained by society to avoid the sacrifice – both in the form of sustained and inflicted casualties – necessary to win:

> My argument is that democracies fail in small wars because they find it extremely difficult to escalate the level of violence and brutality to that which can secure victory. They are restricted by their domestic structure, and in particular by the creed of some of their most articulate citizens and the opportunities their institutional makeup presents such citizens. Other states are not prone to lose small wars, and when they do fail in such wars it is mostly for realist reasons.
>
> (Merom, 2003: 15)

Merom adds that "Essentially, what prevents modern democracies from winning small wars is disagreement between state and society over expedient and moral issues that concern human life and dignity," and "Achieving a certain balance between ... the readiness to bear the cost of a war and the readiness to exact a painful toll from others – is a precondition for succeeding in war" (Merom, 2003: 19).

The argument reduces to the claim that, in small wars, insensitivity to friendly casualties and a willingness to maximize violence against an opponent are necessary for victory; and that *modern* democracies are

from two related problems: (1) weak actors do not always defend with guerrilla warfare (this limits the generality of Mack's theory); and (2) some defenders using guerrilla warfare strategy are defeated quickly (this limits his theory's explanatory power).

structurally constrained in both categories. The particular relationship between society and the state makes democratic strong actors too squeamish to win small wars.

## Problems with the argument

As with the interest asymmetry thesis this one is both carefully reasoned and well supported by historical case evidence. But, overall, it suffers from most of the same problems as the nature-of-actor argument. There are three additional problems.

First, like Mack, Merom restricts his explanatory universe. Mack's analysis restricts itself to asymmetric conflicts between actors in which the weak actor invariably applies a guerrilla warfare strategy. Merom goes one further: asymmetric conflicts in which the strong actor is invariably a "democracy" and the weak actor invariably uses a guerrilla warfare strategy. Merom also follows Mack in claiming that, for the democratic strong actor, small wars are axiomatically "not existential" (Merom, 2003: 21). This may be objectively true, especially in hindsight, but one can hardly think of an example of a democratic state launching a small war it didn't claim (and its leaders and citizens did not in some real measure believe) was of vital importance to its survival; albeit via domino logic.

This in itself is not all that damning for either thesis, because both kinds of asymmetric conflict continue to remain important foreign policy problems for both strong and weak actors. But for the democratic social squeamishness argument, a second problem is that we have important examples of democratic strong actors initiating brutal strategies and still losing small wars (e.g., the French in Indochina, 1946–54; and the United States in Vietnam, 1965–75); as well as authoritarian regimes doing the same thing and losing (e.g., the Nazis in Yugoslavia, 1941–43; and the Soviet Union in Afghanistan, 1979–89).

The authoritarian examples call our attention to a third problem with Merom's argument. It implies that the mechanism of success in small wars reduces to a willingness to deliberately and systematically target enemy noncombatants.[22] Again, the record of success in the use of this strategy is mixed at best. Merom goes wrong by assuming that because

---

[22] It also places too much causal weight for outcomes on the shoulders of strong actors. What if the claim by the weak that they are willing to resist to the death is more than simply propaganda? To the extent that such resolve – most famously represented by the North Vietnamese during their fights with France and the United States in Indochina – is

the strong actor holds additional brutality in reserve, its conduct on the battlefield may still be described as restrained, and when the strong actor later abandons the field that "restraint" becomes the causal focus.[23] There is something to this argument: my own research suggests that in the post-World War II period barbarism was a sound strategy for *winning* a small war yet *losing* the subsequent peace. But Merom seems to rule out the possibility that democratic strong states may hold brutality in reserve – unused – not because their societies constrain them but because they sense, rightly, that the utility of further brutality may be either marginal or even negative.[24] Moreover, democratic states facing insurgencies have another option besides escalating brutality (barbarism) – an option which historically has been both successful and rare: conciliation. Britain experienced success with this option in the Malayan Emergency of 1948, and the United States successfully supported Ramon Magsaysay's reform efforts to overcome the Hukbalahap in the Philippines in 1952.

A final problem with the democratic social squeamishness argument is that it is not well tested. Merom's analysis skillfully brings together political and game theory threads to explain what Mack, for example, assumes: democratic strong actors are politically vulnerable to setbacks on the battlefield. But Merom's analysis ignores the success and failure rates of authoritarian states – states less constrained by (1) dependence of the state on society for military forces; (2) a general preference for measures short of war by society; or (3) by the ability of society, through

---

real, this places strong actors in the position of either having to resort to genocide, or withdrawing. It makes more sense in such cases to look at least as carefully at factors on the "weaker" side as on the stronger.

[23] Merom is hardly alone here. A recent example focusing on the case of US intervention in Vietnam is C. Dale Watson's *The Myth of Inevitable US Defeat in Vietnam*, in which Watson argues that had the United States been less restrained it could have won (Walton, 2002: 5). The problem with this argument, and a weakness in Merom's, is that it deliberately ignores actor restraints that had nothing to do with societal pressure (e.g., "let's do all we can without starting another world war").

[24] This argument goes right back to the first of the modern-era small wars – indeed, the war from which the term itself, *guerrilla*, originated. Napoleon Bonaparte's forces in Spain were harassed and attacked at all turns by Spanish guerrillas from 1807 to 1814, and they responded to these attacks with extremely brutal reprisals, including torture, mass murder, rape, and wholesale property destruction. These only appeared to stimulate even further resistance, creating a spiral of reprisal that did not end until the French left Spain in 1814. So clear was the connection between barbarism and increased social resistance that before pursuing the French into France, Britain's Wellington laid down the strictest restrictions on the conduct of his own troops in French towns (see Fremont-Barnes, 2003: 53–58, 67, 90).

*17*

charismatic representatives, to alter the state's foreign policy or military strategy.

These problems aside, Merom's account of the political vulnerability of democratic small actors in *small wars* is both excellent and timely. It expands on Mack's description of why and how democratic strong actors are politically vulnerable, and offers a useful explanation of why democratic states choose the strategies they do, and why they stick to failing strategies even after they've received a clear indication that their strategy for victory is in fact failing.

## Strategic interaction

My own explanation for weak actor success in asymmetric conflicts is more general. I argue that although relative power, the nature of the actor, arms diffusion, and interest asymmetry all matter, the best predictor of asymmetric conflict outcomes is *strategic interaction*. According to this thesis, the interaction of the strategies actors use during a conflict predicts the outcome of that conflict better than competing explanations. If we think of strategies as complex but discrete plans of action which include assumptions about the values of objectives, as well as tactical and leadership principles and rules of engagement, different interactions should yield systematically different outcomes independent of the relative power of the actors involved.

In Chapter 2, I argue that for purposes of theory building the universe of real actor strategies – blitzkrieg, attrition, defense in depth, guerrilla warfare, terrorism, and so on – can be reduced to two ideal-type strategic *approaches*: direct and indirect. My central thesis is that when actors employ similar strategic approaches (direct–direct or indirect–indirect) relative power explains the outcome: strong actors will win quickly and decisively. When actors employ opposite strategic approaches (direct–indirect or indirect–direct), weak actors are much more likely to win, *even when everything we think we know about power says they shouldn't*. My explanation of strategic choice and the trend focuses on Kenneth Waltz's concept of state socialization: the idea that actors imitate the successful policies and strategies of other actors, while avoiding failed policies or strategies (Waltz, 1979: 127). I argue that socialization of this kind works in regions, and that after World War II the developed and developing world imitated diametrically different patterns of success. When these patterns came to interact systematically, as they did after World War II, weak actors won more often.

18

## Why study asymmetric conflict outcomes?

Resolving the puzzle of how the weak win wars is important for several reasons. First, in terms of US foreign policy in the coming decades, many of the problems of asymmetric conflict – such as catastrophic terrorism, and the necessity, legitimacy, and costs of military intervention in ethnic conflicts and civil wars – will remain vital concerns; particularly because for the foreseeable future the United States will be a strong actor by default relative to any of its potential adversaries.

Recent wars in Iraq, Kosovo, Afghanistan, and again, Iraq, are illustrative in this regard. All were asymmetric conflicts in which the United States, often leading a coalition of states, attacked a much weaker state or non-state adversary. In the first Gulf War (1990), the US-led coalition launched a conventional assault against an Iraqi military bent on defending Kuwait (and later Iraq) with a conventional defense. Iraq was quickly overwhelmed and, having achieved its stated political objective of forcing Iraq from Kuwait, coalition forces declared victory and left.

In Kosovo in 1999, the United States, under the auspices of NATO, attacked Serb-supported forces in Kosovo from the air, hoping to force a halt to well-documented depredations against ethnic Albanians there. This clumsy conventional attack strategy was not directly opposed by Serb fighter interceptors or surface-to-air missile batteries; and it did not prevent Serb-supported forces achieving their objective of depopulating Kosovo of ethnic Albanians and destroying the Kosovo Liberation Army (KLA) as a military force. The three most remarkable features of this war were (1) that NATO was able to justify intervention even though none of its member states was directly threatened by Serb depredations in Kosovo – in essence, NATO violated international law in order to uphold a humanitarian principle; (2) the Albanian refugees came back; and (3) many observers counted operation Allied Force as a resounding success for the independent effectiveness of air power.

In Afghanistan in 2002, US forces attacked the Taliban with a brilliant strategy of providing close-air, logistical, and artillery support to the Taliban's last surviving domestic adversaries, the Northern Alliance. Essentially, the war pitted the Northern Alliance in a conventional attack against a Taliban stuck with a conventional defense. Most analysts predicted a repeat of the Soviet experience of 1979, including failure. But having spent nearly a decade abusing much of Afghanistan's population and bribing potential adversaries with drug money, the Taliban was in no position to launch a popularly based guerrilla defense such as had faced the Soviets in the 1980s. And the US decision not to commit major combat forces prevented the Taliban from rallying religiously conservative Afghanis to the cause of ejecting non-Muslims from Afghanistan. The Taliban lost the war and decamped to Northwestern Pakistan, where today they strike at vulnerable US and government forces and wait and train to take control of Afghanistan once US-supported forces weaken there.

Finally, the second US-led assault on Iraq in 2003 in key ways resembles the Boer War of 1899–1902. Like that war, the world's pre-eminent military power engaged another army in a conventional campaign that, after a few setbacks, quickly ended in an overwhelming victory. But, also like the Boer War, the losers refused to surrender, and instead switched from a conventional to a guerrilla warfare defense strategy. The result has been increasing difficulty for US and Allied forces. These forces were never designed, trained, or equipped for extended occupation duties. They continue to suffer daily casualties from unseen enemies and may, as a result, be increasingly tempted to inflict reprisals on noncombatants. This book explains both the conditions under which the US can win such fights and why it will certainly lose its fight to build democracies in Afghanistan and Iraq so long as it pursues its current strategy (excessively militarized and with the wrong mix of armed forces).

Second, although asymmetric conflicts are the most common type of conflict they are among the least studied by international relations scholars.[25] If there are conflict dynamics unique to asymmetric conflicts, or if an analytical focus on asymmetric conflicts enables us to attain valuable insights into more symmetrical conflicts, then a general explanation of asymmetric conflict outcomes is not only desirable, but necessary, both to reduce the likelihood of unnecessary conflicts and to increase the likelihood of US success when relying on the force of arms to advance its political objectives.

---

[25] See Paul (1994: 4); and Mack (1975: 176). My own survey of all wars from 1816 to the present reveals the following conflict type distribution: asymmetric conflicts = 52 (14 percent), probable asymmetric conflicts = 141 (37 percent), symmetric conflicts = 28 (7 percent), and missing data = 156 (41 percent). The total number of recorded wars since 1800 was 377. Probable asymmetric conflicts include Singer and Small's "extra-systemic wars" (colonial wars numbered 300–454). Missing data include most of Singer & Small's "civil wars" (numbered 600–982). If probable asymmetric conflicts are added to actual asymmetric conflicts, they comprise 51 percent of the distribution of all types of war since 1800. Even without adding probable asymmetric conflicts, however, actual asymmetric conflicts are twice as common as symmetrical conflicts.

Third, the whole question of how the weak win is in itself fascinating. The contests between David and Goliath, Hannibal and Rome at Cannae, Henry V and the French aristocracy at Agincourt, Germany's blitzkrieg into the Soviet Union in June of 1941, and even the World Heavyweight championship fight between Muhammad Ali and George Foreman in Zaire, are remembered chiefly because their outcomes were so unexpected. More recently, we've witnessed the unexpected defeats of US elite forces in Somalia, Russian Federation forces in Chechnia, Israeli forces in Lebanon, and the Taliban in Afghanistan. Explaining how and why these unexpected outcomes happen is itself a worthwhile endeavor. It is an effort that can result in important additions to our understanding of power in international relations theory, as well as a guide to US policymakers struggling to respond to global terrorism.

Finally, a theory of asymmetric conflict outcomes could help us understand how and why weak states respond to strong and strengthening states in the international system (Elman, 1995; Walt, 2002; Nye, 2004). It's an important question, because if the United States – the world's current pre-eminent power – does not act wisely and with restraint, it could well provoke countervailing alliances that eventually overwhelm it or undo its previous economic, political, and military advantages.

For all these reasons developing a theory of asymmetric conflict outcomes is vital.

## Plan of the book

The remainder of the book is organized as follows.Chapter 2 introduces the strategic interaction thesis more fully. It defines key terms, reduces competing explanations to testable propositions, and reports the results of a statistical analysis of all asymmetric wars fought between 1816 and 1998. This statistical analysis supports the strategic interaction thesis.

Chapters 3–7 contain the book's historical case studies of asymmetric conflict. These five case studies were chosen for several reasons. First, each case study is drawn from one of the four major historical periods of analysis: 1816–49, 1850–99, 1900–49, and 1950–99. This helps us track outcomes across large historical trends, and lends a better intuitive fit between the raw statistical data and the facts of each conflict. Second, the cases include variation on key causal variables, such as regime type, arms diffusion, and strategic interaction. Finally, each of the cases contains multiple strategic interactions. Thus, although only five historical cases are examined, together they provide a total of sixteen tests of the strategic interaction thesis.

Chapter 3 examines the fight between the Russian Empire and the Murids in the Caucasus from 1830 to 1859. The Russians won this twenty-nine-year conflict, which involved three distinct strategic interactions. Chapter 4 examines the war between the British Empire and the allied Boer republics of Orange Free State and Transvaal from 1899 to 1902. The British won this three-year war, which was the most costly of their entire colonial history. Chapter 5 examines the conflict between fascist Italy and Ethiopia from 1935 to 1940. The Italians used mustard gas in order to win this war against the vastly outgunned and outnumbered Ethiopians. Chapter 6 examines the fight between the Soviet Union and Afghan mujahideen from 1979 to 1989. The Soviets lost this brutal decade-long war which either killed or made refugees of fully half the Afghan civilian population; and they laid the foundation for the accession of one of the most conservative religious movements in history: the Taliban. Chapter 7 analyzes one of the most complex and important conflicts of the post-World War II era: US intervention in the Vietnamese Civil War. Chapter 8 contains a summary of the book's arguments, its conclusions, and its relevance to international relations theory and foreign policy (in particular, US foreign policy).

# 2 Explaining asymmetric conflict outcomes

I'm a speed demon, I'm a brain fighter, I'm scientific, I'm artistic, I plan
my strategy. He's a bull, I'm a matador...

> Muhammad Ali, Zaire (1974) in Gast (1996)

[T]aking practical account of the area we wished to deliver... I began
idly to calculate how many square miles: sixty: eighty: one hundred:
perhaps one hundred and forty thousand square miles. And how
would the Turk defend all that? No doubt by a trench line across the
bottom, if we came like an army with banners; but suppose we were
(as we might be) an influence, an idea, a thing intangible, invulnerable,
without front or back, drifting about like a gas? Armies were like
plants, immobile, firm-rooted, nourished through long stems to the
head. We might be a vapour, blowing where we listed. Our kingdoms
lay in each man's mind; and as we wanted nothing material to live on,
so we might offer nothing material to the killing. It seemed a regular
soldier might be helpless without a target, owning only what he sat on,
and subjugating only what, by order, he could poke his rifle at.

> T. E. Lawrence (1926)

Actors in a conflict of interests each come to that conflict with three
things: (1) an estimate of the resources immediately available to fight
with, relative to a potential adversary's; (2) a plan for the use of those
resources in pursuit of a specified objective (strategy); and (3) an estimate
of resources potentially available once the battle has been joined (again,
relative to a potential adversary's). As observed in Chapter 1, the
conventional wisdom regarding conflict outcomes is generally derived
from comparisons of each actor's standing armed forces, economic
capacity, and population at the onset of hostilities. In general, the
actor with the greatest amount of these resources is expected to win,
and to win in proportion to its power advantage.

This conventional wisdom is a problem, however. First, relying on it for explanation leaves many conflict outcomes unexplained. Second, as an underlying assumption of policy it can have disastrous consequences. In this chapter, I show that in addition to knowledge of each actor's available resources, explaining outcomes demands an estimate of the consequences of the *interaction* of each actor's strategy. I argue that all actor strategies can be sorted into one of two main approaches – direct and indirect – and that asymmetric conflict outcomes depend on which of two ideal-type interaction patterns obtains. If strong and weak actors use a strategy representing the same strategic approach – direct against direct, or indirect against indirect – strong actors should win as the conventional wisdom suggests. If, however, strong and weak actors employ strategies representing opposite strategic approaches – direct against indirect or indirect against direct – weak actors are much more likely to win than the conventional wisdom allows for. This is the strategic interaction thesis.

## Explaining asymmetric conflict outcomes

The strategic interaction thesis takes Andrew Mack's pre-theory of asymmetric conflict as its starting point. In Mack's model, relative power determines relative interests, and results in a conflict in which the weak actor is systematically more motivated to fight than the strong actor. Relative interests, in turn, determine relative political vulnerabilities: because weak actors are necessarily more motivated to fight and win than strong actors, they will be unlikely to quit short of achieving their political or military goals. Finally, Mack argues that in a long war the high political vulnerability of the strong actor will eventually force it to quit, regardless of whether it has an authoritarian or democratic regime type. This explains why the weak win.

The strategic interaction thesis is a general theory of asymmetric conflict outcomes. It improves on Mack's pre-theory in three areas. First, relative interests determine relative political vulnerabilities, but in the strategic interaction thesis relative interests are not explained by relative power. I argue that actor interests are too complex to be usefully reduced to Mack's simple formula. Not only have many states, for example, maintained an interest in the outcome of a conquest or an occupation far greater than that implied by their relative power, but state interests often shift once a conflict is under way. Second, an actor's regime type matters. It affects the costs and risks of adopting certain

24

strategies (which then alter the likelihood of victory or defeat). Third, and most importantly, the strategic interaction thesis explains why some asymmetric conflicts end quickly while others drag on.[1]

## Interests and vulnerabilities

Interests may be thought of both as a proxy for the probability of national solidarity – that is, broad agreement within a given society and between its elites and its people – and as a description of it. Although prior to the Japanese attack on Pearl Harbor, many Americans opposed US intervention in the war in Europe, since 1945 World War II has come to be regarded as a war fought for the highest of all actor interests: survival (see e.g., Mack, 1975: 183). Survival – or less dramatically, self-defense – is almost universally recognized as a legitimate reason to go to war.

When interests in the use of force are low, this is another way of saying that there is little consensus within a given polity on the need for the risk and sacrifice of war. Any war effort that is undertaken is vulnerable to domestic political opposition should things go wrong. An actor with very high interests will need to be defeated on the battlefield, while an actor with very low interests need not be defeated militarily. This is what is meant by political vulnerability.

The corollary of political vulnerability is what might be called political license, or just license. When interests are high (survival), a polity places few limits on the quantity of resources extracted and mobilized for war, or the way these resources are used. Civil rights can be abridged or suspended, and the laws of war may be ignored (Mack, 1975: 186, 187). The US experience in World War II again serves as an example: Japanese Americans were imprisoned during the war in direct violation of the US Constitution; and Japanese civilians were deliberately targeted by US firebombing campaigns once the Japanese main islands came within range of US strategic bombers.[2]

In sum, actor interests and political vulnerability vary inversely. The higher an actor's interests in the issues at stake, the less vulnerable it will be to being forced to quit a fight before a military decision. The lower an actor's interests, the more vulnerable it will be.

---

[1] Mack attributes protracted wars to the use of guerrilla warfare strategy by weak actors. But he also recognizes that guerrilla warfare strategy is very old, and thus cannot by itself explain why strong actors didn't lose as often in the past as after World War II.

[2] This was true even though, *objectively*, by the time US bombers came into range of the Japanese main islands, no credible case could be made for US survival being threatened.

## Political vulnerability and conflict duration

Even assuming that one actor is much more interested in the outcome than the other, the actor with lower interests can still win. The ideal conflict outcome for an actor with low interests is a *fait accompli*: a victory so swift and so final that before a strong actor's polity can even begin to debate its utility the conflict is already resolved.

It is highly doubtful, for example, that the United States had a high interest in the rout of Cuban-supported insurgents on the tiny Caribbean island of Grenada in 1983. US survival could only have been at stake in the highly dubious domino logic sense, or in the sense of a national identity as "defender of the free world." But the fight in Grenada was over so quickly there was no time for the US public to consider the need to intervene, much less to oppose it, before US victory had become an accomplished fact.

If a *fait accompli* is the ideal outcome for an actor with low interests in a conflict prior to a fight, then the worst outcome would be a protracted war. In a war that drags on there is time to consider the need to resort to arms, the value of the objectives sought by force, the morality of how force is applied, and above all the opportunity costs. Committees and town meetings convene, the press explores all aspects of the conflict, and political and military elites are called upon to justify the expense of what was once called "the appeal to heaven."

This euphemism calls to mind a more subtle reason that delay hurts strong actors – and democratic strong actors in particular. In ancient times many cultures held that the outcome of a fight represented the expressed will of a divine being. This meant that when two parties were aggrieved they could settle their differences by personal combat; it being presumed that victory in combat indicated the will of an all-good, all-powerful, and all-knowing supreme being (Lea, 1968: 86–161), and *was therefore legitimate*. It may well be that this tradition of trial by combat, as it came to be known, has never entirely disappeared from the collective European and North American consciousness. If true, then a war's duration – especially an asymmetric war in which the strong actor's victory is expected quickly – becomes a measure of its legitimacy: if the war is a just one, why is it taking so long? Put differently, the trial-by-combat legacy implies that the chief source of political vulnerability for strong actors has less to do with any assessment of *ex ante* actor "interests" and more to do with the strong association of outcomes with legitimacy, *especially* when there is a gross mismatch in relative material power.

In asymmetric conflicts, as in the Grenada example above, there is a strong expectation that any war will be over quickly. But some asymmetric wars drag on well beyond what was anticipated before the fight. If power implies victory, and a lot of power implies quick and decisive victory, what then explains why power causes quick and decisive victory sometimes but not others?

My answer is strategy. The interaction of some strategies makes the way clear for power to determine the outcome, whereas the interaction of other strategies causes wars to be protracted, thus dramatically abridging power's expected effect on the outcome.

## Political vulnerability and regime type

In his pre-theory of asymmetric conflict, Mack argues that because both authoritarian and democratic regimes face resource trade-offs in wars, political vulnerability constrains strong actors of both types. As Mack puts it:

> Despite these obvious points, my main contention – that limited wars by their very nature will generate domestic constraints if the war continues – is not disproved. In terms of the argument put forward here, "politics" under any political system involves conflict over the allocation of resources. In closed or centrist polities, these conflicts will by and large be confined to the ruling elite–but not necessarily so.
>
> (Mack, 1975: 189)

It is a weak argument, and Mack's discussion previous to this comment supports the claim that on balance an actor's regime type affects actor conduct, and hence, conflict outcomes. As noted in Chapter 1, there are good reasons to assume – resource trade-offs notwithstanding – that regime type affects conflict outcomes. But how exactly? I argue that authoritarian regimes have an advantage in a *particular kind of war*: a war in which the regime's opponents try an indirect defense strategy, such as terrorism, guerrilla warfare, or nonviolent resistance. In such a war, the costs and risks of employing the harshest measures are lower for authoritarian regimes, while the benefits – which don't vary with regime type – remain potentially high.[3] Authoritarian regimes enjoy

---

[3] I say "potentially" because although logically, indirect defense strategies can be more easily overcome by depredations against civilians and other noncombatants than conventional

two advantages over their democratic counterparts. First, authoritarian regimes have much more control over what information reaches their domestic audiences: wars can be made to seem both necessary and fairly fought. That same control over information can also obscure the true nature of the violence to international audiences. Moreover, when evidence of barbarism *does* reach an authoritarian regime's public (or interstate audience) it can be justified as limited reprisal for atrocities committed by an adversary. Second, even when domestic audiences become aware of barbarism, they are in no position to alter state policy or strategy. As Chapter 5 makes clear, Italy's invasion of Ethiopia was aided by both advantages.

In other kinds of war and other strategic interactions, however, there is little evidence to support the claim that authoritarian regimes fight better or win more often than democratic regimes. On the contrary, with the exception of long wars (Bennett and Stam, 1998), democratic states appear to win wars more often than authoritarian states (Reiter and Stam, 1998). Thus, as in this analysis, the proper question isn't "do authoritarian regimes fight more effectively than democratic regimes," but rather, "under what circumstances do authoritarian regimes fight more effectively than democratic ones?"

## Vulnerability and strong actor defeat

Strong actors will more often lose asymmetric conflicts that are protracted. Mack's description of the process by which a strong actor eventually quits the fight serves well here:

> In the metropolis, a war with no visible payoff against an opponent who poses no direct threat will come under increasing criticism as battle casualties rise and economic costs escalate . . . Tax increases may be necessary to cover the costs of the war, a draft system may have to be introduced, and inflation will be an almost certain by-product. Such costs are seen as part of the "necessary price" when the security of the nation is directly threatened. When this is not the case, the basis for consensus disappears. In a limited war, it is not at all clear to those groups whose interests are adversely affected why such sacrifices are necessary. (Mack, 1975: 185–186)

---

defense strategies, the empirical support for barbarism's increased effectiveness is equivocal. For a fuller exposition of the counterproductive consequences of the use of barbarism in asymmetric conflicts, see Arreguín-Toft, 2003.

Merom's thesis takes this argument further still. The key causal relationship is between <u>political will and costs</u>. As Mack and others have pointed out, asymmetric conflicts are those in which, *in general*, the stronger actor will be both more able to absorb unexpected costs and at the same time, paradoxically, more sensitive to unexpectedly increased costs. This is because elites and, in democratic strong actors, publics, have an *ex ante* expectation of quick and decisive (i.e., low-cost) victory. A protracted war is already, therefore, an unexpectedly *costly* war. Again, the key puzzle is why don't all asymmetric wars end quickly?

## The strategic interaction thesis

The essence of the strategic interaction thesis is that there are two *patterns* of strategic interaction – same-approach and opposite-approach – and these determine the likelihood that the strong actor will win or lose. This section explores the logic of this argument.

## Strategy

Strategy, as defined here, is *an actor's plan for using armed forces to achieve military or political goals.*[4] Strategies incorporate actors' understandings (rarely explicit) about the relative values of these objectives.[5] Strategy in this sense should be distinguished from two closely related terms: grand strategy and tactics. Grand strategy refers to the totality of an actor's resources directed toward military, political, economic, or other objectives. Tactics refer to the art of fighting battles and of using the various arms of the military – for example, infantry, armor, and artillery – on

---

[4] The meaning of strategy is both complicated and constantly evolving. Mearsheimer uses perhaps the simplest definition – "the plan of attack" (see Mearsheimer, 1983: 28–29). For a discussion of strategy and its evolution, see B. H. Liddell Hart (1967: 333–346); and J. P. Charnay (1994: 768–774).

[5] This lack of explicitness is an important component of strategy because guessing wrong about how an adversary values its objectives can lead to unexpected outcomes. US strategy in Vietnam, for example, assumed that after sustaining a certain level of casualties, North Vietnam would no longer be willing to support the insurgency in the South. The search for this breaking point, and uncertainty over whether it would have any political utility, bitterly divided the Johnson administration. There may in fact have been a breaking point in Vietnam, but as US Secretary of Defense Robert McNamara concluded in 1967, reaching that point would result in virtual genocide (Rosen, 1972: 167–168; Mueller, 1980: 497–519; Brown, 1980: 525–529; and Karnow, 1983: 454, 596).

terrain and in positions that are favorable to them.[6] Grand strategy, strategy, and tactics all describe different points on a continuum of a given actor's means toward a single end: compelling another to do its will.

The following typology of ideal-type strategies is a useful starting point for analysis:

> *Offense strategies (strong actor):*
>   conventional attack
>   barbarism
>
> *Defense strategies (weak actor):*
>   conventional defense
>   guerrilla warfare strategy (GWS)

Both actors have other strategic options besides those listed here. On the indirect side, for example, strong actors might choose a "hearts and minds" or conciliation strategy over barbarism. Weak actors might choose nonviolent resistance or terrorism instead of a GWS. Moreover, barbarism could be used defensively and GWS offensively (though in both cases they would count as representatives of an indirect strategic approach). In this analysis I assume (1) strong actors initiated the asymmetric conflict in question;[7] and (2), these ideal-type strategies are war-winning rather than war-termination strategies.[8]

## Conventional attack

Conventional attack means the use of armed forces to capture or destroy an adversary's armed forces, thereby gaining control of that opponent's values (population, territory, cities, or vital industrial and communications centers).[9] The goal is to win the war in a decisive

---

[6] This definition is a paraphrase of one from the Littré Dictionary as quoted by Charnay (1994: 770).

[7] Strong actors are often but not always the initiators in asymmetric conflicts. Paul counts twenty weak-actor-initiated conflicts from 394 BC to 1993 (Paul, 1993: 3–4), of which eleven are included here.

[8] In eight asymmetric conflicts (4.1 percent) the outcome was effected by a war termination or conciliation strategy. Conciliation strategies include the use of bribes, offers of amnesty, power sharing, or political reforms, and do not require armed forces to implement. Examples of conflicts ended by a conciliation strategy include the Murid War (1830–59), the Third Seminole War (1855–58), the Malayan Emergency (1948–57), the British–Cypriot Conflict (1954–59), and the Philippine–Moro Conflict (1972–80). In the case of the Malayan Emergency, e.g., see Ramakrishna (2002).

[9] The distinction between forces and values derives from the nuclear war strategy literature; as in "counterforce" (attacking the enemy's forces) *vs.* "countervalue" (attacking the enemy's cities and population) targeting.

engagement or a series of such engagements by destroying the adversary's physical capacity to resist.

In the most common pattern of a conventional attack strategy an attacker's forces advance to capture a defender's values or strategic assets – say a capital city, industrial or communications center, or bridge or fort – and the defender moves to thwart that effort. A battle or series of battles follows, sometimes marked by lulls lasting entire seasons, until one side admits defeat.

### Barbarism

Barbarism is the deliberate or systematic harm of noncombatants (e.g., rape, murder, and torture) in pursuit of a military or political objective.[10] Unlike other strategies, barbarism has been used to target both an adversary's will and its capacity to fight. In a strategic bombing campaign, for example, when will is the target the strong actor seeks to coerce its weaker opponent into changing its behavior by inflicting pain (destroying its values).[11] In a counterinsurgency (COIN) campaign, when will is the target the strong actor may attempt to deter would-be insurgents by, for example, a policy of reprisals against noncombatants.[12] But strong actors in a counterinsurgency can also target a weak actor's physical capacity to sustain resistance by, for example, implementing a concentration camp policy.[13] Historically, the most common forms of barbarism are the murder of noncombatants (e.g., prisoners of

---

[10] See, for example, Walzer (2000: 151). Chemical and biological weapons have been traditionally included in this category because they are inherently indiscriminate. Deliberate destruction of a defender's natural environment (through deforestation, draining of swamps, etc.) is also a violation of the laws of war for the same reason (see Perry and Miles, 1999: 132–135).

[11] The classic work here is Schelling (1966: chs. 1 and 4; see also Pape, 1990: 103–146; and Pape, 1996). In theory it is possible to use strategic air power to target an adversary's capacity to fight by using air forces to destroy or interdict supplies, demolish key communications points (railroad junctions, bridges, and airfields), or arms factories. If it were possible to do so without killing noncombatants this would count as a direct attack strategy. But in practice – even taking into account advances in precision guided munitions – strategic air power is a too blunt weapon, and noncombatants are killed out of proportion to the military necessity of destroying the targets. NATO's strategic air campaign in Kosovo in 1999 is a case in point (see, e.g., Independent International Commission on Kosovo, 2000: 92–94; and Daalder and O'Hanlon, 2000).

[12] Such reprisals typically include executing randomly selected civilians in retaliation for the killing of an occupying soldier (see, for example, Asprey, 1994: 108; and Arreguín-Toft, 2003).

[13] Insurgent intelligence and support networks depend on the participation of sympathetic noncombatants, and concentration camps disrupt these networks (see, for example, Hamilton, 1998: 59; and Krebs, 1992: 41–42).

war or civilians during combat operations); concentration camps;[14] and since 1939, strategic bombing against targets of little or no military value.[15]

## Conventional defense

Conventional defense is the use of armed forces to thwart an adversary's attempt to capture or destroy values, such as territory, population, and strategic resources. Like conventional attack strategies, these target an opponent's armed forces. The aim is to damage an adversary's physical capacity to attack by destroying its advancing or proximate armed forces. Examples include most limited aims strategies,[16] static defense, forward defense, defense in depth, and mobile defense.[17]

## Guerrilla warfare

Guerrilla warfare strategy (GWS) is the organization of a portion of a society for the purpose of imposing costs on an adversary using armed forces trained to avoid direct confrontations.[18] These costs include the loss of soldiers, supplies, infrastructure, peace of mind and, most

---

[14] The British used concentration camps as a counterinsurgency (COIN) strategy during the South African War. Although not intended by the British, as many as 28,000 Boer women and children died in these camps – more than the combined total of combatant casualties from both sides. On the use of concentration camps as a COIN strategy, see Ellis (1976: 111). On their use and consequences in the South African War, see De Wet (1902: 192–193); Pakenham (1979: ch. 29 and 607–608); and Krebs (1992).

[15] The Allied bombing of Dresden is a common example (see Schaffer 1985: 97–99). On the subject of strategic bombing as coercion against Nazi Germany more generally, see Pape (1996: 260–262). In terms of Pape's argument, strategic bombing that targets noncombatants would count as barbarism. When air power is used to target enemy forces, it would count as a conventional attack strategy. Attacks on infrastructure and industry are more problematic: noncombatants are not deliberate targets, but those who use this strategy know beforehand that noncombatants will be systematically killed in such attacks.

[16] An example of a defensive limited aims strategy would be Japan's attack on the US Pacific Fleet at Pearl Harbor in December of 1941. An example of an offensive use of limited aims strategy would be Egypt's attack on Israel in October of 1973.

[17] For full summary descriptions, see Mearsheimer (1983: 48–50).

[18] In Mao Tse-tung's revolutionary guerrilla warfare strategy, a GWS eventually evolves into a full conventional confrontation. In this analysis such an evolution would count as a shift in strategy from an indirect to a direct strategic approach. A related strategy is terrorism, which often has political objectives similar to GWS. The logic of most terrorism mirrors that of coercive strategic bombing. A largely urban phenomenon, terrorism generally seeks either to inflict pain on noncombatants so they will pressure their government to accede to the terrorists' political demands, or to delegitimize a government as a means of replacing it. This implies that the strategy will be most effective when citizens have a say in government policies. On terrorism as an insurgency strategy, see Merari (1993). On suicide bombing as strategy, see Pape (2003).

important, time.[19] Although GWS primarily targets opposing armed forces and their support resources, its goal is to destroy not the capacity but will of the attacker.[20]

GWS requires two essential elements: (1) sanctuary (physical, e.g., swamps, mountains, thick forest, or jungle – or political, e.g., poorly regulated border areas or border areas controlled by sympathetic states), and (2) a supportive population (to supply fighters with intelligence, supplies, and replacements). The method of GWS is well summarized by perhaps its most famous practitioner, Mao Tse-tung:

> In guerrilla warfare, select the tactic of seeming to come from the east and attacking from the west; avoid the solid, attack the hollow; attack; withdraw; deliver a lighting blow, seek a lighting decision. When guerrillas engage a stronger enemy, they withdraw when he advances; harass him when he stops; strike him when he is weary; pursue him when he withdraws. In guerrilla strategy, the enemy's rear, flanks, and other vulnerable spots are his vital points, and there he must be harassed, attacked, dispersed, exhausted, and annihilated.
>
> (Tse-tung, 1961: 46)

GWS is not a strategy for obtaining a quick defeat of opposing forces (Hamilton, 1998: 27). Moreover, because guerrillas cannot hold or defend particular areas (save isolated base areas), they do not provide security for their families while on operations or when demobilized to await new missions. GWS is therefore a strategy that requires placing key values (e.g., farms, family, religious or cultural sites, and towns) directly into the hands of the adversary. Logically then, important costs of adopting a GWS depend on the purpose and restraint of the adversary.[21] When invading or occupying forces do not exercise restraint in the use of force, or when their *political objective* is the destruction rather than coercion of a weak actor's people, GWS can become a prohibitively expensive defensive strategy.[22]

---

[19] On this point especially, see Samuel Huntington's remarks in Hoffmann *et al.* (1981: 7; see also Cohen, 1984: 157).

[20] For general introductions to GWS, see Laqueur (1976); Ellis (1995); Asprey (1994); and Joes (1996). On Chinese and Cuban variations of GWS, see Tse-tung (1961); Katzenbach and Hanrahan (1955: 321–340); Guevara (1961); and Debray (1968).

[21] In March 1900 the British captured the first Boer capital, Bloemfontein. Surviving Boer commanders gathered to decide whether to surrender or keep fighting. They were closely divided, but tipping the balance in favor of continued – guerrilla – war was faith in British civility. The Boer found their faith unjustified (see De Wet, 1902: 192–193).

[22] The question of whether an indirect defense – in particular, nonviolent resistance – can be effective against a ruthless strong actor is taken up by Gene Sharp and others (see McCarthy and Sharp, 1997; Sharp, 2003). The case of Kosovo from 1998 to 1999 suggests

## Strategic interaction

Every strategy has an ideal counterstrategy. Actors able to predict an adversary's strategy in advance can therefore dramatically improve their chances of victory – or at a minimum inflict unexpectedly high costs on an adversary – by choosing and implementing that ideal counterstrategy. Mao, for example, argued that "defeat is the invariable outcome where native forces fight with inferior weapons against modernized forces *on the latter's terms.*"[23] Mao's maxim suggests that when the weak fight the strong, the interaction of some strategies will favor the weak while others will favor the strong.

Building on Mao's insight, I argue that a universe of potential strategies and counterstrategies can be aggregated into two distinct ideal-type strategic *approaches*: direct and indirect.[24] Direct strategic approaches – e.g., conventional attack and defense – target an adversary's armed forces with the aim of destroying or capturing that adversary's *physical capacity* to fight, thus making will irrelevant. They feature soldier-on-soldier contests along with codified rules as to their conduct and a shared conception of what counts as victory and defeat. Indirect strategic approaches – e.g., barbarism and GWS – most often aim to destroy an adversary's *will* to resist, thus making physical capacity irrelevant.[25] Barbarism targets an adversary's will by murdering, torturing, or incarcerating noncombatants. GWS attacks an adversary's will by targeting enemy soldiers, though noncombatants may be targets as well. This constant-if-incremental loss of soldiers, supplies, and equipment, with little chance of a quick resolution, is aimed at the balance of political forces in the stronger actor's homeland. Same-approach interactions (indirect–indirect or direct–direct) imply defeat for weak actors because there is nothing to mediate or deflect a strong actor's power advantage. Barring a battlefield miracle, these interactions should therefore be resolved in proportion to the force applied. By

---

that nonviolent resistance against an adversary bent on genocide will only prove effective when it provokes an armed external intervention (see, e.g., Independent International Commission on Kosovo, 2000).

[23] Quoted in Mack (1975: 176, emphasis in original).

[24] This reduction of strategies to two mutually exclusive approaches is well established in the strategic studies literature. See, for example, Corvisier and Childs (1994: 378); and Liddell Hart (1967: 197, 361–364); see also, Galtung (1976).

[25] For a similar definition see Pape (1990: 106–107). If coercive power is the product of will and physical capacity, then either approach can win: reducing an opponent's capacity to zero makes its willingness to fight irrelevant; and reducing its willingness to fight to zero makes its capacity irrelevant.

contrast, opposite-approach interactions (direct–indirect or indirect–direct) imply victory for weak actors because the weak refuse to engage where the strong actor has a power advantage (i.e., "on the latter's terms").[26] They therefore tend to be protracted, and time favors the weak.[27]

When strategic interaction causes an unexpected delay between the commitment of armed forces and the attainment of military or political objectives, strong actors tend to lose asymmetric conflicts for two reasons. First, although all combatants tend to have inflated expectations of victory (Blainey, 1988: 53), strong actors in asymmetric conflicts are particularly susceptible to this problem (see e.g., Mack, 1975: 181–182; Herring, 1986: 144–145). If power implies victory, then an overwhelming power advantage implies an overwhelming – and rapid – victory. As war against a Lilliputian opponent drags on, overestimates of success force political and military elites to either escalate the use of force to meet expectations (thus overtly increasing the costs of a conflict which were expected to be slight), lie, or look increasingly incompetent. Either way, for democratic strong actors, domestic pressure to end the conflict is likely to increase. The longer the war drags on the greater the chances the strong actor will simply abandon the war regardless of the military state of affairs on the ground.

Second, strong actors anxious to avoid increasing costs – such as declaring war, mobilizing reserves, raising taxes, or sustaining additional casualties – may be tempted to use barbarism because they believe it to be a cost-saving strategy for victory.[28] But in the post-World War II era, barbarism is a difficult strategy to prosecute effectively. Barbarism that is effective *militarily* demands "special" forces, trained and equipped to accomplish their demanding "mission." It demands, above all, thoroughness in its application. Even the Nazis found both demands beyond their capabilities in World War II.

---

[26] In GWS, an attacker's armed forces are physically avoided or only engaged on favorable terms. In a blockade or strategic bombing campaign against a direct defense in a limited war, the strong actor's destructive power is deflected because such attacks invariably place the noncombatant population between attackers and political elites.

[27] On the importance of conflict duration as a cost of conflict, see Mearsheimer (1983: 24); and Katzenbach and Hanrahan (1955: 324–326).

[28] Alexander Downes persuasively argues that both democratic and authoritarian states are likely to employ barbarism in these circumstances because they believe it is a cost-saving strategy (see Downes, 2003). My own research shows that barbarism rarely is effective militarily (it tends to be counterproductive) and is almost always counterproductive politically (see Arreguín-Toft, 2003).

The result was a resistance backlash that dramatically *increased* the costs of Nazi occupation in the conquered territories they administered.[29] But even when *militarily* effective barbarism is risky: for democratic strong actors it carries the possibility of domestic political discovery (and opposition[30]) and for actors of either regime type who are not nuclear powers, it carries the risk of external intervention.

### Strategic interaction: explaining the trend

This is not a book about how and why actors choose the strategies they do. Nor do I offer a general explanation of the reasons some actors shift strategies during a war while others don't.[31] Rather, I take actor strategies as given and then map the consequences of strategic interaction on outcomes.

That said, my explanation for the trend toward increasing strong actor failure is suggested both by the timing of the biggest shift in outcomes favoring weak actors (1950–99), and by the logic of Kenneth Waltz's argument that actors in a competitive international system "socialize" to similar policies and strategies. As Waltz argues, "The fate of each state depends on its responses to what other states do. The possibility that conflict will be conducted by force leads to competition in the arts and the instruments of force. Competition produces a tendency toward the sameness of the competitors" (Waltz, 1979: 127).

---

[29] The Nazis did better at developing forces capable of prosecuting barbarism than they did at achieving a thoroughness in barbarism's application. The few survivors and unindoctrinated witnesses who escaped, e.g., the cruel murdering pits of the *Einsatzgruppen*, spread word of these atrocities, thereby increasing the costs of civil administration and military operations throughout occupied territories. Nazi barbarism raises a problem for the thesis at hand, however, in that, unlike most barbarism, which is intended to be coercive (i.e., a means to an end), the bulk of Nazi barbarism (viz., that aimed at the mentally ill, handicapped, Jews, homosexuals, and Roma) was not intended to coerce but to destroy utterly the groups targeted: it was less a strategy and more an end in itself. Many of these murders – e.g., against Jews in Poland and further east – were initially justified as COIN measures when they were demonstrably nothing of the kind. However, a smaller but real proportion of Nazi barbarism – e.g., in occupied Yugoslavia – was in fact intended to serve a COIN utility in occupied territories. On the creation of the *Einsatzgruppen* and the challenges of training people to mass murder of noncombatants, see Bartov (1992); and especially Rhodes (2002). On the Nazi use of barbarism as COIN strategy in Yugoslavia, see, e.g., Hehn (1979).

[30] Mack correctly emphasizes that barbarism is judged in proportion to the relative power of the actors: weak actors will be forgiven abuses for which strong actors will be hanged (see Mack, 1975: 186–187).

[31] In 77.5 percent of asymmetric conflicts neither actor switches strategies. Winners and losers stay with the same strategy they started the war with.

By "socialization," Waltz means that states imitate each others' successes and avoid what they count as failures. Over time, this means actors will have a tendency to converge on the most successful integration of arms, doctrine, training, strategy, and tactics; where "success" is measured by what won the last big war. I argue that socialization works regionally, and that after World War II different patterns of success emerged in Europe and Asia. In Europe, success in war was measured by a state's capacity to produce and deploy large mechanized and combined arms forces designed to destroy an adversary's armed forces on relatively open terrain; capturing its values without the need for costly battles of annihilation: a blitzkrieg. This model was imitated by the United States,[32] its European allies, and the Soviet Union.[33] In Asia, success was measured by the ability to sustain a protracted conflict against a technologically superior foe on relatively closed terrain: a GWS. Mao's long fight for and eventual conquest of China was a model consciously imitated by Algerian rebels, the Vietminh, the Hukbalahap, Cuban insurgents, Malayan communists, and, to a large extent, Afghanistan's mujahideen.[34] The blitzkrieg model is a direct strategic approach; the guerrilla warfare model, an indirect one. When the two interacted systematically – as they did with greater frequency following World War II – the strong actor lost more often.[35]

The fact that in nearly 78 percent of asymmetric conflicts losing actors don't switch strategies suggests that actors on the verge of armed conflict or defeat are not entirely free to *choose* an ideal strategy. This is true for two reasons. First, forces, equipment, and training – all closely integrated – are not fungible. Each strategic approach will be facilitated by certain kinds of forces and technology and undermined by others. Moreover, the development and prosecution of an actor's

---

[32] See, e.g., Cohen (1984: 179) on this point.

[33] It is true that the major European colonial powers – France and Britain – each possessed large and specialized colonial militaries before World War II. In both World War I and World War II the "colonial" nature of these armies were sometimes cited as reasons why French and British land forces did so poorly in each war, especially in the early phases. But, following the war, during which Britain in particular attempted to socialize to the blitzkrieg standard, the ability of its troops to conduct counterinsurgency operations, while still greater than that of the United States and Soviet Union, was diminished compared to what it had been prior to World War II.

[34] On Mao's revolutionary guerrilla warfare as a template, see Katzenbach and Hanrahan (1955: 322); and Hamilton (1998: 18).

[35] Nationalism proved necessary but not sufficient to account for the success of the GWS pattern against states possessed of blitzkrieg forces. Both GWS without nationalism and nationalism without a GWS will lose to a strong actor's direct approach assault.

ideal strategy or counterstrategy may be blocked by entrenched organizational interests or traditions.[36] Second, actors prioritize threats: if the United States and Soviet Union, for example, identified each other as the primary threat, and both calculated that the most likely area of direct confrontation would be the heart of Europe, then adopting integrated equipment, doctrines, and strategies favorable to winning that sort of war made sense. But the nature of threats can shift faster than an actor – even one as technologically advanced as the United States – can shift strategies. The inertia of decades of preparation to win one kind of war can become a crippling liability when faced with an entirely different kind of war in a different terrain and climate. This is why strong actors – mostly European – lost so many conflicts in Asia in the period following World War II. This is why the United States is currently doing so poorly in its "war" against terrorism (Arreguín-Toft, 2002).

## Main hypotheses: strategic interaction and conflict outcomes

This section explores the logic of four distinct strategic *approach* interactions, and explains how hypotheses derived from each can be usefully reduced to a single hypothesis. The expected relationship of strategic approach interactions to outcomes in asymmetric conflicts is summarized in Figure 3.

### *Direct offense vs. direct defense*

In this interaction both actors make similar assumptions about the priority of values over which they fight. Both can therefore be expected to agree about the implications of a catastrophic loss in battle, the rules of war, or the capture of a capital city. Because nothing mediates between relative material power and outcomes, strong actors should win quickly and decisively.

*Hypothesis 1: When strong actors attack using a direct strategic approach, and weak actors defend using a direct strategic approach, all other things being equal, strong actors should win quickly and decisively.*

### *Direct offense vs. indirect defense*

Unlike direct strategies, which involve the use of forces trained and equipped to fight as organized units against other, similarly trained and

---

[36] See, e.g., Cohen (1984: 165–168); Krepinevich (1986); Asprey (1994: 36); and Marquis (1997).

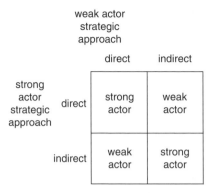

Figure 3. Expected effects of strategic interaction on conflict outcomes (expected winners in cells)

equipped forces, indirect defense strategies (such as terrorism, GWS, or nonviolent resistance) typically rely on forces difficult to distinguish from noncombatants when not in actual combat. As a result, an attacker's forces tend to kill or injure noncombatants during operations, which tends to stimulate weak actor resistance.[37] Most important, because indirect defense strategies sacrifice values for time (see Katzenbach and Hanrahan, 1955: 325–326), they necessarily take longer to resolve so long as weak actors continue to have access to sanctuary and social support.[38] In asymmetric conflicts, delay favors the weak.

*Hypothesis 2: When strong actors attack with a direct strategic approach and weak actors defend using an indirect approach, all other things being equal, weak actors should win.*

### Indirect offense vs. direct defense

Because the overwhelming force available to the strong actor implies success against a weak adversary attempting a conventional defense, an indirect offensive strategy in this context targets a defender's will to resist. Prior to the advent of strategic air power and long-range artillery

[37] Logically it could undermine resistance but empirically, it doesn't (see Arreguín-Toft, 2003).
[38] Although a GWS requires sanctuary and social support, mere access to them in no way mandates its adoption. French forces, for example, had access to both as they faced defeat in the Franco-Prussian War in 1870. France actively considered adopting a GWS after the disastrous defeat at Sedan. Yet threatened with the loss of Paris, France surrendered instead (see Howard, 1961: 249–250).

(such as the V-1 and V-2 rockets of World War II), blockades and sieges were the primary means of coercing adversaries in this way. Today, strategic bombing campaigns[39] and economic sanctions[40] are the most common forms of indirect offense against direct defense *when the attacker is the stronger actor.*[41]

The logic of this interaction could go either way. On the one hand, and as imagined by such early air power theorists as Douhet and Mitchell, the threat of attacking an opponent's population centers and industry – skipping over entrenched standing armies rather than attacking them directly – could by itself coerce that opponent into changing its behavior.[42] It could also turn a defender's people against its own government, making it rational for them to force their leaders to capitulate and spare the citizens further injury. On the other hand, the injury and death of noncombatants – in particular, children – could increase resistance among citizens who might formerly have been opposed to the war or neutral. It might bring them closer to their government rather than alienating them. A defender's government might also disperse key resources more widely, protecting them from future destruction from the air. And, as Pape notes, modern nation states are adept at redistributing the burdens of blockades and economic sanctions away from defense assets (Pape, 1997: 93, 109). Overall, I expect strong actors to lose these interactions because they are (1) time-consuming; (2) tend toward barbarism;[43] and (3), in the post-World

---

[39] Robert Pape has shown that strategic bombing or "punishment" strategies rarely work (and they cannot work against indirect defense strategies, such as GWS) (see Pape, 1996: ch. 6; see also Clodfelter, 1989). If Pape is right and tactical air power is effective as a means to coerce an adversary, then tactical air support that accepts collateral damage should become more common; and "human shield" defense of, say, armored or transport columns, will become an increasingly common countermeasure.

[40] See , e.g., Pape (1997: 90–136). Pape undertakes an updated look at an old debate about the effectiveness of economic sanctions to advance noneconomic political objectives and concludes that such sanctions are likely to be effective only in rare circumstances.

[41] When the attacker is the weaker actor, terrorism and insurgency are the most common forms of an indirect offense against a direct defense. I assume strong actors are the attackers because (a) I am building and testing a theory of asymmetric conflict outcomes, and (b) the strong attacking the weak is by far the most common pattern.

[42] See Douhet (1921); and Mitchell (1925). On the effectiveness of strategic air power in the first Gulf War, see Press (2001). There remains a healthy debate about whether the 1999 air campaign against Slobodan Milosevic's government counts as successful case of coercion by air power. For an argument against, see Daalder and O'Hanlon (2000). For an argument for air power's effectiveness, see Stigler (2003: 124–157).

[43] Strategic bombing campaigns usually start out with the intent to spare noncombatants – often to the point of putting pilots and air crews at increased risk (e.g., by flying lower or

War II period of high nationalism, barbarism tends to be militarily and politically counterproductive (Arreguín-Toft, 2003).

*Hypothesis 3: When a strong actor attacks with an indirect strategic approach against a weak actor defending with a direct approach, all other things being equal, the strong actor should lose.*

## Indirect offense vs. indirect defense

Indirect defense strategies presuppose a certain level of restraint on behalf of attackers.[44] When strong actors employ a strategy that ignores such restraint, weak actors are unlikely to win, both because there would be no one left to win for, and GWS depends directly on a network of social support for intelligence, logistical support, and replacements.[45] Barbarism works as a COIN strategy because by attacking either or both of the essential elements of a GWS – sanctuary and social support – it destroys an adversary's capacity to fight.[46]

---

slower) – but in most cases these campaigns escalate until either noncombatant casualties are simply accepted (as in US bombing of North Vietnam during the ROLLING THUNDER campaign), or they become intended targets (as in the case of the firebombings of Dresden and Tokyo and the atomic bombings of Hiroshima and Nagasaki). A strict interpretation of the laws of war may make a strategic air campaign that accepts "collateral damage" (viz., death or injury to noncombatants) a war crime. The issue is tricky: the laws of war permit collateral damage so long as that damage is proportional to the military necessity of a target's destruction. But where strategic air power has no military utility, and this has been established by bomb damage assessments, then collateral damage subsequent to those assessments would constitute a war crime. It would also count as barbarism, even though "collateral damage" is by definition unintended. This is true because although the specific deaths and injuries caused by the attacks were not intended, they were generally accepted and therefore systematic.

[44] Harry Turtledove explores the counterfactual of what would have happened had Gandhi attempted his nonviolent resistance strategy (an indirect defense strategy akin to GWS and terrorism) against Hitler's Third Reich instead of against the British. In Turtledove's fictional account, Gandhi's resistance is crushed and Gandhi and Nehru are executed (see Turtledove, 2001: 231–262).

[45] Mao Tse-Tung once analogized the relationship between insurgents and citizens in a people's war by likening the fighters to fish and the people to the sea. Effective counter-insurgency would therefore require either altering the terrain (making the sea transparent) or killing, expelling, or imprisoning the people (drying up the sea). Both would count as barbarism (see Mao Tse-Tung, 1968: 284). This interaction is best exemplified by the Serb strategy in Kosovo from 1998 to 1999, prior to the intervention of NATO in Operation Allied Force. In combination with Serb paramilitary forces, regular armed forces of the Yugoslav military engineered the flight of ethnic Albanians so effectively that they destroyed any chance that the KLA would become an effective insurgency within Kosovo.

[46] As noted above, the problem with barbarism isn't that it can't win wars, but that it can only win in special circumstances (comprehensively applied by special forces and in a COIN context) and it almost always results in a lost peace. This is an historical trend which doesn't make itself obvious until the return of the colonial powers to "their" colonies following World War II. Murder, torture, and brutality could deter resistance and cow

*Hypothesis 4: When strong actors employ barbarism to attack weak actors defending with a GWS, all other things being equal, strong actors should win.*

Each of the four interaction outcome hypotheses describes an interaction of either same-approach or opposite-approach strategic interactions. It follows that all four may be tested as a single hypothesis.

*Hypothesis 5: Strong actors are more likely to win same-approach interactions and lose opposite-approach interactions.*

## Alternative hypotheses

As noted in Chapter 1, there are three alternative explanations of both strong actor failure in asymmetric conflicts, and of the trend toward increasing failure over time. Each generates testable propositions.

For example, the logic of the arms diffusion argument clearly implies that better arms for the weak actor make strong actor failure more likely. This in turn implies that arms themselves are an important component of "power," and by extension, the conflicts in question were less asymmetric than they seemed (the weak were less weak when better armed). If true, the high diffusion of military technology to the developing world after World War II might account for the *trend* in strong actor failures as well.

*Hypothesis 6: The better armed a weak actor is, the more likely it is that a strong actor will lose an asymmetric conflict.*

The logic of the nature-of-actor argument also yields testable propositions:

*Hypothesis 7(a): Authoritarian strong actors win asymmetric wars more often than do democratic strong actors.*

*Hypothesis 7(b): Authoritarian strong actors win asymmetric wars in which the weak actor uses an indirect strategy more often than do democratic strong actors.*

The interest asymmetry thesis provides an alternative explanation of asymmetric conflict outcomes in two senses. First, it holds that relative power explains relative political vulnerabilities (power and vulnerability vary directly), and second, it holds that regime type does not matter. It therefore yields two testable propositions:

*Hypothesis 8: Relative material power explains relative interests in the outcome of an asymmetric conflict.*

---

social support prior to World War I. But following World War II the same methods tended to increase resistance, thus increasing the costs of conquest and especially occupation. Strong actors willing or able to follow barbarism through to its extremes (e.g., the French in Algeria under General Massù) could still win wars, but no longer could these methods win the peace.

*Hypothesis 9: Authoritarian and democratic strong actors share roughly equal political vulnerability in a prolonged asymmetric conflict.*

Evaluations of hypotheses 5, 6, and 8 will be included in the concluding section of each historical case study. Hypotheses 7a, 7b, and 9 can only be evaluated across cases. Evaluations of these hypotheses will therefore appear in the overall conclusion to the book.

## A quantitative test of the strategic interaction thesis

Even if the strategic interaction thesis is plausible and logically sound, before it can be pronounced a theory it needs testing. Here I test the strategic interaction thesis in a quantitative analysis of 202 asymmetric conflicts fought between 1816 and 2003. The aim is to determine whether there is a statistically significant correlation between strategic interaction and asymmetric conflict outcomes, but I also test alternative arguments, such as the argument that the weak won wars after World War II because they were aided by the superpowers.

### Coding and cases

The basic method of coding cases was to examine the history of each war in the *Correlates of War* data set. A conflict was coded asymmetric if the halved product of one actor's armed forces and population exceeded the simple product of its adversary's armed forces and population by 5:1 or more. If the strong actor used armed forces to attempt to destroy a weak actor's forces or capture (but not destroy) values, it was coded a conventional attack. If the weak actor used armed forces against the strong actor's forces in an attempt to thwart these attacks, it was coded a conventional defense. A coding of barbarism was reserved for strong actors that systematically targeted noncombatants, employed indiscriminate weapons, or accepted collateral damage in a strategic bombing campaign *after* bomb damage assessments cast doubt on the military necessity of the campaign as a whole. A weak actor was coded as using a GWS if it sought to impose costs on the strong actor with armed force while avoiding pitched battles. Each conflict dyad was coded with one of four strategic interactions (direct–direct, direct–indirect, indirect–indirect, or indirect–direct),[47] before

---

[47] Most asymmetric wars contain a single strategic interaction from start to finish, but a few, such as the South African War or the US intervention in Vietnam, contain multiple-sequential or multiple-simultaneous interactions, respectively. In multiple-sequential

being reduced to one of two interaction types (same–approach or opposite–approach).[48]

The key variable of analysis is strategic interaction (STRATINT) as compared to conflict outcome (OUTCOME). If strategic interaction causes change in conflict outcome, then a shift in the value of strategic interaction across the case universe should be matched by a corresponding shift in *outcome*. The STRATINT variable was coded "0" if the strategic interaction was same-approach (direct–direct or indirect–indirect), and "1" if it was opposite-approach (direct–indirect or indirect–direct). The OUTCOME variable was coded "0" if the strong actor lost, and "1" if it won.[49]

### Strategic interaction and conflict outcomes

Cross tabulations established that strategic interaction and asymmetric conflict outcomes are associated, and that the relationship is statistically significant (see Figure 4).[50]

The results thus support hypothesis 5.[51] Strong actors won 76.8 percent of all same-approach interactions, and weak actors won 63.6

interaction conflicts, strategies change, but in temporal sequence: one side's strategic shift is quickly followed by another's. Multiple-simultaneous interaction conflicts are those in which a single actor or an actor and its allies pursue different strategies against the same adversary within a single theater of operations. The empirical distribution of conflict types is as follows: single, 134 (77.5 percent), multiple-sequential, 29 (16.8 percent), and multiple-simultaneous, 10 (5.8 percent). In this analysis, conflict outcomes are explained by strategic interaction outcomes.

[48] In the main analysis, the relatively few wars with multiple interactions were reduced to single interactions. In multiple-sequential conflicts the final interaction was used to represent the overall conflict: the South African War was coded same-approach because it ended with an indirect–indirect interaction. In multiple-simultaneous conflicts, interactions were averaged: US intervention in Vietnam was coded opposite-approach because although some interactions were same-approach, on balance, the contest was decided by a direct-indirect interaction. The chief consequence of these reductions is a tougher test for the strategic interaction thesis, because collapsing interactions increases the impact of relative material power on outcomes. Because strong actors have a greater material capacity to adapt to failure than do weak actors, collapsing interactions hides strong-actor rather than weak-actor failures. I also tested the thesis using strategic interactions (rather than conflict outcomes) as the dependent variable, thus un-collapsing the data analyzed here. See fn. 51.

[49] Stalemates and ongoing conflicts were coded losses for the strong actor.

[50] Pearson chi-squared (1), 14.56, $p < 0.001$.

[51] An analysis of the relationship between strategic interaction and *interaction* outcomes (as opposed to war outcomes) produces an even more striking finding: weak actors win 23.1 percent of same-approach and 78.4 percent of opposite-approach interactions. This relationship is statistically significant (Pearson chi-squared (1), 40.95, $p < 0.001$). An analysis of the impact of external noncombat support for weak actors did not refute the strategic interaction thesis; even when weak actors received no support, they were still

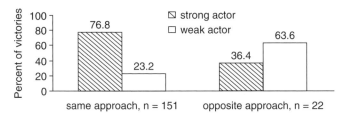

Figure 4. Strategic interaction and asymmetric conflict outcomes, 1800–2003

percent of all opposite-approach interactions. Weak actors were therefore nearly three times more likely to win when fighting strong actors in an opposite-approach strategic interaction.

## Testing an alternative explanation: external support for weak actors

How many of these weak actor victories resulted from external support?[52] Logically, strong actors should rarely attract external support when combating weak actors, whereas weak actors may often attract some support.[53] Weak actors could therefore be winning asymmetric conflicts because they are supplied from outside, rather than because they use a favorable counterstrategy. My data set allows comparison of key causal variables while controlling for external support for the weak actor.[54] The results are summarized in Figure 5:

Figures 4 and 5 are very similar. The fact that weak actors are slightly worse off implies that external support matters, but the key finding is that even when they receive no external support, weak actors are still three times more likely to win opposite-approach interactions than they are same-approach interactions. Essentially, the effects of

three times more likely to win opposite-approach interactions than same-approach interactions (Pearson chi-squared (1), 11.38, $p < 0.001$).

[52] Support in this context means arms, logistical support, and perhaps military advisers, but not combat troops.

[53] The United States received support – including actual combat units – from Turkey during the Korean War and Australia during the Vietnam War. In these contexts, however, support was less about materially affecting the balance of forces available to the strong actor, and more about ratifying and legitimizing US policy.

[54] There were not enough cases of positive external support to make a statistically significant finding. As a result, I report only the relationship of strategic interaction and outcomes when the weak actor received no external support.

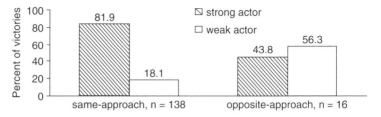

Figure 5. Strategic interaction and conflict outcomes when weak actor received no external support

strategic interaction overwhelm the effects of external support for weak actors.

## Strategic interaction and conflict duration

A key causal mechanism of the strategic interaction thesis is time: same-approach interactions should be over quickly, whereas opposite-approach interactions should be protracted (and weak actors tend to win protracted wars). An analysis of the average duration of same-approach and opposite-approach interactions supports this claim: the mean duration of opposite-approach interactions was 2.27 years; of same-approach interactions, 1.57 years (1.66 years was the overall mean).

## Strategic interaction and long-term trends

In terms of the trend, both opposite-approach interactions and weak actor successes have increased over time: from 1800 to 1849, 5.9 percent of interactions in thirty-four asymmetric conflicts were opposite-approach. From 1850 to 1899, 10.1 percent of interactions in sixty-nine asymmetric conflicts were opposite. From 1900 to 1949, 16.1 percent of thirty-one asymmetric conflicts were opposite, and from 1950 to 1999, 21.1 percent of thirty-eight asymmetric conflicts were opposite.

In sum, the data analysis supports three key hypotheses relating strategic interaction to asymmetric conflict outcomes. First, strong actors are more likely to lose opposite-approach strategic interactions. Second, opposite-approach interaction conflicts last longer than same-approach interactions. Third, the frequency of opposite-approach interactions has increased in rough proportion to strong actor failure over time.[55]

This analysis is limited because some data are missing: many civil and colonial wars recorded neither the quantity of forces committed nor the strategies actors used. Although these defects are balanced by statistical controls, even a perfect data set would support only a correlation between variables, not causation. Thus, although the data analysis might have refuted the strategic interaction thesis, only in combination with a careful comparison of historical cases can the thesis be confirmed.

## Conclusion

Actors in a conflict of interests each come to that conflict with resources, a plan for the use of those resources, and hopes for help from allies or soon-to-be-deployed weapons in development. There is no question that all other things being equal an abundance of resources is good to have in a war. But if the strategic interaction thesis is right, the inter-action of each actor's plan for the use of those resources – whether grand or meager – turns out to be even more important.

### How the remaining chapters are organized

The remainder of this book is taken up with a systematic analysis of five historical case studies. Each case study has the same structure: historical background (including geography and climate), actor interests prior to the fight, how the war was fought, its outcome, and its after-math. The focus of each chapter is provided by each competing argument's expectations: how did each actor's power and regime type affect its interests and strategies? How did comparative military technology work? Was one side politically vulnerable, and if so, how, if at all, did that vulnerability contribute to the war's outcome?

---

[55] The proportion of strong actor defeats as compared to the increased percentage of opposite-approach interactions is greater in the final fifty-year period than in the other periods. This suggests that other factors – such as an established norm of anti-colonialism, a rise in nationalism, the spread of free trade regimes, and interference by superpowers during the Cold War – explain some of the trend. However, as the data make clear, the strategic interaction thesis remains the most important causal variable.

# 3 Russia in the Caucasus: the Murid War, 1830–1859

The Caucasus may be likened to a mighty fortress, strong by nature, artificially protected by military works, and defended by a numerous garrison. Only thoughtless man would attempt to escalade such a stronghold. A wise commander would see the necessity of having recourse to military art, and would lay his parallels, advance by sap and mine, and so master the place.     Veliaminov (Baddeley 1908)

When you do battle, even if you are winning, if you continue for a long time it will dull your forces and blunt your edge; if you besiege a citadel, your strength will be exhausted. If you keep your armies out in the field for a long time, your supplies will be insufficient ...

Therefore I have heard of military operations that were clumsy but swift, but I have never seen one that was skillful and lasted a long time. It is never beneficial to a nation to have a military operation continue for a long time.     Sun Tzu (1988)

Russia's attempt to annex the Caucasus began in earnest nearly two hundred years ago. Since many contemporary studies of interstate politics begin with caveats about the sensitivity of their findings to particular periods of history,[1] it seems worthwhile to say why I think the careful study of so distant a conflict is still useful.

## Appropriateness

Clearly there are many things about the place and time which appear unique to both. The character of warfare two hundred years ago was

---

[1] For example, in *Theory of International Politics*, Kenneth Waltz restricts the explanatory power of structural realism to the post-Westphalian time period; and in *Conventional Deterrence*, John Mearsheimer restricts the explanatory power of his argument to the post-World War II time period. See Waltz (1979), and Mearsheimer (1983).

different from that of the post-World War II era. In the period in question – stretching from the time of the French Revolution to the American Civil War – two differences in particular stand out.

First, the profound sense of honor, duty, and glory associated with war was a major source of motivation for both officers and men. These things strongly motivated a willingness to take risks and make sacrifices; and, most particularly, bravery in battle. Bravery in battle was in turn widely believed to affect combat outcomes, and so it did.

Second, the staggering costs of the Murid War in terms of time (thirty years) and lives (well over half-a-million men) call into question our preconceived notions about the meaning of victory in war; or less prosaically, of the relative costs of achieving a given political objective by military means. Russia's conquest of the Caucasus gave it few new strategic advantages save stability on its southern frontier. The region was costly to control, difficult to traverse and, until the industrial age (which dawned quite a bit later in Russia than elsewhere), its wealth in oil lay fallow.

These differences aside, there remain enough similarities during the time of the Murid War to make it relevant to our larger purpose. There was still an interstate system, with regime types well described as democratic or authoritarian. Weapons technologies were different from today, but strategies were similar, and the interaction between weapons technology and strategy were analogous as well. Most importantly, strategic interaction mattered as much in the nineteenth century as at Hannibal's victory at Cannae in 216 BC, or Norman Schwarzkopf's in the Kuwaiti theater of operations in 1991.

## The Caucasian theater

The idea that as a comprehensive territorial space stretching from the Caspian to the Black Sea, the Caucasus form an unrivaled natural fortress, is repeated by every commentator on that struggle, and on both sides. As Napoleon did before them, and as Hitler was to do after them, the Russians lamented both the difficulties of climate and of the densely forested and sheer mountainous terrain:

> And when the Russians employed the argument so much favoured by later dictators, that they were producing order from chaos and improving the lamentable state of the roads . . . Shamil had his answer ready: "You say my roads are bad and my country impassable. It is well: that is the reason why the powerful White Tzar and all his armies

who march on me ceaselessly can still do nothing against me. I do not compare myself to great sovereigns. I am Shamil – an ordinary Avar." (Blanch, 1960: 129)

In effect, the mountains of Daghestan proper served as a sort of inner keep – a virtually unassailable final barrier to conquest – while the hills and dense forests of Chechnia served as a kind of outer wall or moat – considerable barriers to conquest in their own right (Baddeley, 1908: xxxv).

The lack of roads and the density of Chechnia's beech forests severely restricted the utility of Cossack light cavalry, while at the same time exposing any line of march to an endless series of ambushes. In order to attack and defeat mountain strongholds, the Russians had to bring up sappers and heavy artillery. Yet powder, shot, and field pieces required considerable logistical resources, and these in turn required heavy security. The Russians were slow to adapt, yet adapt they did, though with mixed effect:

> In front of the advance guard, behind the rearguard, and on both flanks of the column for its full length went the sharpshooters, with their reserves and mountain guns. On the level or on open places these flanking lines or chains kept at a good musket shot from the column, but on entering a forest they marched as the ground permitted, striving as much as possible to keep the enemy's fire at a distance, for it was too deadly when directed at a compact body of troops. The soldiers called this "carrying the column in a box." (Baddeley, 1908: 269)[2]

Give up the artillery and supplies, and you increased mobility, but upon reaching the mountain strongholds your troops would find it impossible either to advance or to hold their ground. In the end, Russia adapted to the difficulties of Caucasian terrain in two ways: first, by cutting trees,[3] and second, by building roads and forts.

---

[2] Note that this "column in a box" strategy is the precise analog of the World War I / World War II naval convoy strategy, with the Chechens taking the place of "wolf packs," and the beech trees taking the place of the opaque North Atlantic. The disadvantage of both systems was also similar: more and more combat units had to be tied down to escorting logistical assets; and, worse still, there was simply no glory in the monotonous drudgery of escort duty.

[3] Commentators have argued, in many ways convincingly, that Chechnya and Daghestan fell to the axe, not the sword. The strategy of terrain alteration is a logical, if drastic, counterinsurgency strategy. Yermolov's tree-cutting policies, amounting to systematic deforestation, anticipate the later US strategy of defoliating large areas of South and North Vietnam with Agent Orange; as well as Saddam Hussein's drainage of the southern swamps of Iraq in order to contain and destroy the Shiite guerrillas whose insurgency was based there.

Yet for all their defensive advantages, the mountains and forests did not constitute an unambiguous asset. On the contrary, as Baddeley argues, the difficulties of terrain and climate exacerbated the disunifying effects of ethnicity, language, and the *adats* (Baddeley, 1908: xxii). According to Baddeley, the Murids would win so long as they were able to maintain a politically united front, and alliance defections would ultimately doom them. If true, the terrain of Chechnia and Daghestan presented Shamil with a military advantage but a political disadvantage.

## Background

Russia's conquest of the Caucasus took place in three broad phases. The first occurred during the reign of Peter the Great, following immediately upon the heels of his successful war with Sweden in 1721. Taking advantage of an Afghan invasion of Persia, Peter himself led the expedition south, and his success resulted in the transfer of sovereignty of various administrative districts from Persia to Russia. This phase featured very little military conflict, yet such conflict as did take place foreshadowed what was to come: both in the forests of Chechnia and the mountains of Daghestan, the Russians experienced "difficulties" (Gammer, 1994: 2). Russia's success in this first phase was due to the fact that its conflict was mainly with Persia, not with either the Chechens or the Avars (the main ethnic tribe of Daghestan):

> The whole thing was accomplished in a few months, and in the joy of victory the Russians failed to notice how tremendously pleased the Persians were that they could hand over to the Russians this restless, unprofitable, and, in the last analysis, entirely independent land of brigands. (Essad-Bey, 1931: 213)

The second phase took place during the reign of Catherine the Great. In 1763 she established the fortress of Muzlik in the heart of Kabardia; and after fourteen years of hard struggle, Kabardia was conquered and occupied by a new Cossack regiment, the Mozdok Cossacks. Other wars of expansion were fought during Catherine's reign – Georgia was briefly occupied, then abandoned – but Russian activity in the Caucasus remained half-hearted until just before her death, when the barbarous sacking of Tiflis provoked her into declaring war on Persia. The Russians defeated the Persians everywhere, but Catherine died during the war and her son Paul withdrew Russia's forces from the Caucasus, intending to relinquish all Russian possessions there. He was unsuccessful, however, and after his death in 1800 his son Alexander agreed to accept a dying Georgian monarch's offer ceding Georgian sovereignty to Russia.

It is only in 1800, therefore, that historians mark the beginning of Russia's sixty-year-long attempt to conquer the whole of the Caucasus. The annexation of Georgia, like the later annexation of Manchuria by the Japanese in 1933, provoked a series of escalating military commitments which contained an inexorable expansion logic: in order to hold on to what we have, we have to expand to acquire more resources; but the resources we expend to expand make our new possessions tenuous; and so we must expand again just to hold on to what we have (Snyder, 1991: 3–4, 8).

The period from 1800 to 1815 marked a difficult time for Russia in the Caucasus, but especially in the west. Russia's *de jure* annexation of Georgia proved difficult to achieve *de facto*; and the Empire faced war with the Ottomans, Persia, as well as an invasion by Napoleon's France during this time. Not until the defeat of Napoleon was Russia once again able to turn its sustained attention to its southern flank.

The third and final phase of the conquest of the Caucasus thus begins roughly in 1816, and lasts until the capture of Shamil in 1859. This war eventually came to absorb the complete attention of the Russian Empire; along with the lives of many of its most talented officers, one of its most beloved poets, and hundreds of thousands of its serf soldiers. It is this third phase of the attempted conquest that constitutes the central focus of this chapter.

### Prologue to war: Yermolov, Veliaminov, and barbarism

When Mikhail Yermolov acceded to command of the Army of the South in 1816, his name was already a legend among Russians. Not only was this gargantuan and leonine Russian general revered for his dash and bravery in numerous Napoleonic engagements (he had been awarded the Cross of St. George at the age of 16, and was promoted to colonel after the battle of Austerlitz in 1805), but he is forever remembered as the most beloved of commanders by the soldiers he commanded (Baddeley, 1908: 95).

Larger than life, Yermolov devoted himself unstintingly to his tsar's will and to the glory and security of Russia. Baddeley sums up his goal as follows:

> Yermóloff's central idea was that the whole of the Caucasus must, and should, become an integral part of the Russian Empire; that the exist-ence of independent or semi-independent States or communities of any description, whether Christian, Mussulman, or Pagan, in the

mountains or on the plains, was incompatible with the dignity and honour of his master, the safety and welfare of his subjects.

(Baddeley, 1908: 99–100)

What was his strategy for achieving this end? Yermolov was hardly the first or last to come upon what he considered an ideal counterinsurgency strategy: barbarism. The idea was to divide the region to be conquered into smaller regions, each of which would be attacked and razed piecemeal:

> Baulked, the Russian generals decided on a ruthless system of reprisals. The native population must be broken, crops and villages razed, wells choked, orchards cut down, vineyards trampled. They must be brought to heel. No quarter must be given – not that any was ever asked by the fighters – and the campaign must be brought to a close without further delay. (Blanch, 1960: 23)

Yermolov's strategy was simple: to get at the inner keep (the mountain strongholds of Daghestan) it was first necessary to subdue the Chechens. To that end he began by building a fort called *Grozny* – literally, "menace." Yermolov intended to use Grozny as a base of operations for a succession of raids into Chechnia proper. These raids, as noted above, had the aim of conquering Chechnia by destroying it. The Chechens would either submit to Yermolov and become subjects of the tsar, or they would suffer and die: every man, woman, and child.

For a time it seemed as though Yermolov would succeed. He felled trees, built roads, and completed a line of fortresses stretching from the Caspian to the Black Sea. He razed villages, blasted mountain fortresses to rubble, and forced tribe after tribe to submit to Russia. So great seemed his momentum that, by the end of June in 1820, he declared to the tsar "the subjugation of Daghestan, begun last year, is now complete; and this country, proud, warlike, and hitherto unconquered, has fallen at the sacred feet of your Imperial Majesty" (Yermolov as cited by Baddeley, 1908: 138). Though few could have guessed it at the time his assessment was to prove premature. Success followed on success, and not until 1824 did Yermolov begin to pay heed to rumors of religious fanaticism. Having "conquered" Daghestan, his command witnessed a spontaneous religious uprising in Chechnia.

In December, 1825 Alexander I died unexpectedly, and Yermolov, thinking the tsar's brother Constantine would accede to the throne, swore his and his command's allegiance to Constantine. Unbeknownst to Yermolov, however, Constantine declined to accept the crown, and it passed instead to the tsar's son Nicholas. Yermolov's premature commitment to Constantine woke Nicholas's suspicions, however. Although allowed to continue in the command for another year, the accession of Nicholas I effectively marked the end of Yermolov's career.

Yermolov was eventually dismissed in disgrace; forced even to beg for his own escort home from the Caucasus. His legacy to the contest for the Caucasus is a mixed one. On the one hand, he and Veliaminov invented the Caucasian Corps system, and they built a chain of fortresses which were to serve as crucial bases for the later conquest of Chechnia and Daghestan. On the other hand, his barbaric strategy directly paved the way for the rise of Muridism and Shamil, and for the historically unprecedented unification of the Caucasian peoples into a solid fighting front – a front implacably opposed to Russian sovereignty.

## Russia's interests

During the Murid War the sprawling Russian Empire was ruled from St. Petersburg by two successive tsars: Nicholas I from 1826 to 1855, and Alexander II from 1855 to 1859. Although individual tsars tended to represent opposite political and social philosophies – father seeking reform, son repression, grandson reform, and so on – all the tsars in question shared an absolute secular and religious authority during their respective reigns.

> Russia's great advantage lay in her own system of government, that autocratic power which, coupled with the existence of serfdom, enabled her to fill the ranks of her armies at will, and, yet more important, to secure her conquests by a vast system of land settlement on the Cossack principle of military tenure. (Baddeley, 1908: 236)

This is an argument worthy of elaboration, because in many ways Russia constituted a medieval regime. Only a tiny minority of its citizens were literate, and the serf system amounted to slavery. In effect, Russia at that time had no real "public" which could exercise an independent influence on its foreign or military policies. There was no centralized collection or widespread dissemination of casualty or battle reports. Finally, to the extent that Russia's social and political elites were engaged in the Caucasian campaigns, it is fair to say they were mostly engaged *romantically*.[4]

---

[4] No more visible or durable evidence of this romanticism is needed than Mikhail Lermontov's poems and stories of the Caucasus (see Lermontov, 1966).

Russia's regime type was the very definition of authoritarian. And Russia's interests in the Caucasus were simple: conquest, annexation, conversion, and pacification. These interests had not changed significantly since the reign of Peter the Great, and they did not change during the course of the war.

## Murid interests

In 1816 Russia's adversaries in the Caucasus could best be described as independent tribes and Khanates, each of which resisted Russian advances independently. Although most Christian regions eventually were bribed or browbeaten into swearing loyalty to Russia, Russia's Muslim regions and Khanates were generally dealt with by military means (Gammer, 1994: 6). Regardless of faith, language, or loyalty, however, these areas were generally governed by hereditary ruling families. In formal terms, they were authoritarian regimes; though it should be added that until the advent of Muridism, no single tribe's ruling family enjoyed a degree of authority comparable to that of the Russian tsars. Instead, rulers exercised an authority restricted by ancient laws called *adats*, which among other things specified appropriate rewards and punishments and codes of conduct for the sexes. The *adats* also institutionalized such practices as *kanly* or blood feud, which again, until the advent of Muridism, made unified resistance to Russian advances all but impossible.

After 1830, however, the non-Christian regions and Khanates of Chechnia and Daghestan came under the sway of an absolute ruler, who like the tsar claimed both secular and religious authority. Khazi Muhammad was acclaimed first imam of Daghestan in 1830, and his creed has been called Muridism (see below). Khazi Muhammad was killed in battle at Gimri in October of 1832 (he was survived, in that battle, "as if by a miracle," by a grievously wounded Shamil). In November of 1832, Hamzad Beg was proclaimed second imam of Daghestan. Like his predecessor, he spread the Murid creed, and his military actions were in the main confined to consolidating support among wavering Caucasian tribes. Yet Hamzad Beg, whose treachery was widely blamed for Khazi Muhammad's fall at Gimri, was himself cut down by treachery; and in September of 1834, Shamil was acclaimed third imam of Daghestan. It was a title he was to hold for twenty-five years. It is no exaggeration to say that in terms of absolute authority Shamil's leadership very quickly equaled that of the tsar who was to constitute his main opponent, Nicholas I.

Prior to the advent of Muridism, the Caucasian tribes fought tactically brilliant but strategically uncoordinated engagements with the Russians. Their interests in such attacks were gain or personal fame. After the advent of Muridism, Shamil organized the Murids into a sophisticated order of battle based on a system of tens. Ten "greater" naïbs (famous leaders and devoted followers, the equivalents of generals) commanded 100 "regular" naïbs (unfailingly loyal, the equivalents of colonels), who in turn commanded 1,000 lesser naïbs or murshids (skilled tacticians, the equivalents of captains). Enlisted men and officers alike were motivated by the same burning passion: to free their lands of the infidel, where the term itself combined a secular (ethnic and political) and a religious (non-Muslim) meaning. Instead of gain and fame being the goal of engagements, they became by-products of service to God. The terms of that service were defined by the imam, the mouthpiece of God:

> Muridism was a heady brew of mystic and absolute power, though even after it had become, to the Russians, synonymous with resistance, it was variously interpreted: there were the Murids of the Tarikat who never took up arms, as opposed to the Murids of the Ghazavat who fought a Holy War fanatically. To these last there was no other interpretation of the Prophet's teachings. If to live in peace meant submitting to the Infidel rule, there could be no peace. While the Tarikat abhorred violence and, in the face of force, counseled a withdrawal to some inner spiritual sanctuary, this was not a doctrine which came easily to the fiery Caucasian tribes. Most of them felt that, in this issue, the Tarikat must be modified, or adapted, to meet the more bellicose tenets of the Koran, which promised short shrift to an Infidel foe. (Blanch, 1960: 58–59)

This analysis is remarkable in its reminder that, as a religious philosophy, Muridism in and of itself did not demand armed resistance. It is therefore not the arrival of Muridism in Daghestan, nor its revival in the 1820s, which explain the waxing resolve of the Caucasian tribes to resist imperial Russia. It is the winning out of a particular *interpretation* of Muridism by successive imams which made Muridism the potent force it became – a force which made political unity possible, bribery difficult, and self-sacrifice desirable.

Shamil's accession therefore marks both a shift in the quality of the forces opposed to Russia, and a shift in their interests: from fame, glory, and loot, to the ejection of infidel Russians from the territory of the Caucasus and the establishment of a theocracy to govern the lands from the Black Sea to the Caspian Sea.

## The Murid War

The Russian Empire's population in 1816 is given by Singer and Small as approximately 51 million, of which 800,000 were under arms (Singer & Small, 1983). Gammer gives the total number devoted to the Caucasus at 30,000 in the 1830s, escalating to 200,000 in the 1850s (Gammer, 1994: 24).[5] There are no satisfactory population and armed forces data for the Caucasian tribes,[6] though Gammer gives them at 200,000 and 40,000–50,000 respectively (Gammer, 1994: 22). There is therefore no controversy regarding the relative material power of the two actors: Russia was clearly the strong actor, and the Murids were the weak actor.

The Murid War featured three different strategic interactions. The first interaction, from 1827 to 1845 coincides with the accession of Paskyevitch and Grabbé to command of the Southern Front. Here the overall Russian strategy was barbarism punctuated by direct attacks on Murid strongholds. The Murids pursued a GWS throughout. The second interaction, from 1845 to 1855 coincides with the accession of Voronzov and Freitag to command. The beginning of this period featured a Russian direct attack strategy against a Murid GWS, though it ended with a return to barbarism. Finally, the third interaction, from 1855 to 1859 coincides with the accession of Bariatinsky and Yevdomikov to command. By this time, the main Russian strategy had switched to direct attacks and conciliation while, again, the Murids maintained a GWS.

## Interaction one: barbarism/conventional attack *vs.* GWS

Paskyevitch's tenure began uncertainly. He inherited the beginnings of a nationalist-religious uprising which had for the first time shown that the Russians could be defeated. The start of his command thus

---

[5] Gammer doesn't specify a time period here, but he presumably means during the 1830s. He also notes that more than 80 percent of these troops were regular army units (see below). Note that the lack of any change in relative power, combined with the large shift in the number of troops the Russians were willing to the fight, already suggests that Mack's proposed link between relative power and relative interests is weak at best.

[6] And by "Caucasian tribes" I mean Chechnia and Daghestan only. As will become clear below, these two areas constitute the geographic area during the phase of the asymmetric conflict in which we are chiefly interested.

coincides with both the apparent conquest of Daghestan, and the rise of Muridism (Baddeley, 1908: 237, 239).

The years 1827–30 passed quietly enough in terms of conflict, although, all during this time, the first Murid imams were discreetly gathering strength and adherents throughout the Caucasus. By 1831, however, Khazi Muhammad, first imam of Daghestan, had rallied a considerable body of dedicated troops and begun raids against tribes allied to Russia. His Murids experienced some successes, but overall their first attempts proved a failure. Muhammad was a learned and holy man: he simply lacked the charisma and strategic skills needed to exploit victories and maintain allies.

What emerges from accounts of battles in this early period is the theme of the importance of reputation in attracting alliance support. The Caucasus of the 1830s was a bandwagoning world:[7] success meant allies, defeat meant isolation.[8] Khazi Muhammad's final defeat came in an heroic defense-to-the-death of Gimri aôul, in which he lost his life and, though "mortally wounded," Shamil, his student and chief lieutenant, escaped.

The Russians responded to this religious threat in Chechnia and Daghestan by renewed barbarism:

> Greater Tchetchnia, in turn, was devastated with fire and sword, and a hatred sown and watered with blood, the traces of which are still visible after seventy years. (Baddeley, 1908: 275)

The ultimate effect of such policies was to guarantee the survival of Muridism of the Ghazavat. Russia had not yet gained the capacity to prosecute barbarism on a scale that could damage a Murid insurgency. Shamil recovered from his wounds in a short time and Russia's punitive raids guaranteed a ready audience for his message. From 1833 to 1837 the Murids grew stronger and stronger, uniting more and more tribes and forever demolishing the image of Russians as militarily invincible. Even Russian military victories only strengthened Shamil's grip (Baddeley, 1908: 304–305). Again and again, Russia's COIN strategy – kill everyone and destroy everything – backfired.

---

[7] Bandwagoning means that the more allies you have, the more you will attract; and the reverse is true also, the defection of any ally implies the defection of every ally. On bandwagoning and its interstate implications, see Walt, 1987: 19–21.

[8] This is the essence of the Guevara/Castro *foco* theory: in opposition to Mao's maxim that social organization must precede military adventures, Castro and Guevara held that in Latin America (Cuba specifically), military successes were a necessary precondition of social support. See e.g., Blaufarb and Tanham, 1989: 12.

In 1839, Shamil again escaped almost certain capture after the Russians surrounded and defeated his forces – after frightful losses on both sides – at Akhulgo. By 1840, however, he was once more on the offensive; and from 1840 to 1842, Shamil's Murids made themselves feared by Russia's regiments and allies. Shamil was careful during this period to avoid pitched battles; choosing instead to attack only weak or isolated forces, and withdrawing before help could arrive. From 1843 to 1844 it was therefore Shamil, and not the Russians, who enjoyed the military initiative (Baddeley, 1908: 364).

Paskyevitch, whose strategic plans favored the defensive, tended to play into Shamil's hands. Yet the Murids were not the only ones learning important lessons. On the Russian side, a talented group of Russian junior officers were learning both how to fight, and how *not* to fight, the Murids. In 1845 Paskyevitch was replaced by Count Voronzov.

## Interaction two: conventional attack *vs.* GWS

Arriving fresh from Nicholas's war room with new reinforcements and an impossibly ambitious battle plan, Voronzov's inquiries quickly convinced him of the folly of the tsar's strategy: an all-out offensive aimed at capturing or killing Shamil himself. Yet he was too faithful a servant to challenge his master's will. It was thus almost with a sense of predestined doom that Voronzov set out to capture Shamil in the very heart of Daghestan:

> If God is not pleased to bless us with success we shall nevertheless have done our duty, we shall not be to blame, and we can then turn, somewhat later, to the methodical system which will bear fruit, though of course not so quickly as a victory over Shamil himself.
>
> (Voronzov as quoted by Baddeley, 1908: 387)

Shamil had by this time acquired full mastery of the strategic and tactical requirements of defense against such adventures. His strategy was again a GWS: avoiding direct confrontation with the enemy on his outward march, abandoning even fortifications if necessary to avoid contact, and then attacking the retreating armies when supplies and morale were low, and when exhaustion and frostbite had weakened them:

> His opportunity would come later on when Nature, his great ally, had done her work, and the invaders, worn with toil, weak from privation, uninspirited by successes in the field, would have to face the

> homeward march over the barren mountains of Daghestan or through the forests of Itchkéria. Then indeed he would let loose on them his mobile hordes, break down the roads in front of them, seize every opportunity of cutting off front or rear guard, of throwing the centre with its weary baggage train and lengthy line of wounded into confusion, and give the men no rest by day or by night.[9]
>
> (Baddeley, 1908: 388)

In the event, Voronzov was only saved from complete annihilation by the bravery and foresight of General Freitag who, experienced in Caucasian warfare, had predicted almost exactly the fate of the expedition, and prepared in advance to relieve his superior upon the first hint of danger. This is what happened.

On June 15, Voronzov, opened his campaign to catch Shamil with 21,000 men, and 42 pieces of artillery (Gammer, 1994: 153). Voronzov chased the Murids to Andi Gates, where his spies had assured him Shamil would make a stand. He found the site abandoned and in ruins, its population already evacuated by Shamil. After waiting three weeks at the ruined site, Voronzov then had to decide whether to push ahead in the hope of catching Shamil at another fortress (Dargo), or to return empty handed to Tiflis (Tblisi). Voronzov decided to advance, but the difficulties of terrain, combined with the increasing drain on supplies, soon forced a halt. He compounded his error by sending a body of troops – half the combat strength of each unit in his order of battle – back along the march route to gain additional provisions and evacuate his wounded. This so-called "Biscuit Expedition" proved a disaster. All along the route, long stretched-out columns of Russian soldiers became isolated. Following Suvorov's maxim that "the head doesn't wait for the tail," impetuous Russian vanguards rushed ahead and were cut off from supply units carrying wounded. The Murids then attacked and annihilated the isolated columns piecemeal. As the wounded multiplied, the columns slowed still further.

---

[9] Shamil's strategy was the same as that used by the Russians against Napoleon during his invasion of Russia. Then it was the Russians who avoided confrontation, destroyed crops in the path of the invader, and waited until "General Winter" had weakened and dispersed French formations. Yet here, scarcely thirty years later, was Vorontsov playing the part of Bonaparte, marching toward almost certain destruction at the head of an overconfident, overburdened army. Moreover, Vorontsov had not arrived from St. Petersburg unaccompanied: on the contrary, his reputation and fame provoked dozens of Russia's noble sons to flock to his standard in search of glory in the Caucasus. To the hostile and snowy wastes of Daghestan, these dandies brought elaborate tea services, personal slaves, plush tents and carpets, meticulously tailored uniforms, brandies, pheasants, and fine cigars.

The expedition returned, but it cost Voronzov dearly. Only after reaching Shamil's capital, Dargo, and finding it, like Andi Gates, abandoned and in ruins, did the magnitude of Voronzov's position become clear to him: isolated deep within the mountains, surrounded on all sides by nimble and well-supplied foes, he realized that even to regain the foothills would take a miracle. Quickly he gave the order to withdraw, and the entire formation began the retreat. Almost unbelievably, Voronzov's withdrawal was plagued by the same mindless adherence to maxims which nearly destroyed the Biscuit Expedition. Once again, the columns became separated. Once again, the nimble Murids cut the isolated formations to ribbons. As casualties mounted and food and ammunition dwindled to nothing, Voronzov sent five couriers to seek help from General Freitag. Amazingly, all five couriers reached Freitag, who set off without delay to relieve Voronzov. Gammer gives Voronzov's losses at 984 killed (including three generals), 2,753 wounded, 179 missing, 3 guns, a great sum of money in coins, and all the expedition's baggage (Gammer, 1994: 156). Freitag's foresight saved Voronzov's expedition; and Voronzov, true to his earlier pronouncement, then set about organizing a more methodical destruction of Shamil and the subsequent conquest of the Caucasus. Over the next decade, this involved nothing more complicated or less deadly than the deforestation of Chechnia.

The year 1845 was to mark the high point of Murid power. In 1846, Shamil attempted a conventional military offensive against Russian positions in Kabardia. His hope was that Kabardia's people would rise up spontaneously in support of Muridism, and his bold stroke would completely sever Russian communications while leaving the Murids in control of a continuous geographic space between the Caspian and Black Seas. In the event, Shamil failed, mainly due to the bravery and doggedness of Freitag. Freitag, fully alerted to the strategic consequences of failure, immediately set off in pursuit of Shamil's invading Murid cavalry with a woefully inadequate hodge-podge of garrison troops, Cossacks, and regular army formations. Shamil, isolated from his vaunted intelligence resources, did not realize that the force pursuing him was so weak. Neither, it turned out, did the Kabardians, who waited to see the outcome of the contest before declaring their support. After unexpected resistance at a Kabardian fort, Shamil faced the prospect of being trapped between a stubborn fort, and a "relief force" headed by the much respected Freitag. He withdrew, and later set about fulfilling his promise of prosecuting the steady and methodical conquest of the Caucasus.

## Interaction three: conciliation *vs.* GWS

Into this final period, from 1854 to 1859, marches the last of the famous names among Russia's commanders in the Caucasus: Bariatinsky. Voronzov had set about undermining Shamil's power base in two ways. First, he accelerated the deforestation of Chechnia. Second, he fostered the concentration and development of Russia's artillery. Cleared forests and wide roads made way for the heavy guns, which were then positioned, with frightful losses, so as to batter the Murid strongholds into dust one by one. Moreover, it finally occurred to the Russians that the source of Shamil's foodstuffs, horses, ammunition, and powder was in fact Chechnia. Voronzov therefore tasked Bariatinsky with systematically interdicting the Murids' logistical support, which further weakened Shamil.

Without sufficient supplies, Murid offensives became more and more difficult to mount. This victory drought led in turn to a weakening of alliance support, and in this period once staunch allies began to defect to Russia: at first a trickle, then later a flood.[10]

Bariatinsky, who eventually replaced the aging Voronzov, added the final blow by initiating a heretofore unprecedented policy: clemency. This was a policy the Murids did not expect, and it was one to which they proved powerless to respond.

> Three things brought about Shamil's defeat. The cumulative force of Russian arms ... the leadership of Prince Bariatinsky, who was appointed supreme commander in place of the old ailing Voronzov; above all, Shamil's cause was lost by internal dissensions ... Terror had always been [Shamil's] strongest weapon: it was ever the guiding force in Asiatic warfare. Now Bariatinsky's clemency was proving the stronger weapon. The tribes feared Russian guns – but not Russian vengeance. They had discovered their enemy to be terrible in battle, but magnanimous in conquest. So they ceded over in their thousands, leaving Shamil and his remaining Murids isolated, a diminishing force, withdrawing each day farther into the high mountains.
>
> (Blanch, 1960: 390–391)

---

[10] This implies that a *sine qua non* of effective GWS is a strong degree of social organization which makes bribery and coercion ineffective. The defection of the tribes suggests that Muridism was no substitute for nationalism as we have come to know it in the post-World War I context. For a general discussion of the relationship of nationalism to armed resistance, see Wolf, 1973.

Bariatinsky's clemency strategy was unconventional from the Russian point of view, and it proved effective. Although Shamil lost fewer troops in every engagement than the Russians, his ability to replace these losses constantly diminished. Russia could always draw on resources far beyond Shamil's reach; whereas Shamil's resources, human and material, were constantly and increasingly within Russia's grasp; a fact which, once fully appreciated by Russia, was turned to such advantage that it ultimately led to Shamil's defeat.

It is very likely, in other words, that had the Chechens not already been weakened by decades of punitive raids, the Russians would never have been able to cut the trees. With the forests intact, it would have been as difficult as ever to bring heavy artillery to bear on the mountains. Finally, Bariatinsky's clemency may have been taken for weakness, as Yermolov had previously warned.

## Outcome: Russia wins

The final Murid fortress, Gounib, fell on August 25, 1859. Shamil surrendered, and Blanch argues that he did so this time because only in this way could he guarantee the safety of his family (Blanch, 1960: 408; Gammer, 1994: 286).

Thus did the Russians finally conquer the Caucasus after nearly sixty years of costly struggle. During the course of the conflict Russian military strategy varied depending on the philosophy of the general in command of operations there, as well as the particular tsar ruling in St. Petersburg. After the Napoleonic Wars, the Southern Front's first commander, Mikhail Yermolov, introduced barbarism: a strategy that demanded the use of methods proscribed in European warfare, such as the killing of non-combatants, torture, rape, and the despoiling of wells, crops, and livestock. These things of course happen in every war, but Yermolov made them *policy*. These were adopted by Paskyevitch, and resorted to later by Voronzov as well.

Yet, in every case, barbarism's effectiveness proved mixed. For every short-term military advantage gained, the Russians suffered a corresponding political cost. Ultimately, barbarism made it impossible to coerce the Caucasian tribes; and if they couldn't be coerced, they could *only* be destroyed; and that only at a tremendous cost in lives and treasure.

The three interactions coincide with the fortunes of each side, and explain as much or more than any other factor, the outcome of the war. Yermolov's barbarism worked militarily. Its impact was such that he was able to declare the subjugation of the tribes in 1825. Russia employed an indirect strategy and the tribes had responded with an indirect strategy. Yet Russia had not yet developed the logistical reach necessary to make the barbarism decisive. As a result, the barbarism Yermolov and Paskyevitch unleashed against the Caucasian tribes – isolated and devastated – left smoldering embers. The Murids – Khazi Muhammad, Hamzad Beg, and Shamil, successively fanned those embers into an inferno which nearly succeeded in ejecting the infidel Russians from the Caucasian theater. The greatest successes of the Murids coincided with the period of greatest strategic opposition: Russia employed a direct strategy, and the Murids countered with an indirect strategy. Yet the Russians did not give up. They switched strategies yet again to the indirect strategy of conciliation, to which the Murids had no other answer than their own indirect strategy, GWS.

Bariatinsky's conciliation strategy deserves special mention for two reasons. First, unlike all previous strategies, its aim was more to end the war than to win it. Bariatinsky was the first commander to treat his enemies as warriors and men instead of bandits and savages. He sought to persuade human beings, rather than destroy animals. He treated prisoners in accord with European standards, abolished torture and rape, and provided food and clothing to the women and children of his defeated adversaries. Second, such a policy would have been impossible under Nicholas I. Like his grandfather, Alexander II was a reformer and a firm believer in the power of kindness toward a defeated enemy.

## Analysis: competing explanations of the Murid War's outcome

The Russian Empire won the Murid War, and its victory is in most ways a perfect representative of asymmetric conflict outcomes during the first fifty years of the 200-year period of examination that comprises this book's analytical interest. In keeping with the spirit of the times, it was widely viewed as a conflict which pitted a civilized nation against "unruly savages," and, as such it was one in which few limitations in the quantity or quality (barbarism) were observed. Before comparing the relative explanatory merits of nature of actor, arms diffusion, and interest asymmetry explanations of the outcome, two additional points should be established.

First, relative power appears to have overwhelmed the effects of all competing arguments, including even strategic interaction. That is, the overwhelming advantage of the Russian Empire – and, most importantly, its unflagging resolve to employ those resources for an indefinite period – provides the most satisfying and intuitive explanation of the war's outcome. Second, this extreme cost insensitivity was only made possible by the fact of an absolute ruler and an illiterate population. The distribution of both conditions across time and space is limited, which makes this case a tougher test of competing explanations of asymmetric conflict outcomes.

That said, there are a great many lessons to be learned from how the war was fought independent of its outcome. Strategic interaction explains why victory cost the Russian Empire so much more – in time, blood, and treasure – than any other great power could have been willing to pay under similar circumstances. Regime type proved vital for both strong and weak actors, arms diffusion played a small and unexpected role, and leadership, terrain, and climate were also important parts of the explanation of this particular war and its outcome. Interest asymmetry is not much use in explaining this war.

Assessing the relative explanatory merits of competing explanations of asymmetric conflict requires answering four basic questions. First, what were the interests of the actors prior to the conflict and how are these best explained? Second, what was each actor's regime type, and how did this affect strategy and political vulnerability? Third, what role did military arms diffusion play in the conflict's outcome? Finally, what were the strategies each side employed, what was the rationale given for their selection or change, and how did they affect the eventual outcome of the war?

## Actor interests

Russia's interests were not explained by its material power relative to that of the Murids. Russia's interests appear to have been settled in the geopolitical context of the late eighteenth century, and to have simply continued momentum after that. In the context of Russia as an empire, its interests must best be described as expansion. Less obviously, the fact that Russia's tsars were both secular and religious leaders meant that opposition to the will of the Tsar had the aspect of opposition to God – especially when the opposition came from non-Christians. The very existence of resistance therefore became a *casus belli*.

The Murids fought for their survival, but they also maintained the positive goal of ejecting Russia from the Caucasus. The negative goal could be explained by their relative material power, but not the positive goal.

## Regime types, strategy, and vulnerability

As noted above, Russia's regime type was virtually unique in its day: an essentially feudal empire ruled by an autocrat. How did this affect Russia's strategy and political vulnerability?

The effects on strategy were mixed. On the one hand, debates among Russia's political elites revolved around two questions: (1) when would the tribes be subdued?, and (2) how many men would it take? The question of strategy was largely left up to Southern Front commanders: Yermolov, Paskyevitch, Voronzov, and Bariatinsky. In any case, authoritarian Russia had no need to consult Russian public opinion before committing resources to the fight. Nor would it be held accountable for failure, delay, or barbarism. On the other hand, the personal preferences of the tsars did affect strategy in two cases. First, Nicholas sent Count Voronzov to the Caucasus with both massive reinforcements and a specific plan and timetable for their use. Second, after Nicholas's death, his son Alexander II made it clear that barbarism would not be a strategic option. He fully supported Bariatinsky's use of clemency, bribes, and concessions in order to demobilize Shamil's remaining allies.

In terms of political vulnerability, Russia's regime type effectively precluded this. According to the interest asymmetry argument, we should expect to see even authoritarian regimes subject to trade-off constraints when involved in prolonged conflicts. The practical result is a similar degree of political vulnerability as that expected in democratic regimes. But do we see it here? In fact, Russia was involved in two potentially serious interstate conflicts during the Murid War, and neither caused the expected vulnerability.

Its first fight was with Persia in 1826, just prior to the advent of Muridism. The Persians invaded from the south, and threatened to capture Georgia. Fought on conventional terms, the ponderous Persians were time and again defeated by much smaller Russian formations. The second potential source of Russian vulnerability was the Crimean War (1853–56). This war affected the conduct of the Murid War in two ways. First, and most obviously, the troops mobilized to relieve

Sevastopol were transferred from the Crimea to the Caucasus immediately upon the war's end.[11] This meant a quick and significant influx of fresh troops for Russia. Second, and more importantly, the outcome of the Crimean War removed all hope of relief or support from either Britain or the Ottomans. Gammer and Baddeley both argue that this proved a crushing blow to Shamil's morale, convincing him for the first time that his war with Russia was hopeless, and eventually infecting his forces with resignation (Gammer, 1994: 291; Baddeley, 1908: 459).

In short, we don't see the trade-off's mechanism in this case. There is in fact no sense of political vulnerability either in Russia's willingness to fight in the Caucasus or its soldiers' conduct there, *at all*.[12]

Merom's democratic social squeamishness argument receives mixed support. On the one hand, no comparable democratic regime (and few authoritarian ones) could have sustained such costs in order to defeat Shamil. On the other hand, the proximate cause of Shamil's downfall was not brutality – which had been tried before but had never proven decisive – but kindness.

## Arms diffusion

Military technology played a relatively minor role in the Murid War. In the first interactions of the war, Russian military technology – including firearms, artillery, and even clothing – were much more poorly adapted to warfare in Chechnia or in Daghestan than that of their adversaries. In this sense, their technology was less advanced. Yet, as time passed, this situation improved to the point where Russian military technology equaled that of their adversaries, and in artillery far surpassed it.

As all the commentators agree, artillery proved to be the decisive technology, but its effectiveness depended on very specific circumstances, and on strategy and doctrine (Baddeley, 1908: xxxii). For example, the Russians generally launched campaigns from forts situated in low hills or plains near river systems. Even had the Murids gained artillery capability (as they in fact did briefly), its utility against the Russians in these forts would have required (1) considerable escort

---

[11] And note that Russia's defeat did not weaken the tsar's authority or imply a change of regime.

[12] Again, see Baddeley, 1908: 236.

to counter the Cossack cavalry formations which would be operating in their ideal environment, and (2) the capacity to advance against forts by sap and mine – capabilities neither the mountain Murids nor the forest Chechens possessed. When the Murids did attempt to employ captured Russian artillery against the Russians, they met with disaster. First, their lack of skill with the technology caused them to miss their targets, but, more importantly, Shamyl's insistence on hanging on to the guns once the engagement turned disastrous cost the Murids heavy casualties.

For their part, the Russians were only able to employ artillery effectively after they had deforested Chechnia, and come to accept the high casualty rates necessary to advance and position the guns to destroy Murid fortifications (Blanch, 1960: 90).

## Strategic interaction

If relative power doesn't explain relative interests, and regime type explains political vulnerability (or, in this case, its absence), what best explains the outcome of the Murid War?

I argue that it is strategic interaction, but with an important caveat.[13] Given the disparity in material resources between the two actors, and given the constancy of their interests over time, it is remarkable that the Murid War lasted twenty-nine years. As has been made clear in this case, there are three reasons it took so long to subdue the Murids. First, the terrain and climate made offensive operations very difficult, even assuming the best leadership, training, and equipment. Second, there is the problem of Russian arrogance and incompetence, both of which caused the Russians to underestimate their adversaries. Third, and most importantly, the Murids' GWS systematically sacrificed fortresses for time. When Yermolov prosecuted a barbarism strategy against the Caucasian tribes, Russia won. When, after Paskyevitch, Voronzov switched to a direct attack strategy, the Murids won. And when, finally, Bariatinsky switched to a conciliation strategy, the Russians won. The final strategic interaction, "same approach," ended the war.

---

[13] The caveat is that for authoritarian regimes with large populations, the implied lack of cost sensitivity tends to overwhelm all other factors. Fortunately, the distribution of such regimes is low: China and Iran may be the only contemporary analogues of nineteenth-century Russia.

## Conclusion

The Murid War was an asymmetric conflict between the Russian Empire, and a coalition of Caucasian tribes under the banner of Muridism.

Russian interests were higher than that expected by the interest asymmetry argument. Russia wanted to conquer and annex the Caucasus, and it was willing to spend hundreds of thousands of lives, millions of rubles, and over half a century to accomplish this objective. Russia's dubious possession of Georgia proved to be one of two reasons Russia refused to abandon its crusade in the Caucasus, even after Catherine's decision to leave Russia's possessions there fallow, and Paul's wish to abandon them altogether.[14] As an ally, Georgia's contribution to the war effort was neither inconsiderable nor decisive; though it gave the Russians a huge strategic advantage, lying as it did between another Muslim power, the Ottoman Empire, and Russia's Muslim foes. Access to Georgia's ports on the Black Sea also made it possible to ship supplies and reinforcements from Odessa or Sevastopol.

Its only real strategic interest, therefore, lay in its desire to protect Georgia. It is impossible to argue, however, that the possession of Georgia itself materially or strategically benefited the Russian Empire in any reasonable proportion to the resources Russia was to expend to secure Georgia by conquering the Caucasus.

Murid interests were in establishing their political and religious independence from Russia. To achieve this aim the Murids were willing to fight to the end – and they did.

In sum, hypothesis 8 – relative material power explains relative interests in the outcome of an asymmetric conflict – is not supported in the Murid War. Relative power proved a poor predictor of relative interests in this case – at least on the Russian side. Did relative interests explain political vulnerability?

Russia was simply not politically vulnerable. According to the interest asymmetry argument, its preponderance should have made it

---

[14] The other reason was simple ethnic chauvinism: how dare these "ignorant savages" resist the will of the great white tsar? The language of both the commentators and original sources makes this view of the Caucasians clear: they are constantly referred to as savages, and their behavior is described as cunning where Europeans are described as brave or brilliant. The resistance of these "uncultured children" to the tsar was therefore constructed as an affront to civilization itself.

politically vulnerable. The lack of a serious threat from the Caucasus should have made even an authoritarian Russia sensitive to resource trade-offs, and politically vulnerable in this sense. Yet, during the Murid War, Russia faced two potentially serious interstate conflicts, and neither caused the expected vulnerability. Strong actor regime type therefore matters more than is allowed by the interest asymmetry argument.

Is the nature-of-actor argument therefore a better explanation of the outcome of the Murid War than strategic interaction? No. Regime type remained constant on both sides, but the fortunes of each side varied markedly during the war's three interactions. Regime type had little effect on the strategies chosen or prosecuted by either side. On the Russian side, what may be said is that Nicholas often lent a direct hand in strategic planning, and often with detrimental effects. It should also be added that merit was hardly the basis for assignment to command in the Southern Front: on the contrary, Russian officers with politically unpalatable ideas, or running from debts, or suffering from broken hearts, often ended up in command in the Caucasus. On the Murid side, what may be said is that Shamil's authority for a time transcended all ethnic and territorial cleavages to make possible a sophisticated and effective GWS. Unlike the Russian army, advancement and command in the Murid army was based exclusively on merit. But, as can be readily appreciated, the differences between the two sides are not artifacts of their regime types, which were the same.

Arms diffusion played almost no role in the Murid War, but its limited impact was the opposite of that predicted by the logic of the arms diffusion argument: the possession of modern artillery pieces by the Murids led them to abandon their comparative advantages in mobility and seriously weakened them. Hypothesis 6 – the better armed a weak actor is, the more likely it is that a strong actor will lose an asymmetric conflict – is therefore not supported in the Murid War.

In terms of strategic interaction, the war played itself out in three interactions. During the first interaction, the strategic interaction was same-approach: the Russians pursued a barbarism strategy and the Murids a GWS. The Russians won militarily, but the political consequences of this first interaction led to the rise of militant Muridism. During the second interaction, the strategic interaction was opposite-approach: the Russians pursued a conventional attack strategy and the Murids continued their GWS. The Murids won. But, during the final interaction, the strategic interaction switched to same-approach again:

the Russians pursued a conciliation (indirect) strategy and the Murids, again, GWS. The Russians won, and Shamil went into exile. With one important caveat, then, hypothesis 5 – strong actors are more likely to win same-approach interactions and lose opposite-approach interactions – receives considerable support. The caveat is that the *outcome* of the war was determined more by the unwavering application of unlimited resources than by strategic interaction. On the other hand, the costs to the Russian Empire in time, lives, and treasure is best explained by strategic interaction.

In sum, if we wish to explain why Russia won the Murid War, we cannot rely on relative power alone. Relative power clearly mattered. But what mattered most was strategic interaction.

# 4    Britain in Orange Free State and Transvaal: the South African War, 1899–1902

> They were conquerors, and for that you want only brute force – nothing to boast of, when you have it, since your strength is just an accident arising from the weakness of others. They grabbed what they could get for the sake of what was to be got. It was just robbery with violence, aggravated murder on a great scale, and men going at it blind – as is very proper for those who tackle a darkness. The conquest of the earth, which mostly means the taking it away from whose who have a different complexion or slightly flatter noses than ourselves, is not a pretty thing when you look into it too much. What redeems it is the idea only. An idea at the back of it; not a sentimental pretense but an idea; and an unselfish belief in the idea – something you can set up, and bow down before, and offer a sacrifice to . . .     Conrad, *Heart of Darkness* (1985)

The war between the British Empire and the governments of Transvaal and Orange Free State which began on October 11, 1899, was once called the Anglo-Boer War, or Boer War for short, but historians now call it "The South African War " in recognition of the important role played in it by black Africans.

## The South African theater

European interest in South Africa has its origins in the development of trade contacts with India and the Far East. It was in this context that the first major European economic and security interest – Cape Town – was established by the Dutch East India company in 1652. The Dutch subsequently lost and regained the town, and the colony, until the close of the Napoleonic Wars (1815), at which time Britain finally and firmly established its rule. Britain sought to establish a colony which could safeguard its security interests, while at the same time ameliorating domestic unemployment and unrest. In 1820, 4000 British settlers arrived at Cape Town:

> These nineteenth-century British immigrants, however, did not assimilate into the Afrikaner population as earlier French Huguenot and German arrivals had done. They came from an urbanized, industrializing society in Britain and in South Africa they tended to settle in the towns, the largest of which therefore became predominantly English-speaking. (Smith, 1996: 15–16)

This urban–rural split exacerbated ethnic and linguistic differences, and eventually laid the roots for two convictions. On the British side, immigrants became convinced of their ethnic superiority to local Afrikaners (Smith, 1996: 16). At the same time Afrikaners came to be suspicious that these *Uitlanders* (outlanders) were not interested in sharing power or property in South Africa, but only in capturing it all for themselves. This was especially true after Britain's parliament outlawed slavery in the Colony in 1834. Since slavery was seen then to be vital to the rural economy, many Boer were deeply embittered by this blow to their way of life. The abolition of slavery thus prompted a mass emigration into the South African interior – an emigration now known as The Great Trek (1835–37). Thousands of Boer families took to wagons with all their property, and at great personal risk (many were attacked and killed by the then powerful African tribes such as the Xhosa and Zulu), moved inland, eventually to establish the Boer republics of Natal, Orange Free State, and further north and east, Transvaal.

These were difficult times for the Afrikaners, who ran into hostile and numerous African tribes along the way. From the African perspective, the times were darker still. White settlers poured into their ancestral lands, more often than not killing or enslaving them as they advanced. Atrocities took place on both sides as native Africans were steadily displaced and dispossessed. In 1838, the Boer general Pretorious defeated the Zulu king Dingaan at the Battle of Blood River, and Afrikaners began to concentrate in Natal. By 1843, however, the British had annexed Natal and, five years later, Transorangia (later to become Orange Free State). After a number of sometimes bloody disagreements between the Boer trekkers and the Crown, however, Britain eventually agreed to allow limited autonomy for the two inland Boer republics, Transvaal (1852) and Orange Free State (1854).

There followed nearly three decades of relative peace. In 1870, diamonds were discovered in Kimberley, a town between Orange Free State and Cape Colony (later quickly and illegitimately annexed by Britain in 1871). The "diamond rush" of 1870–71 brought a considerable influx of Uitlanders – which included the then 18-year-old Cecil Rhodes – into the previously pastoral and rural communities of Orange Free State. The miners and prospectors drank and gambled, and were an early shock to the conservative, pious, and hard-working Boer farmers who still constituted a majority within the republics.

These tensions were only aggravated after Sir Theophilus Shepstone announced by proclamation the annexation of Transvaal as a British Crown Colony in 1877. This move was deeply resented by the Boers, who argued that the move was a direct violation of the Sand River Convention of 1852, in which Britain had previously guaranteed their sovereignty.

Disagreements and bitterness aside, Britain's *de jure* sovereignty in South Africa implied British *de facto* responsibility for the security of Europeans within its declared jurisdictions:

> Thus British power succeeded in achieving for the Transvaal state what the Afrikaners had been too weak to achieve for themselves. British annexation may have removed their "sacred independence" but by the end of 1879 it had also secured the Transvaal against its most powerful African neighbours. This crucial development freed the Afrikaners to make a bid to regain their independence during the following year. (Smith, 1996: 28)

In 1879 the British destroyed the Zulus as a military force. The Zulus had been the last major African tribe to resist white imperialism in South Africa. With this last threat to Boer survival eliminated, the stage was set for a major confrontation between the Boer and the British. Although Shepstone's annexation proclamation had promised Transvaalers "a separate government, with its own laws and legislature," after 1879 "the territory was ruled directly, as a Crown Colony, in a tactless, authoritarian way . . ." (Smith, 1996: 28).

As resistance in Transvaal mounted, and threatened to spill into open rebellion, Transvaal's President Kruger waited for the results of a general election in Britain. The election brought Gladstone and the Liberals to power, and Kruger waited for policy to change in accordance with Gladstone's speeches on British policy in South Africa:

> In the Transvaal, declared Gladstone, "we have chosen most unwisely, I am tempted to say insanely, to place ourselves in the strange predicament of the free subjects of a monarchy going to coerce the free

subjects of a republic to compel them to accept a citizenship which they refuse". (Smith, 1996: 29)

Yet, once in power, Gladstone balked: how could he trust the prospect of a South African confederation to the uncultured hands of the likes of Kruger and his cronies? In the event, Gladstone refused to grant Transvaal its own sovereignty and soon the whole region was in open revolt. The three-month war culminated in a humiliating British defeat at the Battle of Majuba Hill (February 27, 1881):

> The battle, in which only a few hundred troops were engaged and where British losses, including the death of Colley himself, accounted for about a third of the total for the whole war, soon acquired great symbolic importance. Like the failure to relieve General Gordon at Khartoum, it came to be regarded in Britain as a blot upon the national honour which Conservatives pointed to as an example of Liberal mismanagement. "Remember Majuba" became the rallying cry with which many British soldiers were to go into action in 1899.
>
> (Smith, 1996: 31–32)

Thus, by 1884, three years after the Battle and two years before the discovery of gold, Transvaal became the South African Republic *officially* in the London Conventions. All the powers of a sovereign and independent state save the right to determine foreign policy (and expand beyond current borders) thus reverted to the Republic.

Then came the discovery of gold at Witwatersrand in 1886. The gold rush which followed had three important effects. First, it led to a massive new influx of Uitlanders. It transformed the demography and economies of the Boer republics. Second, the discovery of gold created for Kruger the problem of maintaining Boer control of the state,[1] while at the same time providing him the opportunity to use the revenues to buttress his state's physical security and independence by purchasing arms and maintaining a state monopoly on dynamite manufacture (Smith, 1996: 54).

---

[1] This problem, which was to become for the British a primary *casus belli*, revolved around the question of the franchise. The Transvaal, for example, restricted the franchise to Afrikaner burghers by means of legal requirements for residency. This meant the burgeoning population (a majority in Transvaal) of Uitlanders were not allowed the vote, and their protests over disenfranchisement, sent even to Queen Victoria herself, allowed Britain to use the franchise issue to disparage the Boers as corrupt and authoritarian in the local and British press.

Kruger also granted a railroad concession (another monopoly) to a Dutch company. Both decisions were to prove crucial during the first interaction of the later war. Third, the gold and diamonds created extremely wealthy (and hence powerful) extra-state interests in the region. The conservative – and by British standards corrupt – government of "peasants" led by Kruger was a constant thorn in the side of the region's great capitalists, such as Cecil Rhodes and Alfred Beit. These wealthy men were hardly shy of using their influence to undermine Kruger, and their meddling ultimately culminated in the fiasco of the Jameson Raid.

On December 29, 1895, Dr. Leander Starr Jameson and 500 Chartered Company[2] police rode across the border into Transvaal in an attempt to spark a rebellion of Uitlanders in Johannesburg, providing a pretext for British intervention in Transvaal. No rebellion occurred, and Jameson's raiders were defeated and forced to a humiliating surrender at the battle of Doornkop.

The main effects of the Jameson Raid were three. First, it provided a powerful impetus to the development of an Afrikaner nationalism which had been sparked at Majuba Hill. Second, it confirmed in the minds of Kruger and Steyn (his Orange Free State counterpart) that Britain was behind attempts to take back Transvaal's sovereignty. Third, it caused Kruger to prepare seriously for war, most especially by building forts and investing in the latest and best military equipment.

## The eve of war: British interests

British interests in the fate of South Africa were overwhelmingly represented by two individuals: first, and foremost, Alfred Milner; second, Joseph Chamberlain, colonial secretary. Milner, as British high commissioner, was the Empire's "man on the spot"; while Chamberlain, as colonial secretary, was responsible for reporting to the queen, Cabinet, and Parliament on all of the Empire's colonial affairs. Milner was convinced of the absolute necessity of a show of military force in order to coerce the Boers into ceding sovereignty (essentially, acceding to annexation); and then later, into abiding by whatever concessions the Boer granted while under such duress (Pakenham, 1979: 77).

---

[2] The chartered company was owned and run by the multimillionaire and then prime minister of Cape Colony, Cecil Rhodes.

Convinced that annexation by force was the only way to assure British control over the two republics,[3] Milner fretted over the prospect of peace:

> What could be more alarming than the prospect of Kruger's conces-
> sions leading to a settlement that he and every British South African
> were certain would prove to be a sham? "Very great feeling of depres-
> sion," he wrote on 23 July, "as I can see no good is coming of the long
> struggle against S.A.R. misgovernment. British public opinion is going
> to be befooled and that is the long and short of it."
>
> (Pakenham, 1979: 82)

This passage highlights the importance key political elites placed on the power of British public opinion.[4] And in this case public opinion was to be "managed" by means of the press, which was believed to exercise a direct influence on British public opinion:

> But Milner's other cronies from his *Pall Mall* days were now in a
> position to show their loyalty, and show it they did . . .
>   All these newspapers taught British public opinion in the last
> few weeks of the dangers of delay, and of being fobbed off without
> a settlement on the franchise. It was *The Morning Post* and *The
> Times*, both staunchly pro-government, that banged the jingo drum
> loudest. (Pakenham, 1979: 86)

Milner exercised a great deal of influence over Chamberlain. He was not only charismatic, but connected. Milner pushed and bullied and threatened and cajoled in order to get his 10,000 troops sent to Natal. Now, under Milner's breathtakingly comprehensive pressure, Chamberlain was to put a particular spin on Kruger's latest proposals which would foreclose any chance of a negotiated settlement:

---

[3] Milner's concept of control included certain good intentions. He believed Kruger and his cronies were anachronisms well gotten rid of, and that Milner's own administration would raise the level of civilization of all the people living in the republics, whether Boer or British.

[4] Here is Pakenham's paraphrase of Milner regarding the threat of a British public undermining "the tough necessities" of Britain's South Africa policies: "Above all, the 'unctuous rectitude' (quoting Rhodes's famous sneer) of the British public must not be allowed to ruin the settlement. No votes for the coloured people in the Transvaal at all costs. There was only one set of laws in the Transvaal that the Uitlanders considered really 'excellent': The laws 'to keep the niggers in their place'" (Pakenham, 1979: 123–124). This passage is important for two reasons. First it counts as evidence of what Mack would call "political vulnerability." Second, the passage highlights the hypocrisy of Britain's position regarding South Africa's blacks. In his arguments to the Cabinet (Pakenham, 1979: 113, 520), Chamberlain went so far as to argue that South Africa's blacks would be better off as British subjects (it was a base lie).

> The final proof of this came from [Kruger's] latest offer. To couple the offer of a five-year franchise with two conditions he *knew* to be unacceptable – on suzerainty and non-interference on behalf of British subjects – this conclusively proved that he did not "want peace". The only way to make him disgorge the franchise was to put a pistol to his head.
>
> The Uitlanders [non-Dutch colonists] were treated like "an inferior race, little better than the Kaffirs or Indians whose oppression has formed the subject of many complaints". (Pakenham, 1979: 91)

But was the franchise really the *casus belli* the British made it out to be? No. Even as a justification for war to the British public, it had serious drawbacks:

> [The franchise] may have served its turn "to get things forrarder" in South Africa and as a "splendid battle cry" to rally the support of British public opinion, but Chamberlain knew that if it came to a *casus belli*, grounds for this would have to be found elsewhere. British public opinion would not support a resort to war over the difference between a seven or a five years' franchise. (Smith, 1996: 314)

In other words, British policymakers were constrained in their arguments and actions by a sense of what the British public would or would not accept. But Jan Smuts and other Boer moderates were not privy to such information, and as a result they crafted a peace proposal designed to assess Britain's true intentions. Britain's rejection of the proposal confirmed to Smuts and Kruger that the franchise was not the real issue, the real issue was instead "British supremacy and Transvaal subservience" (Smith, 1996: 354).

There is another important feature of Chamberlain's arguments to the Cabinet: precedent-setting effects:[5]

> But the issue now went further than the grievances of Uitlanders, or natives. What was now at stake was no less than "the position of Great Britain in South Africa – and with it the estimate formed of our power and influence in our colonies and throughout the world". Such were Chamberlain's formal arguments to the Cabinet. (Pakenham, 1979: 91)

In effect, Chamberlain argued that if Britain didn't threaten the use of force, "others" would think Britain weak and seek to take advantage of

---

[5] In *The Geography of Ethnic Violence*, Monica Duffy Toft elaborates the difficulties multi-ethnic states face in negotiating settlements short of violence with independence-minded ethnic groups when doing so will set a precedent for other groups (Toft, 2003).

that weakness. Keeping in mind that Victorian Britain possessed a sprawling colonial empire, this was a serious consideration. But Chamberlain had a final argument based on his low opinion of Boer culture and resolve. He argued that sending troops would make their use unnecessary because Kruger was bluffing, and faced with force he would back down (Pakenham, 1979: 91–92).

But did the British want war? Did their interests extend so far as to risk an all-out fight with the tiny Boer republics? It's a difficult question to answer, but the question of Britain's war-willingness is important if we accept that a willingness to expend blood and treasure *in a war* is a good indicator of vital interests. The less willing to fight a war, the less vital the interests at stake.[6]

Smith argues that in fact the British did not want war, and his indicator of British intentions is Britain's lack of military preparations for war (Smith, 1996: 337–338). But there is one obvious problem with this interpretation: there may have been other reasons why Britain did not seriously prepare for a war in South Africa. Chief among these reasons is lack of regard for the military capabilities of one's adversary.[7] Smith himself notes that the British were used to "small wars" which required very few troops to prosecute (Smith, 1996: 3). He also makes it clear that the British did not rate the Boer military threat very highly (Smith, 1996: 339). Pakenham takes the argument a step further:

> Only a few days after his arrival Lansdowne cabled to ask his views about the first crucial questions. [Penn Symons's] reply: a mere two thousand extra troops would make Natal safe right up to its northern apex (hemmed in though it was by the two republics).
>
> (Pakenham, 1979: 74)

---

[6] There were economic interests – gold and diamonds – in South Africa which commentators have long argued were the real reason Britain was willing to go to war. The most notable such argument was leveled by the socialist J. A. Hobson, then correspondent for the *Manchester Guardian*. In his influential book, *The South African War: Its Causes and Effects*, Hobson argued that British policy was hostage to capitalist interests, especially those of the "goldbugs," such as Cecil Rhodes and Alfred Beit (Hobson, 1900). Subsequent scholarship has refuted this thesis soundly (see Smith, 1996: 393–412). But even had it not been refuted, the argument would have reduced to the claim that South Africa counted as a vital British interest, one over which it was willing to fight and die.

[7] Another interpretation is that the British were unprepared for *any* military action of a serious nature. For a thorough discussion of Britain's overall lack of preparedness for a major war, see Hamer, (1970: chap. 6). Hamer shows that British lack of preparedness was not specific to the fight in South Africa, but would have been evident in anything *other* than a "small war."

The real question was, what would the Boer do? In September, the two Boer republics could field a total of 54,000 men, whereas Britain had a total of 10,000 men to guard Natal and Cape Colony. If the Boer attacked, would they seek to directly engage these garrison forces in strength, or would they adopt a raiding strategy, pushing only a few thousand commandos into Natal and the Cape? British military intelligence, under the command of Major-General Sir John Ardagh, predicted a raiding strategy:

> How did Ardagh and his department come to this conclusion, that would seem so astounding in the light of events? *Military Notes* gives the answer: the Boers were not regarded as a serious military adversary. As fighting men, they were expected to be inferior to the Boers who had beaten Colley's small force at Majuba. Boer generals, used to fighting Kaffirs, knew nothing of handling large bodies of men . . .
> (Pakenham, 1979: 74–75)

There is, of course, no way to definitively establish Britain's willingness to go to war. However, as these passages make clear, "preparations for war" in this context does not make a good indicator of British intentions. Moreover, the weight of documentary evidence available suggests that whatever Britain wanted, Milner had his heart set on war as the only means of accomplishing British political objectives in South Africa. In short, the British *did* want war, but not the war they got.

## The eve of war: Boer interests

We have established that Britain wanted to annex the republics, take over their political and economic management, and thereby facilitate the establishment of a unified political space – a South African Federation – under British control. What then were the Boer interests?[8]

Essentially, the two Boer republics – Orange Free State under the leadership of Steyn, and Transvaal under the leadership of Kruger – wanted political independence from Britain. In negotiations leading up

---

[8] To be fair and accurate there *were* no "Boer" interests: "Despite the direct and painful testimony of Boer generals and participants on commando, the rifts and divisions on the Boer side tended to be glossed over. An Afrikaner nation did not exist in 1899 and Afrikaners in different parts of South Africa had been moulded in different contexts and states by very different experiences during the course of the nineteenth century. There were more "Boers" in the Cape Colony than in the two Boer republics." (Smith, 1996: 7). However, we may nevertheless discern a common denominator across republics: freedom from British rule.

to war, the Boer proved themselves remarkably pragmatic and willing to compromise on many of the key issues – for example, the franchise – raised by Chamberlain and Milner. Yet by the eve of war two features of this conflict of interests made war inevitable. First, Britain had tipped its hand and made it clear that it would accept nothing less than annexation, while the Boer made it equally clear that although they were willing to redress a number of British grievances, they were not willing to compromise on the key issue of sovereignty. Second, neither side trusted the other's declarations and overtures. To make matters worse, the British dramatically underestimated both the Boer military capacity, and their resolve to use that capacity. The end result was that both sides exchanged ultimatums, and when the conditions of neither were met, the Boer mobilized for war.[9]

## The South African War

Smith provides the most cogent summary of the South African War in terms of its historical importance, and its relevance to our central question:

> The South African War of 1899–1902 was the most extensive, costly and humiliating war fought by Britain between the defeat of Napoleon in 1815 and the outbreak of the First World War in 1914. It involved over four times as many troops as the Crimean War and cost more than three times as much in money. It was a colonial war, by far the largest and most taxing such war fought by Britain during the century of her imperial pre-eminence, and the greatest of the wars which accompanied the European scramble for Africa. The British government resorted to war in 1899 to end a situation of Boer–British rivalry over the Transvaal, where political power was concentrated in Boer hands; to advance the cause of South African unification; and to establish British power and supremacy in southern Africa on a firmer basis. Two Boer republics ... fought for their independence in an anti-colonial war against full incorporation into the British Empire. The combined Afrikaner population, of what were then two of the world's smallest states, amounted to less than 250,000. By March 1900, some 200,000 British and Empire troops were involved in a war in South Africa with Boer forces fielding less than 45,000. (Smith, 1996: 1)

---

[9] Although the Boer initiated the war, this is only of technical interest. Britain is responsible for the war itself: on this there is no disagreement.

There is no controversy concerning the relative power of the two sides in this fight. The UK was the strong actor, while the two Boer republics – even including the possible support of citizens from Cape Colony and Natal – were out-powered well in excess of 5:1.

## Interaction one: conventional attack *vs.* conventional defense

*October–December, 1899*

In the initial interaction of the war the Boer locally outnumbered the British garrisons – in Cape Colony and Natal – by 3:1. Here is Pakenham's characterization of Boer strategic thinking as the likelihood of war became more certain:

> [Smuts] then launched into a feverish plan for a military offensive. Its keynote was a blitzkrieg against Natal before any reinforcements could arrive. The numerical advantage would then lie in their favour by nearly three to one – that is, forty thousand Boers against fifteen thousand British troops. By throwing all their troops against Natal, they would capture Durban before the first ships brought British reinforcements. In this way they could capture artillery and stores "in enormous quantities". They would also encourage the Cape Afrikaners in the interior to "form themselves into a third great republic". The international repercussions, Smuts continues, would be dramatic. It would cause "an immediate shaking of the British Empire in a very important part of it". Britain's enemies – France, Russia, and Germany – would hasten to exploit Britain's collapse.[10]
>
> (Pakenham, 1979: 102–103)

The first half of Smuts's vision seems hardly controversial in light of events. What damned this otherwise fine strategic plan was *time* and the hesitation of Orange Free State's President Steyn. All through September Steyn hesitated as the British troop-ships steamed ever nearer Durban. By the time both republics mobilized it was too late. By 9 October the majority of British troop-ships had already landed at Durban.

---

[10] Although the strategy itself is sound, it is difficult to read this sort of domino reasoning without, first, recalling similar reasoning on the part of the Japanese prior to their attack on Pearl Harbor in 1941; and, second, realizing how common such thinking was in that day. Milner and the British were certainly thinking along similar lines.

And as to Boer tactics, equipment, and training, it must be added that although capable of conventional offensives against regular forces in fortified positions, their organization and training hardly made them ideal prosecutors of Smuts's strategy:

> Their elected civilian leaders were made commandants – appointed, that is, to lead the five hundred to two thousand burghers of each commando in battle. In this commando system, it was no one's job to train the burghers... the men were left to fight as they had always fought – with the tactics of the mounted frontiersman. If the enemy were superior in numbers, they would provoke the enemy's attack, dismount, take cover and shoot, remount and ride away. In European military manuals it was a formula known as "strategic offensive, tactical defensive". The Boers had never seen the manuals.
>
> (Pakenham, 1979: 105)

The war started with attacks by Boer commandos (essentially, mounted infantry with light artillery support) against the British in three areas: Dundee to the south, Mafeking to the north, and Kimberley to the northwest.

The British were dangerously exposed north of the Tugela river in Natal. Britain's general on the spot, Sir George White, wondered whether he should withdraw from Dundee to positions south of the Tugela, and he was answered in the negative by both local military authority (the Dundee garrison's commander, Sir Penn Symons) – who did not consider the Boers much of a military adversary – and by political authority (Natal's governor, Sir Walter Hely-Hutchinson) – because it would encourage the Zulus to revolt (Pakenham, 1979: 109).[11]

The first armed clash of the war took place on October 20 at Talana Hill just outside Dundee in Natal. The Boer were under the command of Lucas Meyer, and the British were under the command of Penn Symons, who was just sitting down to breakfast as the first Boer shells plunged into Dundee. Symons was neither a fool nor a military genius. He organized the defense of Dundee "by the book." His tactics in engaging the Boer were: (1) artillery preparation; (2) infantry attack (ending with a charge with fixed bayonets); and finally, (3) a cavalry charge to "cut off the enemy's retreat." And although a number of his subordinates worried about the target that closely packed troops might

---

[11] Milner later made similar arguments and issued similarly dire warnings regarding the revolutionary potential of the Cape Afrikaners in the event of military defeat or a lack of sufficient military presence in the Cape.

present to sustained and rapid rifle fire, Symons also believed in keeping his infantry in close rather than open order (so as to maximize punch). In this Symons was to prove wrong, but he should not be blamed as careless or incompetent on that account because, as Pakenham notes, "In the whole of Europe there was no body of soldiers that had ever seen the concentrated fire of the magazine rifle, with the muzzle end facing them" (Pakenham, 1979: 132).

In effect, the curtain had just risen on a match between a highly mobile Boer military organization outfitted with dramatically augmented firepower,[12] and a ponderous, hidebound, and overconfident yet superior (in terms of numbers) British imperial army.

In the battle itself, in which the British won the artillery duel (eighteen guns against three), Symons and many of his officers and infantry died forcing the Boer commandos off Talana Hill, only to discover that most of Meyer's commando had escaped on horseback. Unbeknownst to Symons, his cavalry, which was supposed to cut off Meyer's retreat, had run into trouble and surrendered hours earlier. The British thus won the hill, but did they win the battle?

The fight for Talana Hill proved typical of most encounters between the British and Boers up until "Black Week" in December. Although the Boer often had better guns, they were never locally sufficient to alter the outcome of the "second act" of the three-act pattern initiated by Symons and his peer commanders in the early interactions of the war. British infantry tended to rush straight against an entrenched Boer infantry in close order, sustaining heavy casualties against the concentrated firepower of the new Mausers. To the British officers leading their men into battle, the advent of smokeless powder proved to be disconcerting to say the least. To the British, the dug-in Boer were invisible until the advancing infantry were right on top of them. This made it difficult for officers on the ground to disperse, concentrate, advance, and retreat their infantry effectively. The result was high casualties. After fixing bayonets for the final charge, the British usually found their objective abandoned: a few dead Boer and in the distance, a majority of the commando trotting away on horseback. Where the British in fact *had* cavalry, as in the case of Boer General Kock's premature advance against White at Ladysmith, decisive – if brutal – outcomes were

---

[12] Kruger's foresight had armed the Boers with the Mauser '98 – an accurate, reliable, magazine-fed, breech-loading rifle firing smokeless rounds.

possible.[13] However, the British never had a sufficient cavalry presence in South Africa to counter Boer hit-and-run tactics.[14]

In the next few weeks the two forces met in battle after battle, which the British had the worst of. In November, White was trapped at Ladysmith and all pretense of a short war ended. White's internment at Ladysmith was perhaps the greatest British strategic blunder of the war. White had in fact already been ordered to fall back south of the Tugela River in the event of encountering superior forces. His orders, in other words, were to avoid becoming besieged at all costs. How then did it happen, and why?

Essentially, White believed – as all his peers at that time – that the Boer were not a worthy military opponent; and that fighting ability aside, their morale would be so fragile that one decisive British victory would send them packing. Yet he was outnumbered by Joubert, the famous Boer general, by two to one. What made him willing to risk entrapment by offering battle against his specific orders? Pakenham provides an answer worth quoting at length:

> To some extent, [White] was merely expressing the conventional British general's ignorance of the realities of large-scale war. For half a century Britain had fought small wars against the disunited and ill-armed tribesmen of India and Africa. Often these wars had begun with

[13] A British journalist on the scene provides the following description of the cavalry charge against Kock's retreating commando at Elandslaagte: "The charge of two hundred horsemen galloping across a plain is designed to be an irresistible force. It does not stop simply because the enemy would like to surrender ... The charging line of horsemen caught them broadside, like the steel prow of a destroyer smashing into the side of a wooden boat. People heard the crunch of the impact – and saw the flash of the officers' revolvers, and heard the screams of the Boers trying to give themselves up ... Back came the cavalry for a second charge. ('Most excellent pig-sticking ... for about ten minutes, the bag being about sixty,' said one of the officers later.) Again the shouts and screams ... But a story had got round that the Boers had abused a flag of truce and, anyway, the order was: no prisoners" (Pakenham, 1979: 143–144).

[14] Three problems arose in relation to fielding an effective cavalry in South Africa. First, the British found it impossible to get enough horses in theater. They stripped horses from other colonies as far away as India and Australia. But the transport took a heavy toll, and those horses which survived to reach the theater were often too weak to be used as cavalry mounts. Second, the climate and terrain of South Africa was hard on horses, who not only needed extra time to acclimatize, but could not afterward be used in sustained galloping (which killed them). By the time the British understood this, they had effectively destroyed their existing cavalry as a fighting force. Finally, the later British policy of farm-burning (a COIN strategy) had the effect of restricting the mobility of cavalry formations to the railways, because the policy not only destroyed forage for Boer horses, it destroyed forage for *any* horses. In the end, the British gave up trying to employ cavalry, and hit upon the wiser strategy of imitating the Boer by using their horses as mounts for trained infantry.

shattering reverses; small bodies of men, surrounded by savages who gave no quarter, had fought to the last cartridge. In due course, the main British army would come on the scene and inflict a crushing and permanent defeat on the enemy. There was little strategic, or even tactical, maneuvering, by European standards. To transport and supply his men in desert or jungle – that was the chief problem of the British general. The actual fighting was usually simple by comparison. So it had been for Roberts in Afghanistan, Wolseley in Egypt and Kitchener at Omdurman. The campaign might take months, but the decisive battle could be fought in a matter of hours. War was a one-day event, as practised on Salisbury Plain. Hence it was as natural for White to try to deal a knock-down blow to Joubert, as for Symons to try to deal one against Lucas Meyer. (Pakenham, 1979: 155)

White's forces were beaten in the field by the Boer on November 2, and White retreated to Ladysmith, where he and his remaining troops remained trapped until February 28, 1900. By the end of the first week of November 1899, the British had been effectively bottled up in three sieges: Kekewich was stuck with Cecil Rhodes in Kimberley, Baden-Powell was under siege at Mafeking, and White was trapped with his "field force" at Ladysmith. The three sieges significantly complicated the military campaign against the Boers, because White's entrapment (and for political reasons, Cecil Rhodes's in Kimberley) now forced the British to divide their forces in order to relieve the sieges, instead of concentrating them for an irresistible rush toward the Boer capital cities.

### Black Week: December 11–18, 1899

The task of relieving these sieges first fell to the South African theater's new commander-in-chief, Redvers Buller. Lord Methuen, advancing to relieve Kimberley, was repulsed by well-entrenched Boer at Magersfontein on December 11. On December 15, while rushing to relieve White at Ladysmith, Buller was himself repulsed by entrenched Boer under the skillful command of Louis Botha – one of the youngest and most capable of the Boer generals. Three days after this reverse, Buller was relieved of his command and replaced by Lord Roberts, with Lord Kitchener as Roberts's chief of staff.

This last week of reverses came to be known as "Black Week" in the British press. In fact, although the military situation was actually favoring the British at the end of December – they had, after all, taken the offensive, and the Boers, although inflicting higher-than-usual (for the

British) casualties, were in retreat – public outrage over the week's reverses reached crisis proportions. This outrage had in fact become a constraint on Britain's conduct of the war:

> To expand the British army in South Africa was not merely a question of recruiting the troops, hiring the ships, and sending them steaming off to South Africa. It was complicated by two political pressure waves, freak storms of public opinion, now making the windows rattle in Whitehall... The second was ominous for the whole world: a shock-wave of Anglophobia vibrating across the Continent, precipitated by the war, and prolonged by Britain's failure to win it.
>
> (Pakenham, 1979: 257)

Again, perceptively I think, Pakenham continues trying to isolate what lay at the root of British public concern over Black Week. He argues that it was "disappointment in victory so long delayed":

> The people of Britain had had war on the cheap for half a century. Small wars against savages: the big-game rifle against the spear and the raw-hide shield. Small casualties – for the British. To lose more than a hundred British soldiers killed in battle was a disaster suffered only twice since the Mutiny. Now, in 1899, they had sent out the biggest overseas expedition in British history to subdue one of the world's smallest nations. It would have been odd if the public had not shared the government's confidence in a walk-over. The resulting casualties were thought shattering: seven hundred killed in action or dead of wounds, three thousand wounded since October... This was at the root of the public's humiliation. Then the spasm of bitterness passed. (Pakenham, 1979: 258)

This passage highlights two key issues: the context of British casualty sensitivity, and the degree to which pride and shame motivated British actions. And what of British war aims? Now that the costs were mounting, what of the anticipated gains? Paraphrasing Asquith, Pakenham adds:

> But he warned people that it would be "grotesque" to get these reverses out of proportion. He compared the present "humiliations and mortifications" with periods of real national crisis during the Napoleonic War or the Indian Mutiny. How would Marlborough, Wellington or Havelock have survived this ordeal by telegraph – every blow they struck and every blow they received made subject to hourly scrutiny by the public? The struggle now went much deeper than a mere question of "asserting and maintaining our position in South Africa. It is our title to be known as a world power which is now upon trial." (Pakenham, 1979: 258)

If the war had not begun as a vital security interest for the British, Asquith's remarks make it clear that it had now become one.[15] This passage also points to what may be the first media complaint regarding the clash between a public's access to information about the costs and conduct of a war, and the degrees of freedom granted local military authorities in winning it. As will become clear in the next interaction of the war, it would not be the last such complaint.

With the accession of Roberts and Kitchener to command – and more importantly the arrival of massive British reinforcements – the final stage of the first interaction of the war was now set. There were blunders on both sides, but by the end of June 1900, Roberts's "steamroller" had captured Bloemfontein (March 13), Johannesburg (May 31), and finally, Pretoria (June 5). In the euphoria over his capture of Bloemfontein, Roberts issued his first proclamation (March 15): amnesty for Boer regulars (they could keep their property if they turned in their rifles and swore an oath of neutrality) but not for Boer leaders.[16] The three sieges had also been raised; Kimberley (February 15), Ladysmith (February 28), and Mafeking (May 17).

The war was over – or rather, it should have been. But Roberts's triumphant march to Pretoria marked the close of only *the first third* of the war, which was due to stretch on, in much more brutal form, for another two years.


## Interaction two: conventional attack *vs.* GWS

### *Bloemfontein to Pretoria: March–June, 1900*

The second interaction of the war had its genesis, on the Boer side, in failure. Christiaan De Wet – among the most talented of the Boer generals, and in fact the single most talented *guerrilla* leader, – thought through the pros and cons of a Boer shift to a GWS after General Cronje's surrender at Paardeburg:

---

[15] This opinion was shared by the Gladstonian (Liberal) wing's most outspoken member, Henry Labouchère, who "now declared his belief in the doctrine of 'my country right or wrong'. The danger of Britain's being humiliated in front of the other Great Powers, he said, outweighed the moral disadvantages" (Pakenham, 1979: 267).
[16] Roberts believed his capture of Bloemfontein would "knock all the fight" out of the Orange Free State burghers, and "left to themselves, [they would] accept the amnesty, take the oath of allegiance, and disperse to their homes" (Pakenham, 1979: 400).

But [De Wet] had seen enough to realize that, quite apart from the blunders of Boer generals like Cronje, the overwhelming numerical superiority of the British now demanded new strategy from the Boers. Indeed, the commando system was best suited not to large-scale, set-piece battles, but to smaller-scale, guerrilla strikes. A smaller group could make better use of their best asset, mobility; and their worst defect, indiscipline, would prove less of a handicap.

(Pakenham, 1979: 348)

The British had made mistakes too. First, underestimating their adversary, and second, failing to adapt their forces and tactics to exploit vulnerabilities in the Boer method of fighting. But the British, who had, after all, "won," showed little interest in learning from their mistakes. After his capture of the Boer capitals, Roberts returned to a hero's welcome in London. Kitchener replaced Roberts as commander-in-chief in November of 1900, and was not interested in the mistakes of other British generals:

> Kitchener displayed no interest in learning from the mistakes of Buller and Methuen. He probably attributed their own failures, as Roberts did, to their lack of self-confidence. Of the revolution in tactics – of the new, invisible war of the rifle-plus-trench – he showed himself supremely unaware. (Pakenham, 1979: 351)

Other British generals, however, *had* worried about the tactical and strategic difficulties presented by the enemy, terrain, and climate. As early as October of 1899, Buller had planned to build and equip a large force of irregular colonial troops trained to fight like the Boer. It was Buller who had foreseen the problem of lack of mobility, and it was Buller who anticipated the Boer's switch to GWS (and its rationale):

> In this type of pioneering, colonial society, there was no highly organized machinery of administration, and the central government carried little influence or authority. "Time has not yet glorified the seat of Government with a halo of sentiment," wrote Buller. "To every man his own home is the capital. Hence there is no commanding centre by the occupation of which the whole country or even a whole district can be brought into subjection; no vital spot at which a single blow can be struck that will paralyse every member of the body. There are living organisms which can be divided into a multitude of fragments without destroying the individual life of each fragment.
>
> (Pakenham, 1979: 398)

This was part of Buller's warning to Roberts: the Boer were a body with no head. But as we have already seen, Roberts had little faith in Buller's opinion:

> Roberts... stuck to the conventional idea of surrender. Capture the capital and you have cut off the head of the enemy. Their spirit must die too. And he had long intended to use political means – the kind that was often used in Indian frontier wars – to smooth his march to Pretoria. On 15 March he offered an amnesty for every Free State burgher except the leaders. (Pakenham, 1979: 399)

The British were therefore slow to realize their strategy was not going to win the war. They continued to hold to the idea of capturing values and offering limited amnesty as a way to end Boer resistance.[17] The Boer, by contrast, began planning for a new strategy right after the capture of Bloemfontein.

That strategy was GWS. Its chief architect was De Wet, who put forward his arguments for a strategic shift at a war council held just four days after Roberts's capture of Bloemfontein. The strategy had three key elements. First, it needed a new kind of force – one made up exclusively of men who were fiercely dedicated to the Boer cause. After the fall of Bloemfontein, De Wet sent his exhausted commando home on ten days furlough, fully aware that many of them would not come back. But this was by design: those who did return could be counted on. Second, it needed a force which could operate independently of the ox-driven wagon trains which typically accompanied Boer commandos in the field. Third, De Wet urged a switch from attacking concentrations of British troops, to attacking British communications, which were extremely vulnerable. Above all, De Wet argued that even a few small victories could rally the morale of the burghers far out of proportion to their military impact (Pakenham, 1979: 408–409).

The new strategy thus promised new hope – at least of avoiding defeat. Something else – something vital – was not discussed as part of the war council's deliberations: the presumption of British moral conduct in war. One reason the Boer had developed as a mobile military organization – including mobile transport – was precisely due to the character of warfare against native African tribes, who did not often respect the notion of noncombatant immunity. Boer trekkers thus kept

---

[17] This would not last long, however. Within a month, Roberts would detach fully half his forces – 20,000 men – to both guard his communications and begin the process of looting and burning farms as a COIN strategy (see below).

their women and children on wheels, ready to flee their farms on short notice. But since the destruction of the Xhosa and Zulu as military threats, the Boer had become more settled and less mobile. This meant values exposed to the British. But as De Wet makes clear in his later account of the war, it never occurred to the war council to question the safety of Boer women and children under British occupation:

> Many a smart, well-bred daughter rode on horseback and urged the cattle on, in order to keep out of the hands of the pursuers as long as at all possible, and not to be carried away to the concentration camps, which the British called Refugee Camps (Camps of Refuge). How incorrect, indeed! Could any one ever have thought before the war that the twentieth century could show such barbarities? No. Any one knows that in war, cruelties more horrible than murder can take place, but that such direct and indirect murder should have been committed against defenceless women and children is a thing which I should have staked my head could never have happened in a war waged by the civilized English nation. (De Wet, 1902: 192–193)

Of course, not all those attending the war council had such faith in British moral restraint. Louis Botha, commanding the last effective conventional Boer army in the field, objected to the change in strategy on humanitarian grounds:

> But, however practicable, was a guerrilla war a "civilized war"? This was the question that obviously troubled the consciences of the Transvaal leaders, especially Botha, and explains why they clung so long to the strategy of regular warfare on the eastern front. Botha must have read enough military history – Smuts certainly had – to know what a guerrilla war inevitably entails for civilians. Sherman's march through Georgia, the Prussian treatment of the French *franc-tireurs*; they cast ugly shadows on the veld, these international precedents. And a guerrilla war in South Africa, however gentlemanly the main combatants professed to be, threatened to have elements of savagery absent from warfare in more civilized states.[18] (Pakenham, 1979: 500)

---

[18] This is a critical debate. Key members of both sides appeared to accept the idea that a portion – ranging from negligible to complete – of the responsibility for the depredations which often form the heart of COIN operations is often placed on the defenders. So it was during the concentration camps controversy (see below). When cornered in Parliament on the issue of Britain's farm-burning and camp policy, for example, Lord Broderick answered "for the twentieth time, that the policy of sweeping the country had been forced on them by the guerrillas. Some of the women had been assisting the enemy; others had been abandoned by them; none of them could be simply left out on the veld to starve"

On May 3, Roberts resumed his irresistible advance to Pretoria by way of Johannesburg. He detached half his force – 20,000 men – to guard his line of communications and to begin COIN operations designed to deny support to De Wet by disarming Boer farmers and burning "selected" farms whose men were away on commando.

## Interaction three: barbarism *vs.* GWS

This marked the beginning of a COIN strategy which would later harden into barbarism. As Roberts approached Johannesburg, he nego-tiated an armistice with the Boer defenders. They agreed to surrender the town to the British on one condition: that they be granted 24 hours to extract their army (including, it turned out, ammunition, supplies, and gold bullion). In retrospect it seems a blunder on Roberts's part.

Part of the failure, ironically, must be blamed on the very strategy Roberts had set into motion in dividing his forces: barbarism. There is almost always a gap between the initiation of such a strategy and its expected military impact. This creates an early danger that barbarism – in this case, burning farms and forcing women and children into con-centration camps – will stimulate the resolve of the resistance while only having a negligible impact on guerrilla operations. This is what happened here; many burghers had accepted Britain's amnesty offers and returned to their farms, only to find them burned, their cattle dead, and their women and children missing. They were outraged, and many returned to fight with De Wet, Jan Smuts, and Koos De la Rey.

(Pakenham, 1979: 540). The Boers themselves appeared to accept this argument in part, "here was a daunting moral problem. Was it fair to the volk (women and children, as well as the menfolk) to involve them in such a savage kind of war? For the women and children it would be like a return to the dark pages of voortrekker history, when their grandparents had struggled against the Kaffirs: women and children pressed into service, each farm a commissary and an arsenal; their homes looted and burnt; then forced to choose between going as refugees to the cities, or following the laagers into battle" (Pakenham, 1979: 500). The real issue, which would come to dominate international conventions on the laws of war in the next century, was whether, as Pakenham argues, such consequences were inevitable. In Europe's past, dominated as it was by sovereigns who derived their legiti-macy by "divine right," or who occupied the position of defender of the faith, rebellion and heresy were closely related, and neither were protected by the laws of war governing the treatment of prisoners, the granting of quarter, or conduct toward noncombatants in rebel areas. On the contrary, sovereigns, and later states, were permitted to use any force or depredation necessary to crush rebellion and stamp out heresy (Parker, 1994: 43). This slowly changed over the years, so that by the time of the famous Hague Convention of 1899, the matter of rebellion received considerable attention. The issue was not resolved there, however, nor was it resolved in the 1907 convention that followed (Roberts, 1994: 121–122).

For his part, as Roberts advanced, he became frustrated with the delayed victory. Where were the Boer armies to resist his advance? Why wouldn't they stand and fight? All along his advance from Johannesburg to Pretoria, De Wet and the other guerrilla generals harassed his communications, captured his troops and supplies, and generally humiliated his strung-out troops. As a result, Roberts's new COIN strategy was about to take a more systematic and more brutal turn.

Roberts reached Pretoria and marched through its abandoned, dusty streets, on June 5, 1900. During the next five months, as he continued his advance through the last Boer towns to the east, he waited in vain for the approach of Kruger, Steyn, or any of the Boer generals – De la Rey, De Wet, Smuts, or Botha – for terms of surrender. In November he sailed for England, while Kitchener took over as the new commander-in-chief. Under Kitchener's command, the farm burning continued and intensified. It may have made sound military sense, but it was not easy to prosecute – at least not at first:

> The worst moment is when you first come to the house. The people thought we had called for refreshments, and one of the women went to get milk. Then we had to tell them that we had to burn the place down. I simply didn't know which way to look . . .
>
> I gave the inmates, three women and some children, ten minutes to clear their clothes and things out of the house, and my men then fetched bundles of straw and we proceeded to burn it down. The old grandmother was very angry . . . most of them, however, were too miserable to curse. The women cried and the children stood by holding on to them looking with large frightened eyes at the burning house. They won't forget that sight, I'll bet a sovereign, not even when they grow up. We rode away and left them, a forlorn little group, standing among their household goods – beds, furniture, and gimcracks strewn about the veldt; the crackling of fire in their ears, and smoke and flames streaming overhead. (Pakenham, 1979: 466–467)

The practice of burning farms – ostensibly only those of "rebels" but in practice nearly every farm in reach – came to involve much more than just burning farm *houses*. Horses were taken, and cattle were either taken or slaughtered. By the time a British patrol had done its duty, in other words, they had effectively deprived noncombatants of food and shelter. The British decided to solve this problem by putting the women, children, and old men into concentration camps, for their own safety.

93

In theory at least this would have been a brilliant COIN strategy. On the one hand, the British could argue that, after all, they couldn't just *leave* these women and children to fend for themselves against the elements, including black Africans. On the other hand, the real purpose of the practice – to deprive the guerrillas of intelligence and logistical support – could be kept secret (Krebs, 1992: 41–42).

The problem with the theory was that neither Roberts nor Kitchener ever concerned themselves with logistical matters, and for this reason British forces had suffered a far higher percentage of post-battle casualties than usual. To put it bluntly, Roberts had left the management of his field hospitals in thoroughly incompetent hands. That, plus his own "reform" of the system of regimental supply, and the direct actions of the guerrillas themselves, had caused thousands of casualties – not only from battle, but from typhoid. Now these same defects were to strike down and ruin the benevolent justification for the internment of Boer noncombatants. Women and children began to die in the camps, and they began to die in alarming numbers.[19]

The Boer war may count as the first major war in which the literate soldiers of a democratic government participated. Many of the steamers and trains coming from and going to London contained *mail* – letters to and from the homes of regular soldiers in the field. The British public too, as we have already observed, was both literate and able to influence British foreign policy. The British public found out about the conditions in the camps, and the alarming death rate, through the efforts of a well-meaning humanitarian relief worker named Emily Hobhouse.

Hobhouse began her tour of the camps in January of 1901, and what she saw horrified her: poor sanitation, starvation rations, insufficient clean water, and insufferable crowding. By April she had seen enough. She raced back to England to report, and her report proved to be a political bombshell:

---

[19] In May of 1901 there were 93,940 whites and 24,457 blacks in these "camps of refuge." The death tolls had been rising steadily, and alarmingly, for months. In May, 550 died; in June, 782; in July, 1675. By October the death rates were 34.4 percent per year for whites of all ages – 62.9 percent for children in the Orange River Colony, and 58.5 percent for children in Transvaal. "At individual camps like Mafeking, the October figures represented an annual death-rate of 173 percent" (Pakenham, 1979: 548). Pakenham calculates that "at least twenty thousand whites and twelve thousand coloured people had died in the concentration camps, the majority from epidemics of measles and typhoid that could have been avoided" (Pakenham, 1979: 549).

instantly, the sentiment of the country was aroused and had it been allowed its true expression, not only would the camps then and there have been adequately reformed, but very possibly the war would also have dwindled in popularity and been ended.

Government officials feared just such an occurrence.

(Krebs, 1992: 52)

Lloyd George and the Liberals made a great deal of the conditions of the camps, and it is in these speeches in Parliament we find supporting evidence for the claim that even as early as 1900 the British recognized a norm of noncombatant immunity, the violation of which was considered sufficient grounds for a change of government:

> Why pursue this disgraceful policy, he asked; why make war against women and children? It was the men that were their enemies. "By every rule of civilized war we were bound to treat the women and children as non-combatants." The novel method of warfare adopted was all the more disgraceful because it would prolong, not shorten, the war. "We want to make loyal British subjects of these people. Is this the way to do it? Brave men will forget injuries to themselves much more readily than they will insults, indignities, and wrongs to their women and children." He concluded ... "When children are being treated in this way and dying, we are simply ranging the deepest passions of the human heart against British rule in Africa ... It will always be remembered that this is the way British rule started there, and this is the method by which it was brought about". (Pakenham, 1979: 539–540)

In the end, the government did not change. There were three reasons for this. First, the Liberal Party was itself divided on the issue of Britain's war with the Boer. Second, the British public was divided as well: some felt that the Boers were to blame for their suffering and for the conditions in the camps.[20] Others were rightly horrified at the thought of British participation in a system which had such fatal consequences for women and children. Third, the problems of the camps were not mysteries, nor were they expensive to correct. While the political crisis over the camps raged through August, effective reforms

---

[20] Hobhouse's tour was later repeated by special commissions from both the government and the opposition. The government's commission was headed by Millicent Fawcett, who blamed many of the conditions in the camps on the "filthy and superstitious habits" of the Boer women themselves: "Boer women were 'ill-nature[d]', unnatural. British women, it was understood, would not make war. The Boers were seen as primitive, unchanged since their arrival in South Africa from Holland two hundred years earlier. This put them on a lower scale of civilisation than the British, different in what would have been seen as a racial way while they were also a different class – a nation of peasants" (Krebs, 1992: 44).

followed in September. By October the death-rates had stabilized and then began to plummet sharply.

In the meantime, the war itself proceeded apace. Kitchener inherited an army of 120,000 regulars and 20,000 irregulars with which to oppose a Boer fighting force of at most 20,000. He divided his troops into more mobile columns, which he then sent out after the Boer commandos much as one would beat the brush for game. The strategy – essentially a search and destroy mission on a massive scale – was inefficient and destructive. It was inefficient because the Boer were still so much more mobile than the British, and the constant wearing away at them had reduced the average size of effective units to as low as one or two hundred. It was destructive not only of Boer farms and cattle, but of British horses and morale.[21] Kitchener's next innovation was the use of barbed wire and blockhouses to create a massive net covering the countryside:

> On the periphery, the barriers served as offensive, not defensive, weapons; not as cordons to keep out the enemy, but as cages in which to trap them, a guerrilla-catching net stretched across South Africa. By May 1902, there would be over eight thousand blockhouses, covering 3,700 miles, guarded by at least fifty thousand white troops and sixteen thousand African scouts. (Pakenham, 1979: 569)

The blockhouse and barbed wire net was expensive, but combined with all the other measures it finally broke the back of Boer resistance. The farm burning and concentration camps made it impossible for the Boer commandos to replace mounts or replenish their food supplies, and it made intelligence spotty. This resulted in close calls, where only luck and over-riding horses saved many commandos from capture. In addition, the British had begun arming native Africans and employing them as scouts and spies. The effects of this innovation were dramatic: suddenly the ponderous British columns began to find their "game." Finally, Kitchener and his staff hit upon a novel idea: why not stop the practice of shipping Boer women and children off to concentration camps?

---

[21] Here Pakenham quotes Allenby on the hardships of COIN operations: "The struggle, as described in Allenby's letters, took shape and dissolved like a fog. There were no lines or fronts, no battles – mere skirmishes with an invisible enemy, whose only aim, apparently, was to run faster than their pursuers ... The physical strain of the three-month trek, and the moral stain of making war on women and children, left him exhausted and ill" (Pakenham, 1979: 527).

Viewed as a gesture to the Liberals . . . it was a shrewd political move. It also made excellent military sense, as it greatly handicapped the guerrillas, now that the drives were in full swing. Indeed, this was perhaps the most effective of all anti-guerrilla weapons, as would soon emerge. It was effective precisely because, contrary to the Liberals' convictions, it was less humane than bringing them into the camps, though this was of no great concern to Kitchener.

(Pakenham, 1979: 581)

Another problem had already plagued the Boer war effort: what to do with prisoners. Unlike Boer prisoners, who remained prisoners throughout the remainder of the war, British prisoners were often returned to their own lines within hours of being captured:

It is much to be regretted that we were unable to keep them, for had we been in a position to do so, the world would have been astonished at their number. But unfortunately we were now unable to retain any of our prisoners. We had no St. Helena, Ceylon or Bermuda, whither we could send them. Thus, whilst every prisoner which the English captured meant one less man for us, the thousands of prisoners we took from the English were no loss to them at all, for in most cases it was only a few hours before they could fight again. (De Wet, 1902: 227)

It is a tribute to the dedication and skill of commanders such as De Wet, Smuts, and De la Rey that the Boer war effort lasted as long as it did against such overwhelming odds. Surrender terms were signed in Pretoria on 31 May 1902.

## Outcome: Britain wins

Although all concerned agreed that Kitchener would eventually capture or destroy all the remaining commandos, the decision to surrender was far from easy or settled. At the war council that finally decided the issue there were six arguments for why the Boer should seek terms from the British:

no food for women and children, and no means to continue the war; the concentration camps (this was for propaganda purposes; Botha had actually admitted "one is only too thankful nowadays to know that our wives are under English protection"; the "unbearable" conditions caused by Kaffirs . . . Kitchener's proclamation of 7 August, which threatened the confiscation of burghers' land; the impossibility of keeping British prisoners; in short, no hope of success . . . The delegates voted for Kitchener's peace by an overwhelming majority:

> fifty four to six. It was the bitter end, but the alliance stood firm.
> (Pakenham, 1979: 603–604)

Britain had already officially annexed Orange Free State – renamed Orange River Colony – back in May of 1900; and it annexed Transvaal in October of that year. Now the fighting ended, and Milner could at last preside over the formation of a federated South African Republic. Here Pakenham sums up the outcome of the war:

> In money and lives, no British war since 1815 had been so prodigal. That "tea-time" war, Milner's little "Armageddon", which was expected to be over by Christmas 1899, had cost the British tax payer more than £200 million. The cost in blood was equally high. The War Office reckoned that 400,346 horses, mules and donkeys were "expended" in the war. There were over a hundred thousand casualties of all kinds among the 365,693 imperial and 82,742 colonial soldiers who had fought in the war. Twenty-two thousand of them found a grave in South Africa: 5,744 were killed by enemy action (or accident) and shoveled into the veld, often where they fell; 16,168 died of wounds or were killed by the action of disease (or the inaction of army doctors) . . .
>
> On the Boer side, the cost of the war, measured in suffering, was perhaps absolutely as high; relatively, much higher. It was estimated that there were over 7,000 deaths among the 87,365 Boers – including 2,120 foreign volunteers and 13,300 Afrikaners from the Cape and Natal who served in the commandos of the two republics. No one knows how many Boers – men, women and children – died in the concentration camps. Official estimates vary between 18,000 and 28,000. The survivors returned to homesteads devastated almost beyond recognition. Several million cattle, horses and sheep, that had comprised their chief capital, had been killed or looted.
> (Pakenham, 1979: 607–608)

## Analysis: competing explanations of the South African War's outcome

Assessing the relative explanatory merits of competing explanations of asymmetric conflict requires answering four basic questions. First, what were the interests of the actors prior to the conflict and how are these best explained? Second, what was each actor's regime type, and how did this affect strategy and political vulnerability? Third, what role did military arms diffusion play in the conflict's outcome? Finally, what were the strategies each side employed, what was the rationale given for their selection or change, and how did they affect the eventual outcome of the war?

## Actor interests

Britain's interests were not explained by its material power relative to that of the two Boer republics that opposed it. Britain acted *as if* the survival of its empire was at stake. It marshaled three arguments in support of this calculation. First, although the Suez Canal was opened in 1869, because it could be easily closed (sabotaged or mined) in time of crisis, Britain calculated that political control over Cape Town was a vital security interest. Second, because a majority in Cape Colony were Afrikaners, Britain calculated that it could not compromise or back down regarding its efforts to replace Kruger and Steyn with more amenable leaders. If it failed in Orange Free State and Transvaal, it would only be a matter of time before the Afrikaners in Natal and Cape Colony, encouraged by British weakness, facilitated the annexation of Natal and Cape Colony by the two *Boer* republics. Britain would then lose control of its vital port at Cape Town. Finally, British policymakers calculated that failure to put down resistance from such tiny upstart republics would make Britain appear weak to its Great Power rivals, encouraging them to exploit British weakness, and eventually unraveling the tapestry of its empire.

The Boer republics did fight and act as though their survival was at stake – and so it was. The Boer leadership understood early and clearly that Britain's aim was annexation: the end of their political independence and sovereignty.

## Regime types, strategy, and vulnerability

At the time of the South African War, Britain was a democracy. It had a large, literate population with a broad franchise. Its elites worried about public opinion and had to take public opinion into account when formulating public policy (Smith, 1996: 399–400). What then may be said about the relationship between Britain's regime type and the strategies its leaders chose in South Africa?

Chamberlain's and Milner's first difficulty was how to convince the British public of the need to threaten the use of force in South Africa. All during the summer months of 1899, these two men attempted and failed to find a *casus belli* adequate to mobilize public support. Their best effort resulted in the franchise issue – this gained them sympathy, but was insufficient to justify risking British lives over. In the event, as we have seen, they were saved from having to justify the use of force by Kruger's ultimatum and subsequent mobilization. *Self-defense* was a *casus belli* every Briton could rally behind. Had Britain had an authoritarian regime, it could have dispensed with this concern over justifying its actions to an informed and empowered public.

How many troops to send became the second strategic decision which would be constrained by public opinion. Britain could not send too many troops because this would be expensive, and they would moreover imply an interest out of proportion to the stated aim of merely securing Natal and Cape Colony from attack. Besides, what was the need? Part of the propaganda campaign leading up to the ultimatums had caricatured the Boer as backward, venal brutes: one good crack on the snout should be sufficient to send them packing – by Christmas at the latest. The public expected a walk-over, and they expected it on the cheap. An authoritarian Britain could have sent as many or as few troops as it wished, without the constraint of public expectations.

A final strategic decision subject to regime-type constraints was the decision to begin burning farms and concentrating noncombatants into camps. This was a bottom-up decision, started in the field by Roberts as a sort of reprisal for the Boers' refusal to "fight fair" and give up after the capture of Bloemfontein, Johannesburg, and Pretoria. Yet its political impact was such that it very nearly forced Britain from the war. Had Britain been authoritarian, Emily Hobhouse would have been imprisoned or possibly executed as a Boer spy. Her entire family would have been locked up, and her report suppressed.

As to regime type and political vulnerability, nothing emerges more strongly in this case than the sense that British political elites lived in constant fear of, as Cecil Rhodes was apt to put it, that "unctuous British rectitude." Regime type mattered because in democratic Britain there was a gap between what was necessary and what was permissible. In an authoritarian Britain, anything necessary would have been permissible. In democratic Britain this was not the case, and leaders paid more than mere lip service to this constraint. As we have already seen, British interests do not explain its vulnerability in this case. For one thing, its interests were higher than those predicted by the interest asymmetry argument. For another, even though the British public of that day may have agreed that "upstarts must be put in their place," British public opinion made it difficult for Britain to initiate hostilities in South Africa, or to do so with the necessary number of troops. In sum, democratic Britain was vulnerable to certain specific actions which violated the public's sense of right and wrong in a way that an authoritarian Britain would not have been. Yet the necessary condition for the operation of this vulnerability was time. Had the war in South Africa indeed been over by Christmas of 1899, then the public's unctuous rectitude would have had no room to operate. As it was, victory was delayed. This delay was due first, to underestimating the enemy, and second, to the inter-action of the strategies adopted by the British and the Boers in March of 1900: a conventional attack *vs.* a GWS.

## Arms diffusion

In the South African War, the arms diffusion argument appears to gain strong support. After the Jameson Raid, the two Boer republics embarked on a major arms acquisition and modernization program. They gained rifles comparable or superior to those of the British, and their artillery in particular was actually better than that fielded by the British. Moreover, the Boer had not neglected to train their artillerymen to employ their new field pieces effectively (Nasson, 1999: 59). There were, however, two problems regarding artillery that the Boer simply could not overcome. First, they depended upon contracts to re-supply ammunition for the guns which were subsequently bought out by Britain (Nasson, 1999: 59). The Boer succeeded to some extent in manufacturing their own ammunition, but it was never enough to match demand. Second, modern as they were (outranging the British guns in most cases), they were still too few. Once the full British expeditionary force landed and began to move inland, the relatively few guns the Boer had could do nothing to affect the strategic balance of forces. Boer mobility was hampered by the guns and their heavy logistical trains, so that the preferred method of fighting – establishing a well-defended position in difficult terrain, then jumping to horse when overwhelmed – would have been impossible had the Boer continued to rely on their artillery.

The new and highly efficient Mauser rifles Kruger and Steyn had purchased for their burghers were a different story. These proved highly effective throughout the war, but particularly in its opening stages, when British troops were ordered to rush Boer in entrenched positions. The British had never before run into the business end of a breech-loading, magazine-fed rifle firing smokeless cartridges (Pakenham, 1979: 184, 238). It was some time, and not a few bloody engagements, before the British learned tactics that could minimize their soldiers' exposure to concentrated rifle fire from entrenched positions. It is fair to say that they did not learn quickly. But their sheer weight of numbers made it less imperative to learn as time went on: they were taking heavier casualties than anticipated, but until the Boer switched strategies from conventional defense to GWS, they were winning.

## Strategic interaction

The South African War took place in three interactions. In the first interaction, an overwhelmingly superior force of British imperial troops – blunders notwithstanding – decisively defeated their adversaries and captured their capital cities. The strategy employed by the British was conventional attack: they sought to bring the war to an end by destroying the Boer armies in the field (or forcing them to surrender), and by capturing state capitals – Bloemfontein for Orange Free State, and Pretoria for Transvaal. In this first interaction, the two Boer republics countered British strategy with a conventional defense strategy: they sought to block the British advances. Both sides made mistakes, but overall the British had the worst of it. Yet by dint of overwhelming numerical superiority, it became clear that the Boer could not defeat the British with a conventional defense strategy. Indeed, the brighter generals among the Boer recognized their earlier strategy as counterproductive, insofar as the fighting style, training, armament, and discipline (or rather, indiscipline) of the Boer burghers made them poor "regular" soldiers.

Thus, after the capture of Bloemfontein, the Boer switched to a GWS. This shift in strategies marked the opening of the second – and far more brutal – interaction of the war. For the first five months after the capture of Bloemfontein, the British continued a conventional attack strategy. When it became clear that the combination of amnesty offers and capital city occupation would not cause the Boers to surrender, the British switched to a barbarism strategy. Why should we characterize British strategy in this way?

There is some controversy about one aspect of British strategy: the concentration camps. Clearly, the British intended the combination of farm-burning and internment of Boer noncombatants as a COIN strategy. In this sense alone, the policy falls under the heading of depredations against noncombatants. But as always we must qualify such judgments. It is true that the practice of confining Boer women and children led to more deaths – due to malnutrition and plague – than all the battle casualties on both sides combined. But it is equally clear that this particular effect was never intended by the British. Yet after the conditions in the camps were improved, the British then stopped the policy of forced internment in order to deliberately cause hardship to Boer noncombatants and hobble the guerrillas. On balance, local commanders violated the laws of war regarding noncombatant immunity in a systematic way and as a COIN strategy. Moreover, we have sufficient testimony from both sides in parliamentary debates to confirm that, overall, the British accepted the principle of noncombatant immunity as a law of war.[22]

On the Boer side, there were atrocities and violations of the laws of war as well. The three most common complaints from the British were (1) abusing the white flag of truce;[23] (2) the use of prohibited weapons;[24] and (3) the wearing of khaki.[25] Yet at no time did these approach the

---

[22] This was particularly important in this instance because, as is well known, a large portion of the justification of imperialism was the gift of "civilization" brought to those "less civilized." Britain's deliberate violation of the laws of civilized conduct undermined its moral claim to be civilizing the allegedly uncivilized Boer burghers.

[23] Pakenham records a number of claims to this effect, but does not trouble to support or refute such claims. Here is one account, however, which appears to support the British claim in at least one case: "The Boers reappeared with a white flag. They pointed out that the donga was full of wounded, who would unavoidably be shot, if Bullock insisted on fighting. They chivalrously offered to let the wounded be removed, before going on with the fight. Meanwhile, less chivalrously, about a hundred Boers had crept round the side of the donga, and emerged holding their rifles pointed at the heads of the Devons ... Bullock and the rest of the Devons, and the unwounded gunners, were bundled off as prisoners" (Pakenham, 1979: 247).

[24] The Hague Convention of 1899 had prohibited the use of "dum-dum" bullets – at least against European troops (the British had used them liberally in Sudan against the Dervishes). Sanctioned military rounds featured bullets made of lead with a copper jacket (to help maintain the shape of the bullet in flight and to reduce fouling of the rifle barrel). If the points of such bullets were cut or cross-hatched, however, they would become hot in flight and dramatically expand upon contact with a solid body. The likelihood of death when struck with such a round was thus much higher than when struck with a full-jacketed round.

[25] In the later months of the war, Boer commandos were in such a state of poor supply that the soldiers often rode in rags or half-naked. They therefore thought little of liberating the fine uniforms of their captured foes. There is no evidence that Boer commandos sought to use such uniforms to deceive their adversaries (a violation of the laws of war), but Kitchener nevertheless ordered that any Boer caught in khaki be summarily shot. It should be added that by 1900 many British officers and men had begun to adapt their uniforms to the conditions of the veld – especially the headgear (pit helmets were widely abandoned in favor of the floppy Boer veld hats). It is thus probably the case that British soldiers were as often mistaken for Boer, as Boer for British.

scale of British violations. Moreover, such violations as did occur were never deliberate policy on the Boer side.

In sum, the strategic interaction in the first and final interactions of the war was "same-approach." In the first interaction, from October 1899 to March 1900, the British pursued a direct attack strategy which the Boer countered with a direct defense strategy. Facing imminent defeat, the Boer switched to a GWS in the second interaction of the war, from April 1900 to May of 1902. The British responded by switching to a barbarism strategy in the final interaction of the war, from June of 1900. The outcome was that the British won both the first and final interactions of the war, and the Boer capitulated at Vereeniging on May 31, 1902.

## Conclusion

The South African War was an asymmetric conflict between Great Britain – then the world's pre-eminent great power – and two of the world's tiniest states – Orange Free State and Transvaal.

Britain's interests were many, but its willingness to go to war in South Africa was due to its overriding interest: undisputed political control of the four South African republics and, by extension, security for a vital route of communications between Britain and its colonial possessions in India. Contrary to the interest asymmetry thesis, which holds that the stronger actor in an asymmetric conflict will have a low interest in a conflict, Britain calculated that control of Orange Free State and Transvaal was vital for three reasons. First, control of Cape Town was key to maintaining sea communications with India. Second, and related to the first reason, allowing the Boer republics to "dictate" to the British might encourage the majority population of Cape Colony – Afrikaners – to seize control of the Cape. Third and finally, allowing the Boer republics to "dictate" to the British would make the British appear weak-willed in relation to its European great power rivals, thus encouraging interference or intervention from those rivals. Employing a domino-like logic throughout, the British therefore calculated that war was necessary in South Africa.

Boer interests were in maintaining their independence from Britain. The presidents of the two republics guessed that Britain's real interests were not – as they constantly maintained – the franchise rights of Uitlanders and more civil conduct toward "Kaffirs." They guessed that Britain wanted to end their independence, and they were proved right in the end.

In sum, hypothesis 8 – relative material power explains relative interests in the outcome of an asymmetric conflict – is not supported in the South African War. Relative power was a poor predictor of relative interests in this case: at least on the British side. Did relative power and interests explain political vulnerability?

Again, on the Boer side, it is difficult to answer this question. The lack of a solid transnational Afrikaner national identity severely undermined the effectiveness of the later Boer shift to a GWS. Without such an identity, or where such an identity was weak, the Boer GWS was vulnerable to British amnesty offers:

> General Christian De Wet later described these proclamations as "deadly lyddite bombs which ... shattered Afrikanerdom." Some 13,900 of the Boer commandos voluntarily surrendered their arms by July 1900, this figure representing 26 percent of those liable for military service in the two republics, or about 40 percent of the number originally mobilized on the outbreak of war. (Smith, 1996: 7)

We should have expected a "fight for their lives" to have made the Boer defenders much more resolute than this. Yet, on the other hand, when faced with a choice between their political independence and their national survival (a choice which must in some sense depend on a surprisingly benevolent conception of post-war British rule), the Boers chose national survival:

> Six months earlier, the tide had set finally against them – their commandos immobilized and starving, beaten at last by blockhouses and food burning; their womenfolk threatened by Kaffirs. And, to set against all these sacrifices, there was no prospect of foreign intervention, or any corresponding gain. Negotiate now, said Botha and De la Rey and Smuts, while we still have control of our destiny, and can keep the volk together as a nation. Fight on, and the volk will die (or suffer a fate worse than death). The threat was not only to the lives of individuals, but to the continued existence of the nation.
> (Pakenham, 1979: 602)

British political vulnerability may be explained in part by its overwhelming material superiority over the Boer republics. Certainly it explains a large portion of Britain's underestimation of the costs and risks of a war with the Boer. But is relative material capability the best explanation? No. Two other factors play into British political vulnerability and explain it better: regime type and time to objective.

As leaders of a democratic state, British policymakers could not make policy without taking public reaction and judgments into account. In terms of the political theory of the laws of war, there were two loci of vulnerability for Britain: *jus ad bellum* – the justness of Britain's resort to force in South Africa; and *jus in bello* – the justness of its conduct of a war in South Africa. In authoritarian regimes these vulnerabilities are managed by means of control over access to information about both loci, and by the fact that information notwithstanding, there is no mechanism for connecting popular will with foreign policy. As we have already seen, Kruger's ultimatum spared British elites from difficulties over *jus ad bellum*: the British public recognized the legitimacy of self-defense as a justification for the resort to arms. But what of the moral conduct of the war itself? Here is where Britain's regime type made a big difference. The concentration camp controversy created the possibility of Britain's withdrawal from the war short of achieving its political objectives. We have already observed the reasons why this possibility was never realized, but the point is that in an authoritarian Britain withdrawal short of achieving the political objective due to *jus in bello* concerns would not have been a possibility.

Regime type therefore matters more than allowed by the interest asymmetry argument. However, the most important determinant of vulnerability is time to objective. This case makes clear the importance of time to objective in war: it is a positive cost on almost equal footing with blood and treasure. Had the war been over by Christmas – as widely anticipated by British elites and the British public – these concerns over the legitimacy of a resort to force and the moral conduct of war would have had much less space in which to operate. Indeed, in this general category of conflict, we expect wars to be quick and decisive *almost by definition*, since the gap in the ratio of resources available to each actor exceeds five to one. If vulnerability is activated or caused by a delay in time to objective, it then makes sense to ask what caused the delay?

It wasn't arms diffusion. Although the Boer had better arms than the British initially, their possession of a military technology advantage correlates with their rapid defeat, not victory. Thus, although hypothesis 6 – the better armed a weak actor is, the more likely it is that a strong actor will lose an asymmetric conflict – receives some support here, on balance the technological advantage enjoyed by the Boer did not affect the outcome of the war. It marginally increased the costs to the British in terms of killed and wounded soldiers, but only a shift in strategy saved the Boer from defeat in March of 1900.

I argue that it was this shift in strategy to a GWS by the Boer in March of 1900 that explains the delay which nearly forced Britain from the war.

The British won the first interaction of the war, and, after the fall of Bloemfontein, the Boer leadership gathered to discuss surrender or a strategy for continued resistance. After heated debate over the appropriateness of a GWS, and the risks under which it might place Boer noncombatants, the Boer leaders opted to continue their resistance by employing a GWS.[26]

It was five months before the British adjusted to this change in strategy. During this time, Roberts advanced from city to city, capturing each in turn and posting amnesty proclamations. When the Boer didn't give up, and in fact struck back at British communications and isolated units, the British intensified their earlier policy of collective reprisals against Boer noncombatants. They switched to a barbarism strategy, and although this created its own risks in terms of British public opinion, it also proved militarily effective against the Boer – especially by 1901 (Pakenham, 1979: 500–501).

In evaluating the utility and effectiveness of barbarism as a COIN strategy, however, we should keep in mind the evidence that the strategy for shortening the war contained the powerful probability of making a later peace costly or unstable:

> Dundonald agreed that collective punishments were neither fair nor politic. Attacks on the railway were not the work of locals; "and when once these farms were burnt the country round became a desert and their owners inveterate haters of the British."
>
> (Pakenham, 1979: 479–480)

It must remain one of the great counterfactuals of the conflict, but it seems likely that had the British not switched strategies, the war either would have continued for a much longer time, or the continued delay would have itself become a political issue which would have resulted in at least a change of government, and very likely, a settlement short of Britain's *ex ante* political objectives (in other words, a defeat for Britain).

---

[26] The decision also involved a recalculation of Boer interests: was it really the capital cities that represented Boer freedom, or was it something else? Here Pakenham recounts Boer deliberations following the capture of Bloemfontein: "But the man who had inspired Botha and Smuts was Steyn. The Free State President had seen his own capital subjected to the same humiliations two months before, and had realized that it was not a city, but the illimitable veld, that was the true symbol of the volk. When Kruger's despairing telegram reached him on 1 June in his hide-out near Lindley (by an oversight, Roberts had left the telegraph lines to the northeastern Free State intact), Steyn's reply was characteristically blunt. *We* shall never surrender ... Steyn's reply was the most important telegram of the war" (Pakenham, 1979: 457–458).

It is also clear that, as in the Murid War, the barbarism strategy lost in post-war political effectiveness anything it might have gained in war-time military effectiveness:

> And the backward nation of farmers from whose misrule the British were going to save South Africa ended by being granted self-government in the Orange River Colony and the Transvaal. Just eight years later, rallying around an Afrikaner nationalism at least partly fueled by the memory of the thousands dead in the concentration camps, whites in the Cape Colony and Natal joined those of the former republics to become citizens of the Union of South Africa in the beginning of a new era of white government in South Africa. (Krebs, 1992: 54)

In sum, strategic interaction is the strongest explanation of the South African War's outcome. Once it became clear that the capture of the Boer capitals would not force the Boer to surrender, the British had three strategic choices. First, continue with the present strategy, perhaps sending more troops, equipment, and horses to the theater. Second, offer the Boers terms: something which could save face yet end the war. Third, switch to a barbarism strategy: take the gloves off and go after Boer noncombatants, either by holding them hostage or by killing them outright in reprisal for continued resistance. The Boer faced an even starker choice after the fall of Bloemfontein: either give up or switch to a dangerous GWS. They chose a GWS, and the war lasted another two years. During that period, which opened a window of political vulnerability, British policymakers had to face the possibility that outrage over the delay itself, but especially over the concentration camp deaths, might actually force them from the war, or at least force them to make political concessions which would have destroyed the justification for going to war in the first place.

# 5    Italy in Ethiopia: the Italo-Ethiopian War, 1935–1940

We are valiant formations
Of indomitable warriors
Carrying the flags
Into Eastern Africa.
The symbol of glory,
Of peace and civilization
Will be made to shine once more
By the Italic Victory ...
Slavery and barbarity
Are doomed to vanish
The very moment
The Roman eagles appear ...

From an Italian marching song in the Abyssinian campaign

We flung ourselves on the machine-gun nests to clear them out, we hurled ourselves against the enemy artillery. We held firm against their bombs and their containers of mustard gas. We put their tanks out of action with our bare hands. We cannot reproach ourselves with any taint of cowardice. But against the invisible rain of deadly gas that splashed down on our hands, our faces, we could do nothing. Yet I say again that we have no cause to be ashamed: we could not "kill" this rain.                                                    Haile Selassie

The war between fascist Italy and Ethiopia began on 2 October 1935. Italy was the strong actor by a wide margin.[1] It was a sharp conventional engagement between a well-armed and well-supplied yet poorly led Italian army, and the poorly armed and poorly supplied Ethiopian

---

[1] Using Singer and Small's data (1992), the halved ratio of relative material power comes to 24.23 to 1 in favor of Italy.

army. By May of 1936, the emperor of Ethiopia, Haile Selassie, had fled, and the Italians marched triumphantly into Addis Ababa, the capital. Yet the war did not then end. It continued as a guerrilla war from 1936 to 1940, when Britain joined the fight. The Italians surrendered to the British in North Africa on May 5, 1941.

## The Ethiopian theater

Ethiopia lies in the centermost portion of the Horn of Africa. In 1935, it was surrounded by the colonial possessions of four European states. To the southwest and northwest lay Kenya and Anglo-Egyptian Sudan. To the south and east Italian and British Somaliland respectively. To the east and northeast, French Somaliland (Djibouti) and Eritrea (then a colony of Italy).

Ethiopia was thus landlocked. Its main route to the sea was a single railway line running from Addis Ababa, the capital, to the French-controlled port of Djibouti on the Red Sea. It is a country of two distinctive topographies and climates. From Addis Ababa south to the Somalilands stretches a hilly and mountainous country which slowly descends to the Ogaden desert: hot, dry, and flat. From Addis Ababa north to Sudan and Eritrea, stretches some of the most rugged and impassable mountains in all Africa.

The country had but one paved road, which had been built for the emperor's coronation in 1930. The remainder of the country was traversed by means of mule tracks and undeveloped roads, often impassable during the spring and summer rains, which regularly drenched the region from May until September of each year.

Ethiopia's people spoke Amharic, an ancient Coptic Christian dialect, and most Ethiopians were Christians. The state itself consisted of a federation of semi-independent regions each ruled by a noble family, and all under the nominal control of an emperor in Addis Ababa. It was a feudal system. Del Boca provides a description of the capital, Ethiopia's best-developed city in 1935:

> There was only one generator, the generator that supplied electric light and power for the "Little *Gebbi*," the emperor's palace, only one passable hotel, the Imperial, and only one hard-surface road, the one which had been asphalted for Haile Selassie's coronation. There were no drains, no system of waste disposal; all the refuse was simply dumped into the streets and the sky was always black with vultures and crows. (Del Boca, 1969: 31)

Such descriptions, though accurate, would later be used by Italy to justify its conquest and colonization of Ethiopia.

Italian interest in Ethiopia dates from the waning years of the nineteenth century. Having established a viable colony in Eritrea, the Italians decided on a military campaign further inland. On January 26, 1887, a force of 500 Italians were annihilated by a force of 20,000 Ethiopians led by Emperor Yohannes IV at Dogali.[2] This forced the Italians to postpone their conquest efforts for several years.

In fact, after the death of Yohannes and the accession of Menelik II, relations between the two states thawed, and these friendly relations were marked by the signing of a treaty and the gift from Italy's King Umberto to Menelik of 28,000 rifles and 28 cannon. In the Treaty of Uccialli, Menelik recognized Italy's right to Eritrea and agreed to allow Italy to conduct some Ethiopian foreign affairs. But after the Italians chose to interpret the treaty as recognition that Ethiopia had become a "protectorate" of Italy, relations quickly soured. In order to soothe Menelik and convince him of the advantages of protectorate status, in 1893 the Italians made him a gift of 2,000,000 cartridges for the rifles they had previously given him. No sooner had Menelik received the cartridges than he denounced the treaty and began using the threat of Italian invasion to rally the Ethiopian chiefs around him:

> The Italians then very obligingly fostered his efforts to develop Ethiopian nationalism and solidify his own power. Using his treaty denunciation as a pretext, they organized, under the leadership of General Oreste Baratieri, the Governor of Eritrea, an expeditionary force of 17,700 men, a considerably larger force than other colonialist countries were accustomed to using, and marched south into Ethiopia.
>
> (Coffey, 1974: ix)

But the Italians chose an invasion route which appeared poised to cross through Axum, one of Ethiopia's most holy sites and the spiritual center of the Coptic Church. This allowed Menelik to rally more chiefs to his cause, and he assembled an army of more than 100,000 warriors armed with, among other things, the rifles and ammunition the Italians had already given him.

But fielding an army of such size proved difficult for Menelik. His hungry soldiers threatened to desert him when the Italians, already established in an impregnable position at Sauria, decided to end the

---

[2] Such apparently prohibitive odds were the norm on colonial frontiers.

campaign quickly by launching a surprise attack on the assembled Ethiopians.

Baratieri divided his forces into three columns who were all to reach key hills overlooking the Ethiopian positions and then, at the proper signal, descend in a crushing pincer movement to annihilate the Ethiopians. Unfortunately for the Italians, Baratieri failed to adequately scout the approaches and his maps were inaccurate. The columns became separated and the waiting Ethiopians wiped out a flank column before it could reach its assigned positions. The next morning (1 March 1896), as the remaining two columns went into action near Adowa they were unaware that their left flank was entirely unprotected. After being halted by lead elements of the Ethiopian army, the Italians were enveloped and though they fought bravely, 12,000 died before the sun set, ending the battle (the 5000 survivors owed their lives to this Ethiopian tradition of ending every battle at sunset).

This crushing defeat at the Battle of Adowa marked the *only* successful repulse by an African state of a European attempt at colonization.[3] It solidified Ethiopian nationalism and proved an intensely humiliating loss for the Italians – so humiliating that it would still count as a primary *casus belli* for fascist Italy some thirty-nine years later.[4]

In the meantime, Italy licked its wounds, nursed its resentments, and waited. In 1906, it signed a secret treaty with France and Britain, in which the latter two states:

> acknowledged Italy's priority in Ethiopia, with the stipulation that Italy would never hinder the operation of the French-owned railway

---

[3] It also runs counter to the predictions of the strategic interaction thesis: a strong actor and weak actor both used direct strategic approaches and the weak actor won.

[4] Italy's fascist dictator, Benito Mussolini, was 13 years old at the time of the Battle of Adowa, and he personally experienced Italy's humiliation over the defeat (Coffey, 1974: 22). Del Boca characterizes the effects of this humiliation this way: After Adowa, Alfredo Oriani had written:

> We have signed a peace but there will be no peace. We will never give up Africa – the war will be resumed. The defeat seared their minds and the words of the boastful patriotic ditties the soldiers had sung, words such as these stung them like whips:
> Baldissare, hey, beware
> Of these black folk with woolly hair!
> Menelik, you're dead – here comes
> A shower of lead, not sugar plums.
> By and large Italians could not bring themselves to accept the fact that the "barbarous Shoan hordes" had succeeded in annihilating a European army.
> (Del Boca, 1969: 9–12)

from Addis Ababa to Djibuti, or the flow of Blue Nile water from Ethiopia's Lake Tana into the White Nile, which fed England's dependencies, Egypt and Sudan. (Coffey, 1974: 11)

## The eve of war: Italian interests

Benito Mussolini came to power in Italy in 1922, when Italy's King Vittorio Emmanuele called on him to form a government. During the two years it took him to consolidate his power by intimidating or assassinating his opponents, Ethiopia petitioned for membership in the League of Nations:

> When the Ethiopian government, at Tafari's instigation, applied for League of Nations membership in 1923, Mussolini supported the application because he didn't think he could defeat it, even though England opposed it. The British argued that Ethiopia should not be admitted into a society of civilized nations because Ethiopians still practiced slavery... Ras Tafari had already taken steps, not always effective, toward abolishing slavery. His application prevailed and Ethiopia became a League of Nations member. (Coffey, 1974: 13)

Essentially, Britain had argued that Ethiopia was not civilized enough to merit membership.[5] After years of bitter internecine quarrels, Ras Tafari, a powerful Shoan noble, was later crowned emperor of Ethiopia under the throne name of Haile Selassie.

The emperor was an educated, intelligent, and charismatic man who spoke French fluently and planned to reform and develop Ethiopia along the lines of a European state.[6] He was handicapped by his country's poverty, and by the difficulty of establishing and maintaining central authority over the independent princes who ruled Ethiopia's distant regions. Above all, he was distracted by fascist Italy's increasingly obvious acquisitive intentions.

Selassie had attempted to reach an accommodation with Italy in the Italo-Ethiopian Treaty of Amity, Conciliation and Arbitration of August 2,

---

[5] This was a theme which was to underlay all discussions and negotiations among the three European powers. It is difficult to estimate how much this influenced the bargaining, but the memoirs of the participants make it clear it proved to be a major, if at times unspoken, factor (see below).

[6] He maintained a number of foreign advisors close to the throne, including an American, Everett Colson, a Swede, General Eric Virgin, and an Englishman, Sir Sidney Barton (His Britannic Majesty's minister). His coronation on November 2, 1930 was directly modeled on the coronation of King Edward VII in London.

1928, but Mussolini tended to use the more liberal provisions of the treaty to prepare for his invasion of Ethiopia. Del Boca recounts how Mussolini's efforts to build a road from Assab to Dessie was stymied by the emperor (although technically allowed under the treaty), and how Mussolini's propaganda machine characterized the emperor's objection as tantamount to the rejection of civilization:

> The emperor's reluctance to furnish the country which had a common frontier with the most rapid route for an invasion was fully justified, of course, and Mussolini knew it. But from this time on we were the archangelic messengers of light and civilization, the Ethiopians the lowest, most deeply damned race on earth, the personification of all that was evil and abominable. Utterly puerile as this counterblast was, the majority of Italians honestly believed this rubbish was true; consequently, when the hour struck, they gladly acclaimed the act of aggression. (Del Boca, 1969: 14)

From 1930 on then, Italy began preparing for the invasion, conquest, and occupation of Ethiopia. All it needed was a decent pretext for invasion.

The incident which proved to be the "Sarajevo" of the Italo-Ethiopian war took place at the distant outpost of Wal Wal in the Ogaden desert on December 5, 1934. Mussolini had already sent a large expeditionary force to Eritrea consisting of 200,000 troops, 7000 officer, 6000 machine guns, 700 cannon of every caliber, 150 tanks, and 150 pursuit and bomber planes (Del Boca, 1969: 21). But Selassie, clearly understanding Mussolini's intentions, had prudently moved all his armed forces a safe distance away from Eritrea, precisely so as to avoid any chance of a border "incident" which Italy could inflate into a pretext for invasion. He also set about seeking help under the articles of the Covenant of the League of Nations.

But in the Ogaden the Italians had stationed troops at Wal Wal, 60 miles within Ethiopian territory. When a survey commission escorted by Ethiopian troops journeyed to the wells there, they were halted by Somali *Dubats* (African soldiers under Italian command). When the Ethiopians protested that they would not withdraw because Wal Wal was Ethiopian territory, the Italians replied that Wal Wal was Italian territory – part of Italian Somaliland. The Ethiopians at first far outnumbered the Italians, and they refused to withdraw because to do so might be construed as acknowledging Italian claims on the area. Tensions increased, as did Italian reinforcements, until on 5 December

1934, shots were fired and in the mêlée which followed, the Ethiopians were routed.[7]

What was most striking about the incident was the way in which Italy managed it, and the way in which the world powers reacted. Italy instantly claimed it had been the victim of unprovoked aggression on its own territory; it demanded, in the most insulting terms possible, an apology and reparations from the Ethiopians. The Ethiopians protested that they had been attacked by Italians 60 miles within their own borders, and made every effort to downplay the incident, while at the same time refusing to acknowledge guilt or apologize. At the League of Nations, most representatives simply assumed the Italian territorial claims were correct, and Ethiopia was strongly encouraged to accede to Italy's demands.

> Despite a few rumors that Wal Wal might actually be in Ethiopia, most newspapers accepted the Italian assertion that it was in Somaliland, especially after Italy sent a note to the League on December 16 renewing the assertion and decrying Ethiopia's charges.
>
> Eventually, a correspondent in the press room of the League of Nations . . . on or about December 20, did something no one else had thought to do. He looked up at a map on the wall in front of him. It was a map of Africa, issued by the Italian Geographical Institute at Bergamo, which showed that Wal Wal was indeed at least sixty miles inside Ethiopia according to the terms of the 1897 treaty which settled the 1896 war between the two countries.
>
> The Italian delegation, apprised of this evidence, reacted immediately. Baron Pompeo Aloisi, Rome's . . . representative in Geneva, demanded that the map be removed from the press room because it was obsolete. It took no account of certain modifications of the 1897 treaty which were made in 1908.
>
> No sooner had the map been removed than the correspondents, now full of enterprise, went all the way to the League library in the north wing of the main building, where they found an Italian government map of Ethiopia, issued by the Colonial Office in 1925. This map also showed that Wal Wal was at least sixty miles inside Ethiopia.
>
> (Coffey, 1974: 19)

In short, regardless of who fired the first shot, Italy was in the wrong; having invaded Ethiopia and established an armed outpost within Ethiopia's territory. But none of this made any real difference. Italy

---

[7] It was impossible to answer the question of who fired the first shot (Coffey, 1974: 8; Del Boca, 1969: 19), and the battle itself was decided by Italian armored cars, against which the Ethiopians had no effective countermeasures.

continued to bluster, fabricate, and bully; in the end Mussolini used the incident as a way to justify sending more troops and supplies to the theater. The Ethiopians patiently applied for League assistance – even arbitration – but none was forthcoming. The two dominant great powers in the League – Britain and France – each negotiated separate deals with Mussolini in which the end result was to give Italy a free hand in Ethiopia.

What then were Italy's true interests in Ethiopia? The Wal Wal incident is useful in this regard, because as Mussolini's long-awaited pretext for the conquest of Ethiopia, it also prompted the Italians to advance arguments and justifications for that conquest. These come down to three things: reputation, responsibility, and resources.

National humiliation over the defeat at Adowa was deeply felt by most Italians, Mussolini personally,[8] and the military especially. A big reason for the attack and conquest of Ethiopia then, would be to erase that humiliation.[9] Beyond this simple redress, however, there were two other reputation issues at stake: the reputation of Italy as colonial power and the reputation of fascism as a political and ruling ideology within Italy. Italians had also been humiliated by their lack of promised spoils from their "victory" over Germany and Austria-Hungary in World War I (Coffey, 1974: 25).

The responsibility interest centered on Italy's conception of itself – a conception which gained sympathy from Britain and France at the time[10] – as a civilizing European power:

---

[8] Coffey adds that in a secret memorandum Mussolini argued for a *fait accompli* strategy in Ethiopia. Mussolini calculated that so long as British and French interests in the area were respected, he could get away with the conquest: "[Mussolini's] dreams of colonial glory and his bitter boyhood memories of Italy's defeat at Adowa forced him to hope so. 'This problem has existed since 1885,' he concluded in his secret memorandum" (Coffey, 1974: 22). Griffin points out that it is typical of fascism to refer to aggressive colonial myths and aspirations as "problems," which must then be "solved" by military or totalitarian measures (Griffin, 1995: 74).

[9] Baron Aloisi, Italy's representative at the League of Nations, makes this link clear: "There was the earlier defeat at Adowa which would have to be 'washed out in blood'" (Coffey, 1974: 73).

[10] Here is how Britain's foreign minister, Sir Samuel Hoare, put it to the House of Commons: "We have always understood Italy's desire for overseas expansion," he told the House. "In 1925 [it was actually 1924] we ceded Jubaland [a bleak piece of East Kenya bordering Italian Somaliland] to Italy. Let no one in Italy suggest that we are unsympathetic to Italian aspirations. We admit the need for Italian expansion" (Coffey, 1974: 105). This "need" for colonial possessions was therefore a norm of European power politics, and hence a legitimate aspiration for European powers *outside of Europe*. There was another logic at play: precedent setting: "An Abyssinian victory might result in serious

[Mussolini] also proclaimed that Italy could "civilize Africa, and her position in the Mediterranean gave her this right and imposed this duty on her." Then as a warning to other colonial powers he said Italy did not "want earlier arrivals to block her spiritual, political, and economic expansion." (Coffey, 1974: 21)

The negative argument had the form *tu quoque*: after all, Italy was only asking to do in Ethiopia what all the other European powers had done for centuries with impunity (Del Boca, 1969: 26; Coffey, 1974: 59–60, 75).

Finally, the weakest of the three was the resources interest. Mussolini calculated that developing and colonizing Ethiopia would be expensive, and might take as long as fifty years to return dividends. Nevertheless, such arguments were common among Italy's efforts to justify its aggression: "Italy *had no other choice* but to expand." Part of Italy's resources problem had in fact been manufactured by the success of Mussolini's earlier efforts to increase the Italian birthrate.

A final argument has to do with Mussolini himself and his craving for personal power. Coffey argues that part of Mussolini's ambitions abroad were pathological: since he had already acquired as much power from the Italian people as they had to offer, his satisfaction came to depend on gaining power over others abroad (Coffey, 1974: 20). Mussolini recognized all these interests in conquest, but his trump card interest was one we have encountered before: self-defense (Mussolini, 1995: 74–75).[11]

The point is that Italy's preponderance *vis-à-vis* Ethiopia did not reduce its interests in conquest or colonization.[12] It was not greed

disaffections within British possessions. The Abyssinian victory over the Italians at Adowa in 1896, he said, was one of the governing factors which led to the Anglo-Egyptian campaign in 1898, because British authorities then felt strongly that the blow to white prestige in that area required a victorious campaign of whites against blacks" (Coffey, 1974: 112). Of course, the real difficulty with this argument was that Ethiopia and Italy were not yet at war, and preventing war would have been relatively simple (close or threaten to close the Suez Canal). Moreover, Ethiopia was *entitled* to assistance under the provisions of the League Covenant. In other words, to prevent the proposed domino effects of a white defeat in black Africa, all that was necessary was to prevent the war.

[11] When Ethiopia's skillful diplomacy forced Italy to tip its hand, Mussolini, now deprived of the opportunity to realize his *fait accompli* strategy, resorted to a sunk costs variant: the war must go on because Italy has already spent millions of lire on the adventure (see Coffey, 1974: 75, 142).

[12] Mussolini maintained that it was not bad generalship which lost the day at Adowa, but insufficient resources: "For the lack of a few thousand men, we lost the day at Adowa. We shall never make that mistake. I am willing to commit a sin of excess, but never a sin of deficiency" (Del Boca, 1969: 21). Unlike the constraints faced by democratic Britain in the South African War, fascist Italy could send overwhelming forces (and illicit weapons) to Ethiopia without fear of public recrimination.

alone which motivated Italy to seek out a colony in Ethiopia. Nor was the desire to conquer Ethiopia an entirely fascist affair: colonies had long been a dream of Liberal Italy. Italians came to see their conquest of Ethiopia as both necessary and just, and this opinion was distributed across classes and political affiliations in Italy.[13] Most depressing of all, Italy's aims evoked more sympathy than condemnation from other states. The fact of Ethiopia's membership in the League of Nations achieved little more than frequent embarrassment for Britain; and Ethiopia's careful and patient efforts to secure for itself the help to which it was entitled under the provisions of the League Covenant ultimately came to nothing.

## The eve of war: Ethiopian interests

As a state, Ethiopia was considerably less unified than Italy. Its nominal ruler was Haile Selassie, an emperor with titular control over hundreds of allied princes, most of whom jealously guarded their independence but nevertheless remained loyal to the emperor.

Ethiopia's interests were survival, but it is clear from all sources that up until Italian and Eritrean soldiers actually crossed the border into Ethiopia in 1935, and even for some months afterward, the emperor counted on outside intervention from his *de jure* allies: Britain, France, and other influential members of the League of Nations. In other words, many of the early battles – among the bloodiest and hardest fought engagements – were not motivated by a sense of inevitable doom. What then explains Ethiopian interests in the first three months of the war?

The answer is honor: personal, familial, tribal and, possibly, national. All Ethiopian boys were raised on the tales of the defeat of the vaunted Italian army at Adowa at the hands of Emperor Menelik. Ethiopia's barefoot and lightly armed warriors sacrificed their lives bravely and in their thousands as a consequence of this deeply ingrained sense of honor.

---

[13] Del Boca argues that "The vast majority of Italians, particularly the younger generation, hailed the colonial enterprise with sincere enthusiasm. They were fighting for a place in the sun that other great powers had enjoyed for years or for centuries, and to a country as poor and overpopulated as Italy, the conquest of Ethiopia meant jobs and a patch of land for millions of unfortunates" (Del Boca, 1969: 26).

## The Italo-Ethiopian War

The Italo-Ethiopian war began on October 2, 1935, when Haile Selassie reluctantly ordered the mobilization of his 30,000 northern troops to their defensive positions opposite an expected invasion of three Italian armies. The next morning, 250,000 Italian troops under the command of General De Bono crossed into Ethiopia from Eritrea.[14] The war was fought in five strategic interactions.[15]

*Interaction one: conventional attack* vs. *conventional defense*

The fight for Ethiopia began as a contest between the superior (in numbers and technology) forces of Italy and the poorly organized and poorly supplied forces of Ethiopia.

Ethiopia's emperor had forced his eager generals to respect a wide buffer zone between Eritrea and Ethiopia, and so the initial weeks of the war were anticlimactic. The Italians, with advanced radio communications, motorized transport, and total air superiority, advanced by cautious steps from Eritrea toward their first objective: Adowa. They were not seriously opposed.

Military analysts at the time, in fact, questioned Italy's choice of invasion routes. Why advance through some of the least developed and most vehicle-impassable terrain in Africa, when Italy could simply have advanced through the Ogaden from Italian Somaliland right up to Addis Ababa? The answer is that Italian strategy was also guided by the need for revenge: to erase the humiliation of Adowa it was necessary to capture it – preferably after a hard fight and a decisive victory over the Ethiopians. But such was not to be.

In fact, these earliest weeks of the war saw virtually no fighting. The war took on the following pattern. Italian troops, led by the Eritreans, would advance a few miles at a time under cover of air support. Such skirmishes as did take place usually pitted these excellent Eritrean troops against the equally excellent Ethiopians. After the superior firepower of the Eritreans decided the issue, the Ethiopians withdrew, and the

[14] These troops included "two highly efficient [Eritrean] divisions – the 1st and 2nd Eritreans" (Mockler, 1984: 54). The Eritrean divisions were made up of black Eritrean soldiers and NCOs under the command of white Italian officers.

[15] After Italy declared war on France in June of 1940, the Ethiopian conflict became a fight between Britain and Italy. In this sixth and final interaction, the contest was decided by conventional forces using conventional attack and defense strategies. In May of 1941 Italy's forces in Ethiopia collapsed and surrendered. Because the conflict ceased to be asymmetric as defined in this analysis, this final interaction is not discussed here.

Italians advanced cautiously again. The final advance into Adowa was in fact unopposed by the Ethiopians.[16] Anxious Italians, and especially Mussolini, seemed disappointed by the lack of a decisive engagement.

Meanwhile, the emperor set about rallying, organizing, and moving his troops to meet the invader. Ethiopians had no air support and no motor transport. They had very few radio sets, and when they did communicate using these sets, they were forced to do so in the clear (which meant that, combined with total air superiority, the Italians enjoyed strong communications intelligence). Most of the emperor's soldiers went barefoot, and many did not even have rifles, but were armed instead with spears and swords. Many of those who did have rifles, had old ones, or had only a few rounds of ammunition for them. The logistical difficulties of mobilizing a coordinated conventional defense against the Italians were therefore staggering.

In addition to mobilization difficulties, the emperor was being begged by his most loyal generals to oust a number of traitors before they revealed the emperor's defensive plans, or defected at a decisive moment in a crucial battle. But when faced with evidence that one of his generals, Gugsa, was in the pay of the Italians, the emperor refused to take action against him, claiming that many of his generals took money from the Italians but they were all loyal to Ethiopia. Gugsa was a traitor, however, and he had promised the Italians he would bring 10,000 men with him to the Italian side. In November, he made his move, but both he and the Italians were embarrassed to discover that by the time he reached Italian lines his much-vaunted 10,000 men had dwindled to a mere 1200. Gugsa himself proved to be a thorn in the Italians' side, constantly pestering De Bono to advance to Makalle (the seat of Gugsa's family's power).

But De Bono was cautious. He responded to Mussolini's increasingly frequent demands for decisive action by requesting delay after delay before advancing:

> Mussolini's bewilderment and impatience at such telegrams from de Bono was hardly surprising. De Bono had spent almost a year preparing

---

[16] Coffey highlights what would soon become a morale problem for the Italians: "The reason the Third Eritrean Brigade had not been 'employed in the occupation of the valley,' after spearheading the drive to capture it, was that they were black, and the honor of the 'reconquest' of the area, as soon as it had been rendered safe by the blacks, was reserved for the white Italians. The monument whose unveiling he witnessed was inscribed: to the dead of Adowa, avenged at last" (Coffey, 1974: 184). The prowess and battle honors of the black units soon began to cause serious morale problems for the Italians, especially the Black Shirt Divisions (see Coffey, 1974: 262).

for the invasion of Ethiopia. Then, after an unobstructed advance of twenty-five miles into the country in three or four days, during which time his airplanes hadn't been able to find any enemy armies, he had decided it would be too dangerous to continue, even to a place like Makalle, the Ethiopian "defender" of which was now in his employ.

(Coffey, 1974: 194)

Delays in Ethiopian mobilization, combined with excessive caution on the Italian side, best explain the relative lack of action in the theater of operations until December. In November, Mussolini finally grew weary of exhorting a virtually unopposed De Bono to advance and engage the enemy, and replaced him with Badoglio. Unfortunately, Badoglio, who had complained behind De Bono's back that De Bono was not aggressive enough, soon began sending his own telegrams requesting delays and more supplies. Unlike De Bono, however, Badoglio was about the meet the enemy in force.

### The Battle of Tembien

The emperor was no fool. After assessing the terrain, and the strengths and weaknesses of his own soldiers, he determined that the only hope of success lay in a GWS. On the first day of mobilization, October 2, he had advised his generals and soldiers this way:

> "Soldiers, I give you this advice, so that we gain the victory over the enemy. Be cunning, be savage, face the enemy one by one, two by two, five by five in the fields and mountains.
>
> Do not take white clothes, do not congregate as you've done now. Hide, strike suddenly, fight the nomad war, snipe and kill singly. Today the war has begun, therefore scatter and advance to victory."
>
> In these very words lay the key to a possible victory. the Emperor knew if he could persuade his Ethiopian warriors and chiefs to concentrate on guerrilla warfare against the Italians, they might have at least a slim chance to win. But it was not easy to tell an Ethiopian warrior he should sneak up behind his enemy and attack him from the cover of a rock or bush. To these proud men, a war was series of battles or one climactic battle. Each battle should properly be fought in a single day, from dawn to dusk, in an open field, with the winner of the last battle being acknowledged by both sides to be the winner of the war. (Coffey, 1974: 162)

In this passage lay both the possible salvation of Ethiopia, and the explanation of its doom. Ethiopian warriors marched and fought in the open and wore the white *shamma* (a kind of toga) instead of camouflage.

*121*

Selassie was soon forced to acknowledge, therefore, that his ideal strategy could not be pursued for cultural reasons (Coffey, 1974: 311).

By mid December both sides were bracing for their first major confrontation. After directly ordering Badoglio to advance to Makalle, the left wing of the Italian army had advanced and captured the town in November. Enduring constant bombardment from the air, the massed armies of Ras Seyum, Ras Kassa, and Ras Mulugeta attacked the weakest point in the Italian line at Tembien. Suffering frightful losses, they crossed the Takkaze ford and captured a number of key bridges and passes. Within days the advance threatened to cut the Italian army in two, forcing it to retreat back to Eritrea in ignominy.

For the Italians, the situation was as critical as it was unexpected. The poorly coordinated attacks of Ras Kassa and Ras Seyum had proven the bravery and ferocity of the Ethiopian soldiers. They swarmed and destroyed Italian tanks and armored cars, often armed only with spears and swords. Their astonishing local mobility enabled them to fight hand-to-hand, a form of fighting at which they excelled, and against which Italian air support was useless. By January the situation looked grim:

> The trackless terrain was ideal for the Ethiopians and suicidal for the Italians. Only airplanes could get at the advancing Ethiopians in such country. But since they were now learning to spread out and take cover, the airplanes would have to be armed with something more effective than bombs and bullets.
>
> Because of the foresight of Mussolini and De Bono, Badoglio found that he did have something more effective, and though his country had signed an international agreement never to use it, Mussolini, just a few days previously, on the sixteenth, had reiterated an earlier authorization to use it. Badoglio could congratulate himself now for his foresight in banishing the news correspondents to Eritrea. As long as they didn't actually see what he was about to do, they would probably believe him later when he denied having done it. (Coffey, 1974: 263)

There is some controversy over the Italian decision to use gas, and over its existence in theater.[17] The best evidence, however, supports the

---

[17] Del Boca argues that De Bono had refused to avail himself of this option, and that it was Badoglio who took the initiative in its use at the prompting of one of Mussolini's "Roman rages" (Del Boca, 1969: 78). The resort to the use of gas in the south seems especially egregious, because Graziani's 60,000 well-supported troops were opposed by 7000 starving Ethiopians under the command of Ras Desta. Yet Graziani still felt "compelled by necessity" to resort to bombing enemy positions with mustard gas canisters: "A few days after the arrival of the Duce's telegram, on Badoglio's orders, the Takkaze fords were

claim that Badoglio (and Graziani, commander of the 60,000 Italian troops advancing from Italian Somaliland) resorted to the use of mustard gas (yperite) in order to compensate for his own incompetence. The use of mustard gas was a clear violation of the laws of war. The Italians themselves had signed the Geneva Convention of June 17, 1926 prohibiting the use of gas as a weapon of war except in self-defense against a gas attack (Del Boca, 1969: 80). The Italians had earlier justified their shipping of mustard gas (680 tons) to the East African theater by arguing that they needed it for self-defense in the event of an Ethiopian chemical weapons attack (Coffey, 1974: 104). This was implausible, to say the least. Against the defenseless Ethiopians the air-dropped gas crushed the Ethiopian threat to Badoglio's communications. The Italians could now breathe easy again.

*Interaction two: conventional attack/barbarism* vs. *conventional defense*

The use of gas altered the entire character of the war. The Ethiopians had been prepared – psychologically and, to some extent, tactically – to deal with bombing, artillery, machine guns, and even tanks, but they could not fight the gas. Here Ras Imru describes what it was like to experience a gas attack:

> I myself narrowly escaped death. On the morning of December 23, shortly after we had crossed the Takkaze, we saw several enemy planes appear. We were not unduly alarmed as by this time we were used to being bombed. On this particular morning, however, the enemy dropped strange containers that burst open almost as soon as they hit the ground or the water, releasing pools of colorless liquid. I hardly had time to ask myself what could be happening before a hundred or so of my men who had been splashed by the mysterious fluid began to scream in agony as blisters broke out on their bare feet, their hands, their faces. Some who rushed to the river and took great gulps of water to cool their fevered lips, fell contorted on the banks and writhed in agonies that lasted for hours before they died. Among the victims were a few peasants who had come to water their cattle and a number of people who lived in nearby villages. My chiefs surrounded me, asking wildly what they should do, but I was completely stunned. I didn't know what to tell them, I didn't know how to fight this terrible rain that burned and killed. (Del Boca, 1969: 78–79)

drenched with mustard gas, while Graziani – in his own words – 'terrorized the inhabitants' of the villages scattered round Jijiga by dropping on them container after container of poison gases" (Del Boca, 1969: 78).

It was not just soldiers and retreating soldiers who were gassed in these aerial assaults, but lakes and streams and pastures as well. Ethiopian soldiers relied for food on livestock they drove with them to the battle site. The mustard gas killed not only women and children but also these cattle, by the thousands. Medical facilities were only the most rudimentary, and such as there were had become subject to frequent air attacks by Italian bombers. Since many of these hospitals were staffed by volunteers from "civilized" countries, such as Sweden and Britain, Mussolini had ordered these strafings and bombings to scare away witnesses to his use of gas. This created the rather ridiculous situation in which the Italians were committing one war crime (attacking clearly marked Red Cross hospitals) in order to conceal another.

The Italian response to the increasing evidence of both practices followed a typical pattern. It began with outright denial: that the claim that photographic evidence had been fabricated,[18] or that reporters were in fact communist agents. As evidence mounted, Italy argued that it had been forced to do some of these things, but on a small scale; and that they were justified as reprisals against Ethiopian atrocities (Del Boca, 1969: 81).[19]

Whether Italy was believed or not, the end result was that a much-hoped-for great power intervention on Ethiopia's behalf never happened. Instead, the war dragged on, with the desperate Ethiopians fighting a losing battle against a rain of death from the air.

---

[18] Del Boca relates a chilling story which supports the argument that many in the Italian military didn't know about Italy's resort to gas. It seems a general in Italy's military intelligence service and his aide had been snooping into the mail of a London news correspondent when they came upon some suspicious photographs: "they found several photographs of Ethiopians whose bodies were covered with sores. These photographs struck them as extremely suspect and a few minutes later they were on my desk. I looked at them and took them straight to Professor Castellano, then the leading authority on tropical diseases. He examined them and confirmed what I had suspected – there could be no doubt, he said, that the sores on the bodies of these Ethiopians had been caused by mustard gas. We stared at each other in deep embarrassment. After an awkward silence, Castellano added, 'Still, leprosy produces almost identical sores,' and he handed me a few photographs of lepers so that I could compare them with the others. As I could not spot the difference, I suddenly made up my mind: I would substitute the pictures of the lepers for the original photographs and let the package go on its way" (Del Boca, 1969: 80). This later enabled the fascist propaganda machine to declare the photographs, which later appeared in print, as "fabrications" intended to falsely malign the honor of Italian arms.
[19] Tales of Ethiopian atrocities had become a major fascination for average Italians. Alleged abuses included mutilating Italian corpses (in particular, cutting off their genitals), and especially the use of dum-dum bullets. The Italians also claimed that Ethiopian soldiers were using Red Cross hospitals as shelters from air attack.

Although the use of mustard gas killed or injured noncombatants as well as combatants, its use in this interaction of the war was directed against Ethiopia's soldiers. In other words, it was used in order to coerce Ethiopia by destroying its capacity to fight, not to punish Ethiopia by destroying its will to fight. In this sense, Italian strategy must best be described as conventional attack supplemented by barbarism.[20]

After four more battles, and the liberal application of mustard gas on retreating Ethiopian armies, the only remaining organized opposition between Eritrea and Addis Ababa was the emperor's Imperial Guard. After consultations with his advisors and surviving generals in which he attempted and again failed to convince them to adopt a GWS, Selassie decided to march to meet the Italians at Mai Chew with the best-trained and best-supplied forces Ethiopia could field. His plan was to feint a frontal assault against the Italian main position and then swing around with his main force to attack a weak point in the Italian left. The plan might have worked, but it depended on surprise and a degree of timing difficult to achieve under even the best of circumstances. In the event, the Italians intercepted a radio transmission containing all the details of the emperor's planned attack, and they altered their defensive arrangements to counter it.

The morning of the battle, March 31, 1936, the Ethiopians moved into position against the waiting Italians. Even with foreknowledge of the Ethiopian plans, the Italians were nearly overwhelmed in a few places. However, the tide of battle soon turned, and the emperor was forced to retire.[21]

As at all of the other battles, the Italian air force liberally doused the retreating Ethiopians with wave after wave of mustard gas mixed with high explosive. The retreat became a rout, and the emperor fled to

---

[20] This is supported by Sbacchi's argument that the fascists considered mustard gas to be "a means of legitimate warfare" (Sbacchi, 1985: 73).

[21] Del Boca argues that the Italian need for a decisive engagement was so great that many felt actual disappointment over the low Italian (read: white) casualty figures in the battle: "While no words can do justice to the heroic stand made by the Alpini and the gallantry of the Italian officers who set a shining example to their men," the "battle for the empire" was in fact won by the colored troops who shed their lifeblood so generously for the common cause. This afforded little comfort to Mussolini who hoped to certify that, through the state, his people had acquired a strength as solid and durable as cement. Indeed, for the next few months, he was filled with bitter disappointment. Denis Mack Smith interpreted his feelings correctly: "The Duce grieved over the fact that the fallen Italians had not even numbered 2,000 and that the war had been won at too low a price to reinvigorate the national character to the extent Fascism required" (Del Boca, 1969: 172).

Addis Ababa, closely pursued by the Italians. On May 2 he quietly slipped out of the capital with his wife and family on a train bound for Djibuti. The war was over and Ethiopia had been crushed.

### Interaction three: barbarism vs. GWS

But the war was not over. It should have been, and might have been, but for the continued use of mustard gas in the hunt for the emperor's remaining loyal generals. As noted above, the aerial application of mustard gas (especially from sprayers attached to the wings) was a far from discriminate weapon. Its use during the war itself had already stirred much resentment and caused terrible tragedies in Ethiopia. Now the Italians had won the war, but they continued to use yperite as a counterinsurgency weapon,[22] and many of Ethiopia's water resources were rendered deadly as a result. Livestock and mules continued to die, as did ordinary men, women, and children entering streams to wash themselves or their clothing.

On July 28, 1936, after almost two months of relative peace, a group of resistance leaders launched a four-pronged assault on the capital. It was repulsed, but after the rains ended in November, Graziani, the newly appointed viceroy of Africa Orientale Italiana (or Italian East Africa: AOI), ordered the capture or destruction of the rebel leaders. Italian columns fanned out into the countryside. By December, all the remaining resistance leaders had been captured: all were shot on Mussolini's orders save Ras Imru, whom Graziani, uncharacteristically, spared.

But Graziani's brutal methods soon backfired. Resentment built to the point that an attempt was made on his life. On February 19, 1937, Graziani was seriously wounded by a hand-grenade fragment during the assassination attempt. In fury and anger, the Italians ordered the most brutal of reprisals: for three days the capital city became a hunting ground, as soldiers, Black Shirts, and even common citizens vented their fury and frustration by killing, raping, and burning at will (Del Boca, 1969: 221–222).

Unable to find his would-be assassins, Graziani took the opportunity to murder the entire Ethiopian intelligentsia, every member of the Young Ethiopian Party, and all the officers and cadets of the Holeta

---

[22] "Not only was gas used throughout the war, but afterward as well to break down the resistance of the Ethiopian patriots, as we know from a telegram dated September 11, 1936, sent by Graziani . . . 'Today our air force will carry out reprisals, dropping various asphyxiating gases between those who have submitted and those who have not . . .'" (Del Boca, 1969: 82).

[military] Academy (Del Boca, 1969: 222). Graziani's methods were heartily approved in Rome, but

> the wish was nevertheless expressed that the executions be carried out in the utmost secrecy with no witnesses present, an instruction that, needless to say, was never followed. The apparent rebuke rankled Graziani, who wired back in order to justify himself, "I cannot deny that some Ethiopians have shouted as they faced the firing squad, "Long live Ethiopia!" I beg to state, however, that executions ordered in consequence of the attempt on my life are invariably carried out in isolated spots where no one, I repeat, no one can witness them.
>
> (Del Boca, 1969: 222–223)

But of course they were witnessed. Worse still, on May 20, 1937, Graziani ordered 297 monks of Debra Libanos, Ethiopia's most famous monastery, to be shot. The enormity of this atrocity had the opposite of its intended effect: instead of cowing the population, it incensed them.[23] Italian outposts came under fire, and convoys were ambushed and destroyed. Whole regions, in particular Gojjam and Beghemder, rose in revolt.

In addition, Graziani appeared to have become mentally unbalanced by the attempt on his life and his failure to find the assassins. He reportedly locked himself into his bedroom at night, and had an entire battalion assigned to his personal security. By November, his eccentric behavior and his counterproductive policies eventually prompted Mussolini to replace him with the duke of Aosta – a man reputed to be humane as well as intelligent.[24]

### Interaction four: conventional attack vs. GWS

The duke inherited an impossible situation. His intention had been to attempt to reverse the revolts by a combination of direct military action against the most powerful opposition, combined with an amnesty and a halt to summary executions. But the Ethiopians had ceased altogether

---

[23] Mockler explains the consequences of the accumulation of brutalities: "Killings and atrocities, however, no longer acted as a deterrent, for the [Ethiopians] had been driven to desperation. The internal feuds and quarrels which had made so many of them accept, if not welcome, an alternative to their Shoan rulers, were submerged in the face of a common enemy. Their leaders had been treacherously killed. Their clergy had been treacherously massacred. Like any race faced with extermination they instinctively rebelled" (Mockler, 1984: 184).

[24] It is not clear why Mussolini chose the duke of Aosta to replace Graziani (Mockler, 1984: 186). All agree that Graziani needed to be replaced, and that the duke would have been the best candidate for the position, had not Graziani already "poisoned the well" with his brutal pacification policies.

to trust the Italians. To get that trust back was possible, but only after years of hard work and consistent policy. Mussolini was hardly likely to be patient in this regard, and the duke's main military advisor, General Cavallero, was soon complaining behind the duke's back to Rome that the duke's lenience was counterproductive.

In March through April of 1938, the Italians launched a series of major military campaigns intended to crush the rebellions in Gojjam and Beghemder. The invasion of Gojjam was undertaken by 60,000 troops, and appeared to achieve all its aims. But no sooner had Gojjam been declared pacified than new threats appeared.

Cavallero decided to try a different strategy. Instead of deploying regular forces in overwhelming numbers as at Gojjam, he created three flying columns or *Gruppo Bande* which he dedicated to the capture of Abebe Aregai, one of the most exasperating of the resistance leaders, who had been trying for months to relocate his forces in the much more forbidding terrain of Menz.[25] The fighting, which lasted from the end of the rains in October to December of 1938, proved inconclusive.[26] Aregai succeeded in reaching Menz and joining Dejaz Auraris, and both survived repeated Italian efforts to destroy them. The Italians withdrew.

If Graziani's pacification policies sparked a unified rebellion against Italian rule, the duke of Aosta's more lenient policies and more conventional assaults had not proven effective at solving the military problem. At the close of 1938, Ethiopia was still in full revolt. Its resistance leaders were still at large, and the sixty-five Italian battalions in Ethiopia were forced to live inside their forts. In March of 1939 the duke was recalled to Rome for "talks." Meanwhile, Hitler invaded Czechoslovakia, and Europe began to brace itself for war.

### Interaction five: conciliation vs. GWS

In Ethiopia 1939 was a different sort of year. There was no repeat of the previous year's intensive military campaigns against intransigent rebel leaders for two reasons. First, the costs of such operations in terms of

---

[25] Menz was the heartland of the Shoan kingdom. It rose 10,000 feet above sea level, and occupied 850 square miles of plateaux. Its governor was a respected Shoan noble named Dejaz Auraris, who was another of the resistance leaders the Italians desperately sought to capture or kill.

[26] Part of the problem was that although Cavallero's *bande* were more mobile and independent, they lost proportionately in firepower. Much of the fighting which took place from October to December, therefore, was virtually hand-to-hand. Although casualties were high on both sides, it proved impossible to achieve decisive results in this way.

money had become staggering. The previous year's operations alone had cost three times as much as the entire bill for the administration and development of the colony, and the results had been inconclusive.

The second reason was a new focus on preparations to defend Ethiopia in the event of a war breaking out between the European powers. Mussolini did not intend to draw on support from Ethiopia in the defense of Italy, but he made it clear that in the event of war Ethiopia was on its own. For this reason, the Italians spent much of the year and proportionately more of their resources organizing an army for the defense of the AOI from an attack by British or French forces. As a result, Italian efforts against rebellion in Ethiopia shifted emphasis from coercion to bribery, amnesty, and negotiation. Ironically, now that they had given up trying to win a COIN war against the Ethiopian resistance, this combination of policies proved to be more effective than anything the Italians had so far attempted.

As the year came to a close, Europe was at war, but although Poland had fallen, the situation in Europe had stabilized. Italy remained neutral, and as a result, tensions between Britain, France, and Italy in East Africa eased.

## World War II in East Africa

By 1940, the only significant resistance leader still holding out was Abebe Aregai. The Italians spent the first part of the year attempting to gain his trust by bribes, promises of amnesty, and promises of independence after submission to Italian rule. These negotiations ended in March, however, after the Italians were warned that the planned submission of Aregai was in fact an ambush.

In April, Germany invaded Norway and in May, France. In June, Italy declared war on a defeated France, prompting Britain's Prime Minister Winston Churchill to call Mussolini "the jackal of Europe."

Italy's declaration of war instantly transformed the strategic map of North and East Africa. In June of 1940, the AOI had 250,000 troops supported by 200 aircraft, as compared to Britain's 10,000 troops and 20 aircraft (Mockler, 1984: 208). A major concern for the British was being sandwiched between Italy's considerable armies in Libya and the AOI in East Africa. But the Italians were not thinking about offense in the Spring of 1940:

> "I saw the Duke of Aosta this morning," [Italian Foreign Minister Ciano] wrote in his Diary for April 6. "He tells me that for him it is

not only impossible to take the offensive but will also be extremely difficult to hold his actual positions because the Anglo-French are now well-equipped and ready for battle and the population, among whom rebellion is still smouldering, will rise as soon as they have the sensation that we are in trouble." (Mockler, 1984: 208)

The French in Djibouti were prepared to join with their British allies in the defense of East Africa. But they were soon knocked out of the war, and Djibouti's commander was forced to become a passive bystander in the Anglo-Italian fight.

That fight did not last long. Although the British had hoped to spark a rebellion in AOI by the return of Haile Selassie [27] (supported by British-led guerrillas along the lines of T. E. Lawrence's adventures in Arabia), the fight itself was soon reduced to a series of conventional strikes and counterstrikes, with the British initially getting the worst of each encounter. In August of 1940, the Italians even succeeded in routing British forces in British Somaliland.

But Italian success in Somaliland emboldened them to try their luck against Egypt from Libya. These forces, under the inept leadership of a rehabilitated Graziani, advanced several miles into Egypt, but stopped at Sidi Barrani. In December, the British Army of the Nile counter-attacked, and the Italians were shattered: "At one stroke the threat to Cairo and the hope of linking the two halves of Italy's African Empire were removed; and at one stroke Italian morale dissolved" (Mockler, 1984: 307).

The collapse of Italian morale was not confined to North Africa. The impact on the AOI was devastating – all the more so because the defeated Italian troops had been led by none other than Graziani:

> But it was, naturally, among the Ethiopians that the defeat of Graziani had the greatest effect. He had been their conqueror and, as Viceroy, their tyrant. As the victorious Army of the Nile pressed on and in its turn invaded enemy territory to capture first Bardia and then Tobruk with fresh hordes of prisoners, George

---

[27] Interestingly, Mockler argues that the British were embarrassed and concerned by Haile Selassie's return to the Middle East. Their early concern was that his presence would provoke an attack on Sudan by Italy (Mockler, 1984: 226). After some thought, however, it occurred to the British that after all, they were at war so then the issue became, how best to use Selassie for their own ends. This was not clear either. Britain was dramatically outgunned in Egypt, Sudan, Kenya, and British Somaliland: all places where they expected Italian attacks. And attack the Italians did, though they never pressed their advantage. It then occurred to the British that the way to take the pressure off was to seriously foment rebellion within Ethiopia.

Steer[28] issued leaflet after leaflet with photographs of long lines
of Italian captives. (Mockler, 1984: 309)

In 1941, it was the revitalized British who took the initiative, and
Italian forces everywhere in East Africa collapsed. Haile Selassie was
returned to Ethiopia on 20 January, 1941 and, after a series of sharp
battles, British forces with Ethiopian support forced the Italians to
surrender. On May 5, 1941, five years to the day since Badoglio had
marched triumphant into Addis Ababa, the emperor once again took
his seat on the lion throne.

### Outcome: Italy wins, or does it?

The Italo-Ethiopian War ended when Britain entered the war in North
Africa against Italy in 1940. At that point the Italians become obsessed
with the British and begin pursuing a war-ending strategy with the
Ethiopian resistance. The Italo-Ethiopian war is subsumed by World
War II. Had Britain not entered the war, Italy would have won in the
short term but lost in the long term. Italy did win interaction five, but
only with the promise of years of heavy bribes could it have maintained
its victory, and Italy's economy could never have supported such a
policy for more than a year.

What emerges most clearly from this case is that Italy in 1935
possessed a supremely incompetent military. It was so ineptly led
that its effectiveness must go down in the annals of military history
as one of the poorest of the period. The Ethiopian emperor had worked
out an ideal defense strategy which took advantage of Ethiopian
strengths while minimizing its severe weaknesses, but his generals
would not listen. They insisted on opposing a conventional Italian
attack with a conventional Ethiopian defense, a defense which
included observing the peculiar (and in this case debilitating) custom
of ending all fighting at sunset. The Italian military's incompetence,
especially evident in the early interactions of the war, forced a stark
decision: risk high losses and setbacks in a hard fight for Addis Ababa,
or cheat by using mustard gas against an adversary with no defense
against it and no capacity to respond in kind. The choice of mustard
gas facilitated Italy's short-term military aims but – especially after
Selassie's flight from the capital – undermined its political goal of

---

[28] Steer had been responsible for all counter-AOI propaganda efforts, including a highly
successful Imperial Proclamation (or *Awaj*), in which the emperor had declared his
imminent return, and had called on all loyal Ethiopians to desert and resist the Italians.

establishing a viable self-sustaining colony. It stimulated rather than reduced resistance, and it increased the costs of the subsequent bribes necessary to keep Ethiopia's princes from leading attacks against Italian troops in AOI.

## Analysis: competing explanations of the Italo-Ethiopian War's outcome

### *Actor interests*

Italy's interests in the conquest of Ethiopia had little to do with its power relative to Ethiopia. It might be more accurate to argue that its interests were explained by Italy's power relative to other *European* powers. Italians in general, and Mussolini in particular, clearly felt that the other European powers had not accorded Italy the respect due a European state, especially one which had been an ally during the Great War. Italy's interest in Ethiopia reduced to four elements. First, a need to redress past humiliations by a decisive military victory over the only Africans to successfully repel a colonizing European power. Second, a need to confirm the "virility" of fascism as an ideology by a hard-fought military victory: defeat or even significant delay could undermine the legitimacy of Mussolini's fascist regime and in this sense, Italy's survival was at stake. Third, a civilizing mission or duty, which Italy sought to undertake to prove to the world its status as a true light of civilization. Fourth, a powerful and growing sense of *necessity* due to overpopulation and unemployment. The combination of these four elements made Italian resolve to see the conflict through much higher than that which could be predicted by a gap in the relative material power of Italy and Ethiopia.

Ethiopia's interests were survival, and, recognizing its weakness *vis-à-vis* Italy, Ethiopia consciously sought the aid of other states in pursuit of this interest. Foreign advisors found it difficult to understand why, in the face of such overwhelming force, the emperor refused to back down and accept Italian demands without a fight. But Ethiopian imagination had been as fixated by the victory at Adowa as the Italians had been about their defeat there. Ethiopia's noble houses believed they could repeat their victory again if the Italians chose to invade. Early on, the emperor himself counted on two things. First, he counted on the intervention of the League of Nations to prevent an all-out war. Second, he hoped to fight a GWS in the event of war, which the League would almost certainly act to stop. Neither of these hopes were realized, but Ethiopia never surrendered to Italy.[29]

### Regime types, strategy, and vulnerability

In 1935, Italy had an authoritarian regime type. Italian foreign and domestic policy were under the complete control of Benito Mussolini.

The effects of regime type on strategy are clear in this case. Because Mussolini had complete control over the Italian press (and some control over foreign press access to the battle space), the invasion of Ethiopia presented strategic options which would have been more risky when prosecuted by a democratic regime. Specifically, although Italy had signed the Geneva Protocol prohibiting the use of chemical weapons in war, it was clear that early on Mussolini planned to use such weapons in Ethiopia, and, moreover, he was confident that he could get away with it. How could this be, in 1935, when all of the European powers now boasted mass-literate populations and extensive and sophisticated press corps?

To get away with barbarism required managing three kinds of witnesses and two audiences. The three sorts of witnesses were Italian newsmen, foreign correspondents, and foreign aid workers. The two audiences were Italians and other states. The fascists had a strategy for each group.

Italian newsmen were carefully selected and briefed before going to the Ethiopian theater:

> "Before we left Italy," wrote Bruno Roghe ... "we were received by the Hon. Dino Alfieri, then Under-Secretary of State, who greeted us, wished us luck, and gave us the exhortation that our press cards warranted: we were to be lively and concise in our reports so as to bring out in our style of writing the latest prerogatives of the Italian undertaking, vibrant with youth, unshakable determination, and single-mindedness of purpose." In other words this was an invitation to glorify the war, to exalt every incident into a shining example, to give voice, in fact, to a paean of unqualified praise, unmarred by the faintest shadow of doubt, the least trace of criticism.
>
> (Del Boca, 1969: 62)

---

[29] The fact that Ethiopia never formally surrendered to Italy had at least one crucial effect. The laws of war prohibit the execution or mistreatment of captured soldiers, but provide few if any such protections to "rebels." Had Ethiopia officially surrendered to Italy, the legitimacy of Graziani's executions of rebels would have been debatable. As it was, they were a clear violation of the laws of war as signed by Italy and the other European powers at Geneva.

Foreign correspondents were often fascists in their own countries, and those who weren't often experienced "technical difficulties" filing their reports.[30] Others were intimidated, or forbidden access to key areas or battles.

Finally, foreign aid workers were initially the target of intimidation tactics. Italian planes were ordered to buzz Red Cross field hospitals and to strafe near them in order to frighten the hospital administrators into leaving. When this failed, the Italians took to directly attacking such facilities, claiming their attacks were justified reprisals for Ethiopian violations of the laws of war. When evidence did leak out, and it did, the Italians had other strategies for dealing with such crises (see also Sbacchi, 1985:63):

> These were the Ethiopian charges [use of mustard gas, attack of Red Cross units, attacks on civilians], but the Italians, anticipating them, had already found a way to cloud them and confuse the issues. On December 26, the Italian government had sent a letter to the League of Nations charging the Ethiopians were using dumdum bullets. And on January 16 [the Italians] sent the League a letter reiterating the dumdum charge and adding to it a charge that Ethiopian soldiers were protecting themselves from bombardment by hiding under Red Cross flags. Wasn't that considered sufficient justification for bombing Red Cross units? It was considered sufficient justification in Geneva, anyway, for allowing the Ethiopian charges and Italian countercharges to balance themselves out. (Coffey, 1974: 275–276)

There are two crucial points to be made here about the Italians getting away with mass murder. First, they had a specific strategy in place for preserving the secrecy of their barbarism, and that strategy presupposed an authoritarian regime type. Second, the use of mustard gas *in the particular context of Ethiopia in 1935*, combined with a more vigorous conventional attack strategy, ended the war in time to avoid international intervention. As a result, Italy's victory was nearly a *fait accompli*. The question of Italy's use of mustard gas was not formally raised in Europe until March 30, 1936. At that time, it was agreed that it couldn't be discussed until a formal inquiry could be launched, because, as Lord Halifax put it, it would be wrong "to prejudge a matter so grave and so vitally affecting the honor of a great country [Italy] ... The first step

---

[30] As noted above, the Italian intelligence service specialized in interdicting unfavorable evidence.

must be to obtain the observations and comments of the Italian government" (Coffey, 1974: 317).

When it became apparent to everyone that the Italians were not only
using gas, but using it liberally and against noncombatants, the question again came up, this time at Geneva on April 8, 1936:

> When a question was raised about Italy's use of gas, most of the
> delegates agreed that efforts should be made to collect reliable infor-
> mation on the subject. But Pierre-Etienne Flandin, the French Foreign
> Minister, objected. He asked if any inquiries had been made into
> atrocities committed by Abyssinians, including the use of dumdum
> bullets.
>
> At a private meeting after the committee's first morning session,
> British Foreign Secretary Anthony Eden attacked the implications of
> Flandin's remarks. There was, Eden insisted, "a distinction between
> the irresponsible atrocities of undisciplined military forces and the use
> of poison gas which could not be other than a governmental act."
>
> Flandin agreed. He said the Italians were "very stupid" to use this
> form of warfare, but he doubted "the wisdom of issuing a formal
> condemnation at a moment when an attempt was being made to
> bring hostilities to an end, for this might disturb the negotiations."
>
> The Committee of Thirteen decided at a meeting later that day not to
> inquire into the Italian use of poison gas. (Coffey, 1974: 324–325)

By April 8, fully a week had passed since the last Ethiopian army in
the field had been smashed at Mai Chew. The war was already over.

In sum, Italy's authoritarian regime type made it much simpler to
avoid the risk of public disaffection and international intervention
when Italy resorted to a barbarism strategy. Still, even authoritarian
Italy was not entirely able to hide its barbarism from the world or its
own people. The fact of nonintervention can best be explained by the
context of the day, in which the goal of European stability had come to
mean so much to Europe's leaders that they were willing to sacrifice
every principle of morality and justice on its altar.

The impact of Italy's regime type on its political vulnerability to
military setbacks is clear in at least one important respect. As already
observed above, Mussolini had control of all the Italian public's access
to information about the course of the war and its conduct. Every letter,
photograph, and newsreel sent home was scrutinized and sanitized.
But among Italy's political elites, the course of the war and the frequent
setbacks Italian forces suffered early on, should have, according to
Mack, resulted in political vulnerability due to trade-offs among elite
interests. They did not. Mussolini determined what resources would be

expended to conquer and develop Ethiopia and that ended the matter. In fact, Mussolini himself makes the proposed link between authoritarian regime type and political vulnerability clear:

> On July 6, [1935], at Eboli, he had allowed himself to venture beyond prudence in an address to four Black Shirt divisions which were about to embark for Africa. Speaking from the back of a truck, he had completely exonerated Italy's soldiers of 1896 for their defeat at Adowa, blaming instead the "abject" government in Rome at that time. With his Fascist government in power, he assured the Black Shirt troops, their efforts in the field would get full support at home.
>
> (Coffey, 1974: 103)

There were trade-offs, of course, but these took the form of personnel transfers: generals sacked or promoted. But although there were intrigues and arguments, the basic aim of Ethiopia's conquest and colonization was not questioned: not by the Italian people, and not by the fascist political elite.

In sum, Italy's authoritarian regime type made its resort to barbarism more likely, and reduced the probability that it would be forced to withdraw from the fight due to domestic political pressure or interstate intervention.

### Arms diffusion

In none of the five historical cases analyzed here was arms diffusion a less plausible explanation for weak actor success than in the Italo-Ethiopian War. As noted above, the Ethiopians had few rifles, and fought for the most part barefoot. Paradoxically, this gave them greater mobility in the tough mountainous passes leading from Eritrea to the central plateau upon which Addis Ababa sat. For their own part, the Italians and their Eritrean allies tended to move in motorized columns. This gave them some advantages in terms of the artillery they could carry but these advantages were on balance overwhelmed by the disadvantages of having to move and maintain communications along poorly made roads and across innumerable ideal ambush sites.

The decisive technology proved to be airplanes. The Italians had them, the Ethiopians didn't. Once the Italians got organized, they were able to use their air force to spot concentrations of Ethiopian soldiers and thus degrade the Ethiopian ability to catch the Italians in surprise ambushes. This was especially devastating because the Ethiopians refused to fight at night, when the Italian air advantage could have been nullified. When air-dropped mustard gas was added to the reconnaissance function of air power, the military contest quickly became one-sided.

### Strategic interaction

The Italo-Ethiopian war provides five independent tests of the strategic interaction thesis. In this case, there were some surprises.

In the first interaction of the war, the strong actor should have won quickly, because Italy chose a conventional attack strategy and Ethiopia a conventional defense (same-approach). Yet not only did the Italian offensive bog down even before coming to grips with the enemy, but an Ethiopian counteroffensive threatened to drive the more numerous Italians back into Eritrea. The explanation for this outcome is poor Italian military leadership and an unwillingness to risk casualties. These factors, in this interaction, overwhelmed the expected effects of a same-approach interaction.

In the second interaction, the strong actor should have won, because Italy continued its conventional attack strategy against an Ethiopian conventional defense. Italy did win, but it won with the help of mustard gas. In the Ethiopian theater, mustard gas proved to be a powerful force multiplier. Although the indiscriminate nature of air-delivered mustard gas makes its use barbarism under my definition, in this interaction of the war Italy used gas to destroy Ethiopia's military capacity, not its will to resist. In this interaction, then, the use of gas does not indicate a shift in strategy so much as tactics. The interaction remains same-approach and the outcome was as expected.

In the third interaction, the strong actor should have won, because Italy employed a barbarism strategy against an uncoordinated Ethiopian GWS (same-approach). In this case, the use of gas was combined with the summary executions of noncombatants, rape, and reprisal killings, all intended to coerce the will of the Ethiopian resistance. It is difficult to assess with any certainty the outcome of this interaction, because it was so brief. As noted in Chapter 4, in a barbarism strategy there tends to be a gap between when the strategy is first put into effect and when it begins to yield military dividends. Although the Italians had been using gas against Ethiopian troops (and, inadvertently, noncombatants) for some time, the real initiation of a barbarism strategy dates from the accession of Graziani to the position of viceroy in 1936, and especially after the attempt on his life in February 1937. But, in November, Mussolini replaced Graziani "just as he was getting started." The accession of the duke of Aosta to the position of viceroy caused a shift in strategy once again.

In the fourth interaction, the weak actor should have won, since Italy pursued a conventional attack strategy against an Ethiopian GWS (opposite-approach). And, as predicted, the Ethiopians not only survived Italian attempts to destroy them but began to contest many of the areas formerly under Italian control. But, ironically, the very expense of the effort to use large conventional units to chase Ethiopian guerrilla leaders prompted yet another shift in strategy.

In the fifth interaction, the strong actor should have won, because Italy switched from attempting to coerce Ethiopian resistance to trying to bribe it (conciliation *vs.* GWS: same-approach). As predicted, Italy did win, or might have won, had not World War II intervened. The accession of the duke of Aosta to viceroy had prompted a major thaw in British–Italian relations. The duke liked the British, and the British admired and respected the duke (Mockler, 1984: 187–188, 194). Yet Mussolini's decision to enter the war against France and Britain instantly changed all that.

In sum, by the logic of the strategic interaction thesis, Italy should have won every interaction of its contest in Ethiopia save one (interaction four: conventional attack *vs.* GWS). Yet it lost interaction one (conventional attack *vs.* conventional defense). The reason it lost when it should have won is poor leadership. The five interactions of the Italo-Ethiopian War, the nature of the strategic interaction in each interaction, and outcomes are summarized in Table 1.

## The problem of leadership

The effects of strategic interaction were overwhelmed in the war's first interaction by the incompetent Italian generalship. Italy's generals in Africa were to become as famous for their incompetence as for their brutality. Many Italian officers were brave and many were competent, and none of Italy's enemies have faulted the bravery or skill of the individual Italian soldier. But the generals – De Bono, Badoglio, Graziani, Cavallero, Trezzani[31] – have been condemned to live in military infamy. Mockler offers the following curious explanation:

[31] Trezzani took over from Cavallero on April 20, 1940. Mockler characterizes him this way: "He was one of the few Italian senior officers who had never served in a colonial campaign, or indeed in the colonies at all. His career had been that of a professor at the School of War. His interests were in tactics, his approach one of detached calculation. He was Badoglio's man – imbued with skepticism before he ever set foot in Africa... If the Italians had deliberately decided to choose a general whose prime characteristic was his capacity for lowering the morale of the troops he was to command, their choice could hardly have fallen on a better man" (Mockler, 1984: 209).

Table 1. Strategic interaction and outcomes: the Italo-Ethiopian War, 1935–1940

|  |  | strong actor strategy | weak actor strategy | strategic interaction | actual outcome |
|---|---|---|---|---|---|
| Phase | 1 | conventional attack | conventional defense | same-approach | Ethiopia wins |
|  | 2 | conventional attack/barbarism | conventional defense | same-approach | Italy wins |
|  | 3 | barbarism | GWS | same-approach | Italy wins |
|  | 4 | conventional attack | GWS | opposite-approach | Ethiopia wins |
|  | 5 | [conciliation] | GWS | [same-approach] | [Italy wins] |

> It seems to me that, consciously or subconsciously, the memory of Adowa and of General Baratieri's end must have been preying on the minds of all Italian generals in Africa. Only this can explain their reluctance ever to move forward till they had overwhelming superiority totally assured and lines of communication totally safe. Only this can explain, and perhaps excuse, their inability, even then, to move forward at more than a snail's pace. So many missed opportunities cannot but have been pathological. They were certainly disastrous.
>
> (Mockler, 1984: 254)

The true test of this thesis would be to assess Italian military leadership in other theaters of war – say Greece or Russia. Were Italian generals more aggressive or more generally competent? They were neither.

One is tempted to argue that Italy's top generals were merely Mussolini's fascist cronies with epaulettes, and the incompetence which resulted was therefore the inevitable concomitant of an authoritarian regime. But this is unsatisfactory. The French military had its share of cronyism and incompetence and it was a democracy. Moreover, fascist Germany fielded the most effective military leadership the world had ever seen.

## Conclusion

The Italo-Ethiopian War was an asymmetric conflict between fascist Italy and imperial Ethiopia. Italy won.

Italian interests reduced to revenge for the defeat at Adowa in 1896, a need to legitimize fascism as an ideology, responsibility for "civilizing" a barbarous black African state in the Horn of Africa, and resources with which to ameliorate its poverty and population problems. Ethiopian interests reduced to survival and honor.

Relative material power did not explain relative interests in the case of the strong actor, Italy. Relative material power may explain Ethiopia's interests, however. How, if at all, did regime type explain the strategies or political vulnerability of the strong actor? Hypothesis 8 – relative material power explains relative interests in the outcome of an asymmetric conflict – is not supported in the Italo-Ethiopian War.

As we have seen above, Italy's strategic choice was affected by its regime type. Mussolini was always concerned about the possibility of foreign intervention – economic or military – and he counted on being able to manage information about his intentions and conduct in the war in order to forestall such intervention. He understood the risks involved in his decision to make mustard gas – a prohibited weapon of war – available to his commanders in Ethiopia. Italy's resort to barbarism in fact presupposed the total management and control of information on the conduct of the campaign.

In terms of political vulnerability, Italians, regardless of political affiliation or class, all shared the dream of having a thriving colony in Africa.[32] Mussolini demanded it as Italy's right. Italy's preponderance in material power should have made it politically vulnerable to military setbacks – if not by the weight of public opinion then at least as a consequence of trade-offs among fascist political elites. But although Italy experienced stunning setbacks during its Ethiopian campaign, and although evidence of Italy's use of mustard gas did leak out, this didn't happen. Regime type therefore matters more than allowed by the interest asymmetry argument. But if nature-of-actor and interest asymmetry arguments cannot explain the outcome, can arms diffusion or strategic interaction?

Arms diffusion can't. Bluntly, the Ethiopians did not receive arms of any quantity or sophistication until the British entered the war in 1940. For this reason, hypothesis 6 – the better armed a weak actor is, the more likely it is that a strong actor will lose – is not tested here. Prior to the war, Ethiopia's emperor had been counting on diplomatic support and even military intervention from his fellow League members in Europe. Ethiopia was too poor and too proud to import arms as the Boer had done prior to their fight with the British.

Strategic interaction best explains the outcome of the war, though even strategic interaction is not proof against poor Italian leadership. With one exception, each strategic interaction of the war contained an interaction which favored an Italian military victory. The first interaction of the war featured a conventional attack *vs.* a conventional defense, and Italy appeared poised to lose this fight due to bad generalship. The stalling of the Italian advance, combined with effective Ethiopian counterattacks, led in the second interaction of the war to a shift in strategy. Italy employed a conventional attack strategy aided by a super-weapon against an Ethiopian conventional defense. This

---

[32] For a contrary view, see Sbacchi, 1997. Sbacchi convincingly recounts a broad Italian opposition to Mussolini's planned "adventure" in Ethiopia, but fails to provide a sense of how widespread such opposition in fact was. In addition, Sbacchi's account suggests that once Italians became convinced of military success in the initial months of the war, Italian public opinion shifted to support the invasion unconditionally.

strategy proved highly effective militarily, and Ethiopia's organized resistance collapsed within a few months. The Italians won.

But the very methods used in Ethiopia's conquest – and especially the post-war policy of summary executions and continued use of mustard gas on "rebels" – sparked renewed resistance. The Italians might have won this third interaction of the conflict, but before it could register a military impact Mussolini cancelled it.

The fourth interaction of the war reverted to a conventional attack against any organized resistance. Only where Ethiopian forces sought to engage the Italians directly, as at Gojjam, were the Italians successful. In the remainder of the country the Italian conventional attacks were countered by a GWS, and the Italians lost. The costs of such operations were prohibitive, and the combination of those costs and the perceived need to become security self-sufficient in the event of war in Europe, led to a final shift in Italian strategy.

This fifth interaction of the war introduced a conciliation strategy for Italy, opposed by an Ethiopian GWS. Conciliation proved the most effective of all the strategies the Italians had attempted since marching into Addis Ababa in May of 1936. Only one rebel leader held out, and it seemed likely that but for the outbreak of World War II even Abebe Aregai would have been forced to flee Ethiopia or submit. The Italians would have almost certainly won the war in the short term.

But World War II changed all of this. The contest in Ethiopia ceased to be between occupying Italians and an Ethiopian resistance, and became a fight between the British and Italians fought in Ethiopia, Sudan, British Somaliland, and Kenya. At first, the Italians launched conventional attacks against British defenses, and they succeeded almost everywhere. However, they failed to exploit their victories, and after the collapse of Italy's armies in Libya and Egypt, the British launched a series of conventional attacks against Italian defenses. The British had hoped to coordinate these attacks with a British-sponsored "general uprising" in Ethiopia. Yet although they had devoted enormous resources to finding and funding a "Lawrence" for Ethiopia – Orde Wingate – Wingate's and Haile Selassie's triumphant re-entry into Ethiopia were superfluous to the outcome. The Italians fought hard in the north, but again suffered from poor leadership. While, in the south, a British probe toward the port city of Kassala in Italian Somaliland resulted in a complete rout of vastly superior Italian forces. Within one month, British forces invading from the south had rolled up the Italians and entered Addis Ababa.

On balance then, in four of five interactions, hypothesis 5 – strong actors are more likely to win same-approach interactions and lose opposite-approach interactions – was supported.

In sum, if we wish to explain why Italy lost the Italo-Ethiopian war, we cannot rely on relative power, regime type, interest asymmetry, or arms diffusion. With the exception of arms diffusion, these factors clearly mattered. But what mattered most was strategic interaction and Italian military leadership. Once it became clear that the capture of Addis Ababa would not force the Ethiopians to surrender, the Italians had three strategic choices. First, continue with the present strategy, perhaps sending more troops, and equipment to the theater. Second, offer the Ethiopians terms: something which could save face yet end the war. Third, switch to a barbarism strategy: take the gloves off and go after Ethiopian patriots and their families, either by holding them hostage or by killing them outright in reprisal for continued resistance. In the event, the Italians chose the third option. From then on, the Ethiopians maintained a GWS. But the Italians shifted and innovated a number of times, painstakingly improving their advantage until World War II came to Africa and swept them away.

# 6  The United States in Vietnam: the Vietnam War, 1965–1973

> Everything rotted and corroded quickly over there: bodies, boot leather, canvas, metal, morals. Scorched by the sun, wracked by the wind and rain of the monsoon, fighting in alien swamps and jungles, our humanity rubbed off of us as the protective bluing rubbed off the barrels of our rifles. We were fighting in the cruelest kind of conflict, a people's war. It was no orderly campaign, as in Europe, but a war for survival waged in a wilderness without rules or laws; a war in which each soldier fought for his own life and the lives of the men beside him, not caring who he killed in that personal cause or how many or in what manner and feeling only contempt for those who sought to impose on his savage struggle the mincing distinctions of civilized warfare – that code of battlefield ethics that attempted to humanize an essentially inhuman war.
>
> Caputo (1996)

US military intervention in Vietnam began soon after the French defeat at Dien Bien Phu in 1954. The full commitment of US combat troops, however, did not occur until eleven years later. When US Marines came ashore at Da Nang in 1965 the US population was about 194 million, while North Vietnam's was approximately 19 million.[1] US and North Vietnamese armed forces totaled approximately 2.5 million and 256,000, respectively. Adding in allies who contributed combat troops (negligible), multiplying population and armed forces, and dividing the strong actor's total by two results in a relative force ratio of about 53:1 in favor of the United States. Even allowing for the fact that the United States did not actually devote half its "power" to the

---

[1] These figures are taken from Singer and Small, *Correlates of War*, war number 163.

conflict,[2] this was an asymmetric conflict and the United States and its allies were the strong actor.[3]

## The Vietnamese theater

The place we now call Vietnam has been known by many names: Cochinchina, Annam, and Indochina to name only the most prominent. Some of these place names corresponded to countries with borders similar to those of contemporary Vietnam and some included portions of what are now China, Laos, and Cambodia. The rich history of this land and its people – and in particular the strong relevance of that history to the events that unfolded in Indochina following the end of World War II – cannot be adequately captured here, but three key aspects of that history bear emphasis in this introduction.

First, the terrain and climate of Vietnam has always made it a forbidding place in which to conduct warfare of any type, but especially the kind of large-scale conventional warfare for which the United States was best prepared in 1965. Vietnam is both suffocatingly small and intolerably porous; open to the west along an impossible-to-seal border with Laos and Cambodia, and open to the east to the Gulf of Tonkin and South China Sea. Vietnam's economic and cultural life are dominated by its two river deltas. To the south, Vietnam's geography is dominated by the Mekong River delta. There are vast marshes, impenetrable jungles, mangrove swamps, countless rivers, and at times a sticky, sweltering heat such as few can imagine without actually having experienced it. In the Central Highlands there are thickly rain-forested hills and valleys; and to the north, still more mountains, covered with rain and monsoon forest, and cut by deep valleys whose rivers drain into the second of the country's two major river delta systems – the Red River delta.

Second, Vietnam's social, political, and military institutions were shaped by its terrain and climate, as well as by its predominant form of agriculture: wet rice farming. Wet rice farming demands cooperative labor, and as a result the Vietnamese developed a strong collective spirit and a militia tradition of defense against invasion (Karnow, 1983: 98–99).

---

[2] The logic of the relative power estimate does not require calculating how much of a given actor's power resources were applied to the fight. What matters is the resources an actor could have applied to win the war. On this point, see Schelling (1966: 142–143, 172).
[3] Even if we assume, for the sake of simplicity, that the contest was between only the United States and North Vietnam, the ratio shifts to 49:1 in favor of the United States.

Third, over the centuries Vietnam has been invaded often. Important ethnic divisions between North and South Vietnamese were most often shelved during foreign invasions. The Vietnamese people were therefore effective "nationalists" hundreds if not a thousand years before the rise of nationalism in Europe.[4] Frequent invasions resulted in both a loathing of would-be foreign conquerors (see e.g., Karnow, 1983: 58), and a strong military tradition. That military tradition often favored an indirect defense, utilizing the advantages of terrain and climate to wear down more powerful invaders rather than meeting them head-on in pitched battles. Here Stanley Karnow recounts the strategy of a thirteenth-century Vietnamese general defending against a Mongol invasion:

> The Vietnamese, commanded by the illustrious Tran Hung Dao, repulsed each offensive. Like outnumbered Vietnamese officers before and since, he relied on mobile methods of warfare, abandoning the cities, avoiding frontal attacks, and harassing his enemies until, confused and exhausted, they were ripe for final attack.
>
> (Karnow, 1983: 101)

Climate and terrain abetted this strategy, but in no way mandated its adoption. In its nineteenth-century struggles against France, for example, Vietnamese emperors and their generals were more often brought into direct engagements with their French attackers and in those fights invariably lost.[5]

But defeating the Vietnamese in battle never proved decisive. Again, this was partly because the Europeans had military technology specialized for winning major battles, not for maintaining control of hostile populations in difficult terrains and climates. By 1893 the French, after much difficulty and expense, had consolidated their control of what they came to call French Indochina: Tonkin (North Vietnam), Annam (South Vietnam), Cambodia, Laos, and Cochinchina. World War I soon followed, and Asian intellectuals, including Ho Chi Minh,

---

[4] Vietnamese nationalism was not monolithic, save during *foreign* invasions. During the Vietnam War, South Vietnamese communists had a national identity separate from that of Northerners. What united them strongly during the war was the presence of foreigners on Vietnamese soil (see Connor, 1969: 51–86; Karnow, 1983: 462, 534; and Herring, 1986: 271).
[5] This happened in large measure because in earlier fights between the Northern Trinh and the Southern Nguyen, France sold "modern" weapons to both sides. Modern weapons (breech-loading rifles, e.g.) rewarded different tactics and strategies, and encouraged the Vietnamese to confront their adversaries head-on. This proved disastrous, as even small French forces could always defeat larger formations of similarly armed and trained indigenous soldiers.

applauded US President Woodrow Wilson's passionate advocacy at Versailles of national self-determination as an antidote to future wars. Ho and others in Asia eagerly awaited the end of European colonialism. But when the victors – Britain and France – refused to dismantle their Asian empires, secret societies and revolutionary groups began to form and agitate. In 1930 the French brutally suppressed a nationalist uprising in Yen Bay, just north of Saigon. But, unlike elsewhere in Asia, French repression in Vietnam only succeeded in uniting their adversaries (Karnow, 1983: 58), giving them stronger incentives to resist French rule.

Like Mao in China, Ho recognized the opportunity provided by the Japanese conquest of Indochina. He reorganized the Indochinese Communist Party in order to capitalize on Vietnamese nationalism and to forge a broad alliance capable of seriously hurting the Japanese in Vietnam. As a result, many of these underground groups became affiliated or incorporated into the Indochinese Communist Party. These groups sharpened their insurgency skills against the Japanese occupation, and, during this time, came to view the United States as a natural ally. By late 1944 Vietnamese resistance led by Ho and his allies had become troublesome enough that Japan decided to "grant" Vietnam's independence under a puppet ruler, the Vietnamese Emperor Bao Dai. In March of 1945 Bao Dai declared Vietnam's independence. But his rule was short lived. In August, assuming Ho's claims to leadership of Vietnam had Allied support, Bao Dai abdicated and handed control of Vietnam to Ho Chi Minh, who proclaimed the Democratic Republic of Vietnam (DRV) on September 2, 1945.

The First Indochina War began in 1946, following the return of the French to Vietnam, Laos, and Cambodia. The tale of France's failed attempt to re-conquer and pacify Vietnam, the intrigues of the 1954 Geneva Conference on the fate of Indochina, and the decade of political and economic blunders (on both sides) that followed the Geneva Conference make interesting reading, but there is no space for a detailed review here. There are important points to take away from each experience, however.

First, by 1945, Vietnamese resistance to French rule had become truly nationalist and truly widespread. The French could not recognize that it was already too late to win enough "hearts and minds" to make reoccupation of Indochina a rational pursuit. Japan's invasion had forged a national resistance, and that resistance could not be as easily broken as before the war. Contrary to US assessments at the time, French military forces were on the whole well trained, well equipped, and skillfully led. But they were never sufficient in numbers to quell Vietnamese resistance to French rule. The French struggled in vain, and their efforts to defeat the Viet Minh eerily prefigure later US struggles to accomplish the even more limited goal of securing South Vietnam.[6]

Second, the DRV was soundly betrayed by China's Zhou Enlai at the negotiating table in Geneva. Far from the unified Vietnam the DRV felt it had earned on the battlefield following its victory over the French at Dien Bien Phu, backroom negotiations between China and France forced the DRV to accept both partition and a delayed election to determine Vietnam's ultimate fate. Further negotiations – the Soviet Union's Molotov intervened – forced a division at the 17th parallel, and set the date for elections in the summer of 1956.

### *The eve of war: North Vietnamese interests*

From 1945 until the end of the second Indochina (Vietnam) war in 1975, the DRV's interests remained the same: drive all foreigners from Vietnam, unifying the country under *Vietnamese* rule. Since the DRV considered those working with and for the United States to be effectively "foreign," this also meant the "liquidation" – as communist doctrine put it – of South Vietnam's government and its military.[7]

By 1959 the DRV had shifted emphasis from political agitation to preparation for war. It sent 4000 troops to the South and began formal construction of what would later be called the Ho Chi Minh trail: a serpentine supply route linking the North to the South through Laos and Cambodia. It also began smuggling arms to the South by sea. In 1960, the DRV established the National Liberation Front to coordinate the war in the South. By 1961, Viet Cong (VC) forces had begun escalating attacks against Diem's government in the South. Assassinations of village leaders and provincial officials had risen from 1200 a year in 1959 to 4000, and had provoked Diem into replacing them with military men, loyal to Diem but ignorant of the communities they were tasked to

---

[6] French *agrovilles*, for example, later became South Vietnamese/US "strategic hamlets"; and French *jaunissement* later became US "Vietnamization" under Nixon. In 1950, the French had to struggle with a skillfully led, perfectly dedicated foe supplied and supported by China. By 1965, US and South Vietnamese forces had to deal with the same problem: a line of supply that extended from China through North Vietnam to South Vietnam via the Ho Chi Minh trail.

[7] Frederick Brown makes the point that to the DRV the continued existence of a South Vietnam under foreign control was tantamount to a threat to its survival (see Brown 1980: 526).

serve and protect. In 1963 the DRV and VC began more aggressive and larger-scale actions against South Vietnam (henceforth the government of Vietnam or GVN). In January, a well-planned assault on VC forces at Ap Bac went horribly awry, as GVN soldiers effectively refused to fight and were severely mauled by the VC.

On the eve of Indochina's second war, the DRV maintained its passionate – even maniacal – interest in unifying Vietnam under Vietnamese rule. In pursuit of this objective, the DRV possessed *two* distinct armed forces: a conventional military (the North Vietnamese Army or NVA) and a nationalist guerrilla military (the VC).

### The eve of war: South Vietnamese government interests

As early as 1955 the GVN was well on the way to becoming synonymous with the person of Ngo Dinh Diem. If the fact that the DRV was ruled by the iron will of one man – Ho Chi Minh – is to be taken as a criticism, then that criticism cannot be spared the GVN under Diem.

The extent to which this was true makes it much simpler to explain why Vietnam was ultimately unified under the DRV and not the GVN; Diem, and the nature of his leadership remain controversial subjects to this day. A few scholars of the period claim that the picture of Diem as an eccentric autocrat is an unfair caricature promulgated by disenchanted US journalists, while most characterize him as a true Vietnamese nationalist, yet a man increasingly convinced of his own indispensability in securing a non-communist future for Vietnam. As a result, Diem's priorities on the eve of war were in his survival as Vietnam's sole ruler, not, as so fervently hoped by his ally the United States, the survival of South Vietnam as a viable, secure, and independent noncommunist state (the two goals often diverged, and Diem appeared unable to appreciate the difference). Diem's interest in securing his personal control over Vietnam (first South, then North) led to a steady restructuring of the GVN and its military. Ministers and officers were increasingly advanced based on loyalty to him or on a known grudge against a rival, rather than on merit or combat experience. In the decade stretching from the Geneva accords to the eve of the second Indochina war, this had the effect of reducing the GVN's military capabilities to the point where it was capable *only* of repressing domestic opposition and securing Diem against the machinations of his rivals in the South. This was made starkly clear to the United States at the debacle at Ap Bac in 1963.

Yet the success of Diem's efforts to secure his rule paradoxically supplied its greatest threat. Under a real and ever-escalating assault

from the DRV, Diem's often brutal suppression of dissent visibly weakened South Vietnam's defenses. By 1963, even loyal officers with little
interest in risking their lives in "adventures" against the VC in the
Mekong delta were aware that allowing Diem to continue might
mean South Vietnam's – and by extension, their own – destruction at
the hands of the DRV.

Diem's restructuring of the GVN had taken the better part of a
decade, and by the early 1960s US diplomats and military advisors
were well aware that it might take a decade of hard work to reconstruct
a GVN capable of capturing broad public support – a necessary precondition for fighting and winning a major war against a dedicated,
well-supplied, and increasingly skilled foe. This is why the decision to
oust Diem was so controversial at the time. If, as some in the Kennedy
administration believed, Diem had to go (Diem's repressive measures
had become the focus of increasingly irrepressible South Vietnamese
public outrage), then who would replace him and what positive difference could his replacement make?

Diem was murdered on November 1, 1963 and replaced by General
Nguyen Khanh. Instead of beginning the difficult work of repairing the
GVN and building a coalition of social and economic forces capable of
an effective defense against the VC, however, Khanh's first priority was
securing his *own* rule. Corruption and incompetence continued,
prompting the United States, now under the leadership of Lyndon
Baines Johnson, to further escalate its support. That support would
begin with the president's approval of covert sabotage and espionage
operations against the DRV, and eventually include the commitment of
US combat forces in March of 1965.

### The eve of war: US interests

US interests in the outcome of the war between the DRV and the GVN
remain a source of contention to this day. In the simplest terms, however, there is broad agreement about three key aspects.

First, US interests in Vietnam were colored by the personal political
interests of one man, President Lyndon Johnson. Johnson's true ambition as president was the passage of a package of social programs he
dubbed "The Great Society." Johnson had become president in 1963
after John F. Kennedy's assassination in Dallas, and had immediately
set about working toward his election as president in November of
1964. Although Johnson was aware that prior to Diem's assassination
President Kennedy had planned to withdraw some 16,000 US military

advisors from Vietnam, the assassination of Diem put those plans on hold while the president's national security team reevaluated the costs and benefits of a withdrawal from Vietnam. Moreover, Johnson was well aware that his chief rival, the Republican nominee, Senator Barry Goldwater, would attack him as a "liberal" who was soft on defense. For this reason alone Johnson continued to support covert military action against the DRV, including secret sabotage and espionage operations against DRV military facilities.[8] His immediate political objective was to provide enough support to stabilize Vietnam and defend against Goldwater's accusation that he was soft on communism. Once elected, he planned to reassess Vietnam: perhaps escalating a US commitment or perhaps engineering a withdrawal.

Second, the United States was never interested in seeking the direct overthrow of the DRV. It remained content with a Vietnam divided across a DMZ just as Korea had been divided and for the same reason: it feared China's entry into the war and a possible escalation to, as Johnson put it, "World War III." US interests were in this sense, and only this sense, accurately described as "limited." In 1965 the United States viewed the survival of the GVN as worth fighting and dying for, under the condition that (a) it wouldn't be too costly a war, and (b) in support of the theory that the fall of the GVN would very likely lead to the collapse of other noncommunist regimes in Southeast Asia, perhaps overwhelming Japan and India and ultimately threatening more vital US interests in Europe and the Western Hemisphere.[9]

Third, the deployment of US combat forces to Da Nang in 1965 was viewed by the president as crossing a threshold, but not to the degree that with hindsight seems so obvious today. As would happen so many

---

[8] It was these operations, an accidental coincidence of an Op-Plan 34-A sabotage attack against the DRV, and a top-secret DeSoto electronic espionage mission being undertaken by the USS *Maddox*, that led to the first Tonkin Gulf incident of August 2, 1964, in which three DRV patrol boats attempted to attack the *Maddox* with torpedoes, but were driven off with minor damage. A second attack was alleged, and at the time genuinely believed, by the United States on August 4. Subsequent analysis and extensive research has revealed that this second attack, which prompted Johnson's military retaliation and the Tonkin Gulf Resolution (August 7, 1964), never actually happened. On this last point see Moisie (1996).

[9] After 1968 it became increasingly clear that the survival of the GVN was not worth the cost of securing it, but by then the United States had another rationale for staying – prestige and precedent setting. The United States had said the GVN would stand, and even those in the administration now long convinced of the hollowness of the domino argument could agree that a US failure in South Vietnam might endanger vital US national interests elsewhere or in the future.

times later, Johnson and his advisers were attempting to use US military forces to send careful and clear messages to the North – "we don't seek to overthrow you but we refuse to permit your support of 'aggression' against the GVN" – never fully comprehending how badly these "messages" would be translated. These force messages were invariably thought of as necessary and limited escalations which were likely to yield quick and positive political results. When they did not, the president and his team tended to respond – not by questioning the *process* of communicating by the use of military strikes – but by sending yet another "clarifying" message.

Overall, the United States went to war in Vietnam to stabilize an ally and prevent what it then believed to be the first step in a Soviet-inspired, Chinese-supported, communist takeover of Southeast Asia. In 1965, the Johnson administration believed that US military power and technology could make it possible to secure the GVN without a major escalation or a declaration of war. With the power to punish the DRV from the air and destroy the VC on the ground, most in the administration believed the only question unresolved as the Marines waded ashore at Da Nang was, "how much punishment would they take before calling it quits in the South?" (Mueller, 1980: 500).

## The Vietnam War

The Vietnam War is one of the last century's most complex military and political engagements. US military intervention, for example, involved four overlapping strategic interactions: (1) barbarism (ROLLING THUNDER) against a conventional defense; (2) a conventional attack against a conventional defense (the main-force units war); (3) conventional attacks against a GWS (the guerrilla war in the South I); and (4) barbarism against GWS (the guerrilla war in the South II).

### Interaction one: ROLLING THUNDER, 1965–68

The first strategic interaction of the war began in March 1965 with a US strategic bombing campaign, later named ROLLING THUNDER.[10] Its main goal was to destroy the willingness of North Vietnam to support

[10] On the origins of the ROLLING THUNDER campaign, its purpose, and collateral damage to noncombatants, see Karnow (1983: 397, 458). On relative US moral restraint in ROLLING THUNDER, Karnow (1983: 653). For a dedicated analysis of ROLLING THUNDER and its failure, see Thompson (1980); and for a theoretical treatment that anticipates the strategic interaction thesis, see Pape (1996: ch. 6). Pape's overall argument

the guerrilla war campaign against South Vietnam, and as its name implied, the campaign was expected to take time:

> Instead of a coordinated air campaign...which would destroy the enemy's ability to wage war and break their will to resist, air operations over the North were designed as a diplomatic "slow squeeze" signaling device. As Secretary of Defense Robert S. McNamara said on February 3, 1966, "US objectives are not to destroy or to overthrow the Communist government of North Vietnam. They are limited to the destruction of the insurrection and aggression directed by North Vietnam against the political institutions of South Vietnam."
>
> (Summers, 1995: 96)

The United States sought to inflict enough pain on North Vietnam to compel it to stop supporting the VC in the South. North Vietnam's defense against ROLLING THUNDER was conventional: it sought to thwart US military attacks on its infrastructure and forces by means of fighter aircraft and an increasingly dense radar and surface-to-air missile defense network supplied to them by the Soviets.

US Air Force generals and their civilian leaders shared a theory about the general effectiveness of strategic bombing as a strategy. Strategic bombing should have both hampered North Vietnam's war effort (interdiction) and coerced its leadership into giving up (pain). When neither expectation was met, military and civilian elites faced a stark choice: either reject the theory, or blame failure on some flaw in implementation. The Air Force chose to emphasize flaws, while the Johnson administration was increasingly split: some agreed that the United States was hitting the wrong targets, or not hitting the right targets hard enough, whereas others – including eventually Defense Secretary McNamara – concluded that strategic bombing against the DRV could not work. McNamara's reports indicated that the military value of ROLLING THUNDER's destroyed targets was zero.[11] Bombing that accepted collateral damage subsequent to this recognition was therefore barbarism: the deaths and injury to individual noncombatants

---

is that when air power is used to target an adversary's armed forces, it generally wins, and when used to target an adversary's values (including infrastructure), it generally fails. Insofar as punishment and denial represent indirect and direct strategic approaches, respectively, Pape's argument, as Mearsheimer's (1983) before it and mine after, is an argument for the independent causal impact of strategy on conflict outcomes, (see also May, 2000). May explains French defeat in the Battle of France in 1940 as a function of strategic interaction: the Germans simply had a better strategy.

[11] Its political utility was less than zero: it increased international and domestic opposition to the US war effort, and although the North Vietnamese feared and hated the bombing, they never considered altering their war aims as a result of the pain it inflicted.

and their property were not specifically *intended*, but they were collectively deliberate and systematic.

ROLLING THUNDER continued until a week before the November 1968 US presidential election. It was an interaction in which a strong actor (the United States) employed an indirect strategy against a weak actor (North Vietnam) using a direct strategy, and lost.[12]

## Interaction two: the main-force units war, 1965–1969

The main-force units war featured a series of pitched battles between regular units of North Vietnam and of the United States and the South Vietnamese Army (ARVN). In a series of engagements that lasted throughout the war, US forces proved overwhelmingly successful at destroying NVA and VC main-force units.

Examples of this interaction, which opposed a strong actor conventional strategy with a weak actor conventional strategy, include Operation STARLITE (August 1965), the Battle of Ia Drang (October–November 1965), MASHER/WHITE WING (January–March 1966), and Phase II of Operation ATTLEBORO (October–November 1966).[13] As the ground war continued into 1968, the frequency of these interactions dwindled, and US forces in the South focused increasingly on the problem of counterinsurgency.

Part of the decreasing frequency of this interaction reflected actor learning: North Vietnam's leadership analyzed main-force unit engagements carefully, and concluded that US forces were so adept at combining maneuver and firepower that, unless the encounter took place between dramatically mismatched forces (as at landing zone Albany in November 1965), NVA and VC main-force units would invariably be destroyed. In the context of Mao's warning above, native forces were fighting with inferior weapons on US terms; and as predicted, they lost.

As the loser in this interaction, the North began to innovate tactically and strategically. In tactical terms, NVA units attempted to "cling to the belt" of US or ARVN forces (Karnow, 1983: 463), getting so close so

---

[12] No one involved in the campaign on the US side considers ROLLING THUNDER a success, although it is fair to say that the reasons proposed to explain the campaign's failure have been numerous and controversial. From the military perspective, the consensus is that the campaign failed because it misapplied military means to a political end. For a more thorough discussion and analysis of ROLLING THUNDER's target and impact, see, e.g., Thompson (1980); Herring (1986: 147); Clodfelter (1989); and Pape (1990).

[13] These examples are drawn from Summers (1995); and Marc Leepson (1999).

quickly that allied forces could not benefit from close air or artillery support. In strategic terms, the North shifted more of its resources into the guerrilla campaign in the South.

### Interaction three: the guerrilla war in the South I, 1965–1973

Guerrillas in the South waged their campaign with considerable skill, and were countered with a mix of professionalism, passion, sadism, and incompetence. In this dimension of the conflict more than any other, US efforts were heavily filtered through, and constrained by, the GVN.[14]

In US army areas of responsibility, the first attempts to defeat the VC insurgency involved search and destroy missions. In these counter-insurgency (COIN) missions, regular army units, acting on local intelligence that located enemy unit concentrations, would seek to make contact with these concentrations and destroy them. Large-scale examples of this interaction include Phase I of Operation ATTLEBORO (September–October 1965), Operation CEDAR FALLS (January 1967), and Operation JUNCTION CITY (February–May 1967), but the interaction repeated itself on a smaller scale throughout the war. Forces were killed on both sides, but the strategic balance slowly shifted to favor the VC, largely because US forces relied heavily on indirect firepower – tactical air and artillery support – a consequence of which was considerable death or injury to noncombatants (Asprey, 1994: 881).

Not all US COIN efforts failed outright or succeeded through barbarism. US Marine Corps forces in the mountainous northernmost area of South Vietnam, for example, pursued a COIN strategy combining local and highly motivated (but poorly trained and equipped) villagers with direct support from US Marine combat platoons. These combined action platoons (or CAPs) operated on an "inkblot" principle: secure a village or hamlet, then patrol out in widening circles until intersecting with another CAPs' secured area. The strategy had two major disadvantages, however. First, although it protected South Vietnamese citizens from immediate danger of terror attacks by VC guerrillas, it could achieve success only in the long term – and time favored the VC (Asprey, 1994: 848). Second, although militarily

---

[14] The record of performance by ARVN units is mixed. Some units and their commanders are extolled for their bravery, skill, and loyalty, while many are remembered only for their cowardice, incompetence, and venality (see, for example, Karnow, 1983: 441; and Summers, 1995: 80).

effective, CAP success only highlighted the inability of the South Vietnamese government to protect its *own* citizens.

The United States lost this interaction. Its combat forces had been trained and equipped to fight a uniformed regular adversary using massive firepower, not an invisible enemy that refused to meet it in battle.[15] The indiscriminate impact of the US Army's (and the ARVN's) heavy reliance on artillery and air support progressively alienated potential allies among South Vietnam's people. As losers, however, US forces were not slow to innovate a strategic response.

*Interaction four: the guerrilla war in the South II, 1965–1973*

US strategic innovation aimed at seriously damaging the VC guerrilla campaign in the South took two forms. The first was the Strategic Hamlets program, and the second was the Phoenix program.[16]

The US Strategic Hamlets program reactivated the French *agroville* program. In this version, South Vietnamese villagers were forcibly evacuated from their homes and relocated to fortified hamlets.[17] Where implemented effectively, this program had the military benefit of severely damaging VC intelligence and supply networks, at a political cost of turning US public opinion against the war, as nightly news images showed wailing peasants being forced to leave their villages. But the program was rarely implemented effectively. In most cases corrupt officials failed to deliver weapons and embezzled funds and supplies intended to make the hamlets functioning and secure communities (Karnow, 1983: 257). As a result, the program alienated the people whose goodwill the United States and South Vietnam needed to win the war: forced to leave their homes and then abandoned, many South Vietnamese turned against their government and became active supporters of the VC. By decreasing the program's COIN benefits and increasing its political costs, the South Vietnamese government's corruption and incompetence rendered the Strategic Hamlets program a disaster.

The second US innovation was the Phoenix program, whose aims and legitimacy continue to provoke sharp debate (Asprey, 1994: 910–911).

---

[15] This is Krepinevich's central thesis, (see Krepinevich, 1986: 4; see also Cohen, 1984: 166–167).

[16] "Phoenix" was the code name for a US assassination program that targeted VC leadership.

[17] On the Strategic Hamlets program in Vietnam, its logic, and its successes and failures, see Karnow (1983: 255–257); Herring (1986: 85–86, 88–90); and Sheehan (1989: 310–311, 540, 687).

The overall military view is that Phoenix was a legitimate military operation. It relied on special intelligence to target and destroy VC leadership, and it proved to be the single most successful strategic initiative pursued by US forces during the war.[18] To most observers, participants, and historians, however, the sustained effort to kill non-combatants raised troubling questions about its legitimacy as an extension of US policy, or as a COIN strategy, regardless of its effectiveness.

Overall, the United States won this interaction. The Strategic Hamlets program was never implemented properly, so its contribution to US success in this interaction was negative. By contrast, the Phoenix program, which eviscerated the VC command infrastructure in the South, may even have provoked the North into its premature and disastrous direct confrontation with US regular forces during the 1968 Tet Offensive. Because both strategies systematically and deliberately targeted noncombatants, both must be counted as barbarism – albeit barbarism at the milder end of the violations spectrum.

### Outcome: North Vietnam loses, then wins

The DRV won the Vietnam War, losing the military contest with the United States by 1969, but delaying its defeat long enough (and at a horrible cost) to force the United States to abandon the GVN (1973). From March to April 1975 the NVA crushed the ARVN on the battlefield. The accession to command of US forces of General Creighton Abrams (July 1968) and his subsequent reforms and innovations – leading to the virtual collapse of the VC/NVA military threat to South Vietnam – proved irrelevant to the outcome, save to the extent to which its continuing reconstruction (see e.g., Sorley, 1999) rehabilitates US military honor.

## Analysis: competing explanations of the Vietnam War's outcome

The outcome of the Vietnam War should stand as a puzzle in IR theory for two reasons. First, as with all the unanticipated outcomes explored

---

[18] There is little question that Phoenix effectively disrupted the capacity of the VC to continue their GWS in the South. Even the North Vietnamese admit this: "Nguyen Co Thach, Vietnam's foreign minister from 1975, admitted that the Phoenix effort 'wiped out many of our bases' in South Vietnam, compelling numbers of North Vietnamese and Viet Cong troops to retreat to sanctuaries in Cambodia" (Summers 1995: 148; see also, Karnow, 1983: 534; and Herring, 1986: 232).

in this book, the DRV's victory is puzzling in that the most powerful actor, the United States, lost a war against a weak actor, the DRV. Second, the DRV won the war *even though, unlike weak actors in every other case examined here, it lost on the battlefield.*[19] How can these puzzles be explained?

### Actor interests

A first explanation is that the DRV won because, as all observers came to know, it was profoundly dedicated to the outcome it sought. As a nation, the DRV appeared to forge itself into the living embodiment of the sentiment "better a dead lion than a live jackal." Better, in other words, to be annihilated as a people than to live under foreign rule. There was always, during the war, a sense of disbelief about this sentiment (possibly on the DRV side as well), and a reasonable concern that it represented more the propaganda of a desperate regime than the true aspirations of a people – a people very often divided historically. But the balance of evidence supports the argument that the dedication of the people of the DRV and their VC allies in the South, was nearly unprecedented historically.[20] General Abrams may have destroyed their ability to reunify Vietnam and even set it back another twenty years. But even under those circumstances the DRV showed no signs of injury to its *willingness* to unify Vietnam, whether it took another twenty, fifty, or a hundred years. In short, the roots of DRV resolve had less to do with its "survival" as framed by IR theory (i.e., less to do with it being the weak actor), and more to do with a two thousand year history of nationalist opposition to foreign rule, regardless of the balance of forces.

---

[19] To clarify, the DRV lost on the battlefield to the United States and the United States withdrew in 1973. The DRV won on the battlefield against the GVN in 1975, but by then few could have been surprised at the outcome.

[20] If willingness to absorb casualties and continue pressing ambitious political demands is an indicator, then the DRV is in rare company. As Mueller puts it, "the Communists lost some 2.5–3 percent of their prewar population in the war in battle deaths. How does this compare with other wars? It is almost unprecedented ... scarcely any of the hundreds of participants in the 100 international wars in the last 160 years have lost as many as 2 percent of their prewar population in battle deaths. The few cases where battle deaths attained levels higher than 2 percent of the prewar population mostly occurred in the two world wars in which industrial nations fought with sophisticated machines of destruction for their very existence. In World War II ... Germany and the Soviet Union each lost some 4.4 percent of their prewar populations in battle deaths. In World War I, Germany lost 2.7 percent, Austria-Hungary, 2.3 percent, France 3.3 percent, Rumania, 4.7 percent, and England 2.0 percent" (Mueller, 1980: 507–508).

Compared to this the interests of the United States must at first seem trivial. The United States sought only the survival of the GVN. But by 1965 the United States had come to view the survival of the GVN as a *necessary* part of its larger overall strategy to contain communism. Containing communism, in turn, was a vital national security interest because if it could not be contained – if it spread – it could either directly threaten US vital interests (stability in Europe, or oil in the Middle East, for example), or escalate to another world war capable, in the thermonuclear context, of ending all life on the planet. US interests in the outcome of the Vietnamese civil war were therefore far higher than suggested by the interest asymmetry thesis (Karnow, 1983: 377–378), but not as high as those of the DRV and VC. The United States did fight in Vietnam, initially, because many in the Kennedy and Johnson administrations believed that if they didn't fight the communists in Vietnam sooner, then they'd be force to fight them in Europe or the Western Hemisphere later. For the United States, Vietnam was a "limited" war not because South Vietnam's fate was a peripheral US interest, but because US political elites believed that the use of force in *proportion* to US interests might provoke Chinese military intervention and lead to a third world war.

Hypothesis 8 – relative material power explains relative interests in the outcome of an asymmetric conflict – is therefore not supported in the Vietnam case. The problem with actor interest asymmetry as an explanation of the outcome of the Vietnam War, however, is not that it is poorly explained by relative power, but rather that it doesn't explain potential outcome variation. In 1968, the United States was still committed to the idea that the GVN's survival was a vital US national security interest, under the theory of protecting US credibility (rather than the earlier domino theory). In other words, both actors were equally committed, independent of the nominal balance of coercive forces, and on top of that the United States had won the military contest on the ground. Given its high interests and its physical capacity to continue escalating the use of force against its weak adversary, the United States shouldn't have been as politically vulnerable as it was. Yet the United States *was* politically vulnerable, and that political vulnerability functioned just as Mack's thesis predicts: it forced the United States from the war.

## Regime types, strategy, and vulnerability

If interest asymmetry is a poor explanation of the puzzles of DRV victory, maybe regime type is a better one. Perhaps the DRV won because its authoritarian structure made it possible to completely control information from the battle space, and enabled it to engage in more brutal – and hence, more effective – tactics, than its democratic foe.

It is true that the DRV maintained an extraordinary degree of control over information about the outcomes of battles, and about the degree to which its enemies resorted to brutal conduct.[21] In general, the DRV lied to its people. It lied about nearly every aspect of the war, from the conduct of US and ARVN forces, to casualties suffered – their own and those of their adversaries. The DRV's efforts to control information from the battle space came at a significant cost in resources, and was aided by the fact that most common soldiers in the NVA and VC were not literate, and therefore could not write letters home in which alternate versions of events could compete with the DRV line. This was equally true of the ARVN but *not* of US forces, whose letters home eventually accelerated a "credibility gap" already being widened by journalists in theater.

There is also ample evidence that neither the DRV nor its VC allies observed the Geneva Conventions regarding the treatment of noncombatants in war – ranging from surrendering soldiers, to prisoners of war and enemy soldiers wounded in combat (many of whom were tortured and then murdered, or simply murdered on the spot). The argument that in Vietnam, in particular, a willingness to act with deliberate brutality was necessary to win, is captured nowhere better than in the words of the fictional Lieutenant Colonel Walter E. Kurtz in Francis Ford Coppola's 1979 film *Apocalypse Now*:

> It's impossible for words to describe what is necessary to those who do not know what horror means . . . I remember when I was with Special Forces . . . We went into a camp to inoculate the children. We left the camp after we had inoculated the children for Polio, and this old man came running after us and he was crying. He couldn't say. We went back there, and they had come, and hacked off every inoculated arm. There they were in a pile. A pile of little arms. And I remember I, I cried. I wept like some grandmother . . . And I thought: my God, the genius of that. The *genius!* . . . And then I realized they were stronger than we because they could stand it. These were not monsters. These were men – trained cadres – these men who fought with their hearts, who had families, who had children, who were filled with love. But they had the *strength*, the strength to do that. If I had ten divisions of

---

[21] See Tin (2002: 30–32). Bui Tin supports the argument that the democratic structure of the US government made it highly vulnerable as compared to that of the DRV.

those men our troubles here would be over very quickly. You have to have men who are moral, and, at the same time, who are able to utilize their primordial instincts to kill, without feeling, without passion, without judgment. Without judgment, because it's judgment that defeats us.

The weakness of this argument is that the GVN was also authoritarian and fully willing to "do what was necessary" to win, and yet the ARVN was always said to be a hindrance to military effectiveness rather than an aid. In the calculation of US forces and diplomats in theater, the ARVN were in fact the *most* brutal yet the *least* effective forces engaged against the DRV/VC in the war. Also, US forces proved to be just as brutal on several occasions (the My Lai massacre being only the most famous and most public of many such "incidents"), and as observed above, accepted considerable collateral damage in strategic bombing raids designed to coerce the DRV through the infliction of pain. Yet the military effectiveness of the bombings was negligible. Had it escalated to the point of destroying the Red River dike system (killing up to a million DRV civilians), Bui Tin, then a colonel in the NVA, argues that the results would have been catastrophic for the United States:

> Such a tragedy would... have offered Hanoi an incomparable occasion for whipping up anti-American sentiments throughout the world, for arguing for large-scale international aid and support, and for rallying the whole socialist bloc.
>
> My feeling is that when you take into consideration the sociopolitical and psychocultural makeup of the Vietnamese, destroying the dikes would have worked in Hanoi's favor. The government would certainly have been faced with many difficulties and the people would have suffered untold hardships, but their war effort would not have diminished... (Tin, 2002: 34)

But the strongest argument in favor of the effectiveness of regime type is the structure argument; the structure of the DRV and GVN – both authoritarian regimes – did not permit public disaffection with the war or how it was fought to affect policy. But the structure of the US government – a democratic regime – did permit public opinion to affect US policy. Mack, Merom, and others correctly identify this as political vulnerability, and specify how it operated to force the United States from the war *despite* a military victory in theater.

The most important consideration here, however, is whether the United States failed because it was a democracy. The answer is no, on two counts. First, if democracies are to be associated with more restrained conduct on the battlefield (historically not a sound association), then the United States may, as Merom asserts, have lost because it couldn't "escalate the level of violence and brutality to that which can secure victory" (Merom, 2003: 15). It is difficult to argue, however, that the United States and ARVN were not brutal enough, considering that as a proportion of pre-war population, the DRV lost from 2.5 to 3 percent – higher even than that suffered by Japan in World War II (Japan lost an estimated 1.4 percent in that war).[22] Second, it is hard to argue that the United States in Vietnam was *more* politically vulnerable, given its high interests in the outcome, than it was in the first Gulf War of 1990, in which the rationale given for US military intervention was only the preservation of a "new world order" (nothing said about dominos). Yet the United States and its allies, who together inflicted tens of thousands of casualties on their hapless Iraqi adversary while sustaining only hundreds of casualties themselves, won that war quickly and decisively, forcing the Iraqis to agree to humiliating terms of surrender. Thus, political vulnerability drives democracies from wars when it can't affect authoritarian regimes, but only when there is a gap in time between the commitment of armed forces and the achievement of political objectives. This is what happened in Vietnam. Thus regime type is necessary but not sufficient to explain the DRV's victory. A full explanation demands accounting for why some asymmetric conflicts are over with quickly while others drag on.

### Arms diffusion

Arms diffusion is not a good explanation of US defeat in the Vietnam War for two reasons. First, the DRV's acquisition of armaments from the Soviet Union and China did make a difference (especially to the air defense of key installations in North Vietnam), but only at the margins.[23] Second, the battlefield impact of access to better arms was often negative (Johnson, 1968: 442, 443). The DRV's acquisition of new arms

---

[22] Numbers are from Mueller (1980: 509).

[23] A good counterargument would be that given "low" US interests in defeat of the DRV, increasing costs at the margins was sufficient. But US interests were not low. Moreover, the most serious costs imposed on the US were in the form of (a) outraged public opinion following reports on the collateral damage of US bombing strikes in the North, and (b) improvised booby traps and mines against US forces in the South. If Bui Tin and others are correct, a lack of any conventional air defense of the DRV might have caused the United States even greater problems by accelerating the trend toward increasing negative public reaction to high-tech, high-altitude attacks against a "poor, defenseless, backward"

tended to encourage premature escalation to direct confrontations with US or US-supported ARVN units, and this invariably proved disastrous. Moreover, the lack of dependency on locals for logistical support made it possible for the cadres to terrorize wavering South Vietnamese peasants (summarily executing "informants" and so on) in direct opposition to Maoist dicta concerning the necessity of treating peasants with respect. The legacy of this abuse would haunt the VC following the loss of so many of their cadres in the ill-fated Tet Offensive of 1968. The DRV was forced to send replacements from the North, but these men could not reconstruct the intimate web of relationships with the peasants and terrain of their predecessors. In addition, the new cadres were haughty toward the ethnically distinct "Southerners," and this, along with the disaffection brought about through previous years of terrorization, made it impossible to re-establish a viable insurgency in the South after 1968. On balance then, absolute increases in armaments hurt more than helped the DRV war effort.

Hypothesis 6 – the better armed a weak actor is, the more likely it is that a strong actor will lose an asymmetric conflict – is therefore not supported in the Vietnam case.

### Strategic interaction

If it is true that actor interests and regime type are themselves insufficient to account for the DRV victory in Vietnam, it is nevertheless obvious that they are necessary. But the best explanation of the war's outcome is strategic interaction. Strategic interaction explains how the high resolve of the DRV/VC, along with the regime-affected political vulnerability of the United States, combined to force the United States from the war as and when it did.

According to my account, however, it is difficult to assess the cumulative impact of the four [24] strategic interactions that made up the war.

country. Ironically then, the DRV's use of Soviet anti-aircraft technology might count as yet another example of advanced technology imports hurting, rather than helping, a war effort.

[24] Lewis Sorley (1999) argues that the war had yet another crucial phase after Tet, in which US forces shifted strategies under their new commander, General Creighton W. Abrams. In terms of the strategic interaction thesis, this would count as "Phase 5: Guerrilla War III/ indirect – indirect/US wins: abandons Vietnam/war ends." The difficulty with Sorley's argument is measuring the effectiveness of Abrams's talented leadership in the context of a VC recently devastated by Phoenix and Tet, and a similarly routed NVA. If, as many assert, the North had retreated to lick its wounds after Tet, then US military effectiveness would appear high regardless of its strategy. For this reason, and because its inclusion would add little in the way of a test of competing explanations, I do not include the interaction in this analysis.

These interactions and their contribution to the outcome of the war are summarized in Table 2.

The United States won two and lost two; and the impact of the interactions on the war's duration also seem equivocal. Shouldn't this imply a tie? Perhaps. But considering US public and elite expectations prior to the fight, even a tie must count as a failure from the US perspective, because anything other than a quick victory was going to be politically unacceptable. Keep in mind that US strategy was aimed, and aimed publicly, at intimidation – at coercing the DRV by force and the threat of even more force to stop supporting the war against the GVN in the South. In World War II, the United States had been fighting a war many Americans believed to have been a *real* war: a war for survival against a powerful, technologically fearsome, and unambiguously evil enemy. For the United States, that war lasted three long years (1942–45). If three years is a long time in a "real" war, how much longer must it have seemed in Vietnam, a far away place with a poor, weak, "backward" and hence sympathetic enemy? Three years into its war of intimidation against the DRV, the United States and the GVN were attacked boldly and on all fronts by the DRV and VC. Clearly, whatever else was working in Vietnam, and regardless of the military outcome (NVA/VC defeat), US hopes of intimidating the DRV were bankrupt, and the American people knew it.

Strategic interaction explains two things that Mack's and Merom's theses can't. First, as demonstrated in the Vietnam case, relative power in an asymmetric conflict is a poor predictor of relative interests (resolve, if you will) in the outcome of an asymmetric contest. Even when facing weak actors, strong actors – whether superpowers or middling powers, whether authoritarian or democratic – justify their attacks against weak actors in terms of survival of some sort. This can be by means of domino logic (the additive power of otherwise small defeats could eventually constitute a direct survival threat), precedent-setting logic (if we don't hold here, an imagined audience will conclude we can't hold anywhere, and vital interests will be put in jeopardy as a result), or by reference to some cherished identity or principle (one thinks, e.g., of Margaret Thatcher's justification for attacking Argentina over the Falklands/Malvinas Islands in 1982; or George Bush Sr.'s declaration of a need to protect a "new world order" by forcing Iraq from Kuwait in 1990). The point being that these causes need not be objectively existential. It is enough that they are metaphorically existential, at least in the initial stages of conflict. If the war is over quickly, then the

Table 2. Summary of strategic interactions and effects in US intervention in Vietnam, 1965–73

|   |   | Strategic interaction | Innovation effect | Duration effect |
|---|---|---|---|---|
| 1 | Rolling Thunder | indirect–direct | United States loses: abandons strategy | lengthens war |
| 2 | Main force war | direct–direct | North loses: withdraws, then escalates (Tet) | shortens war |
| 3 | Guerrilla war I | direct–indirect | United States loses: switches to barbarism (Phoenix) | lengthens war |
| 4 | Guerrilla war II | indirect–indirect | North loses: escalates, then withdraws | shortens war |

metaphorical justification will likely stand. If it is protracted – a function of strategic interaction – however, the metaphorical justification will be challenged. In sum, strong actors are not vulnerable in small wars because such wars are less than existential. They are vulnerable because the time it takes to defeat an objectively weak adversary calls into question the legitimacy of the interests, regardless of their bases in reality or metaphor.

Second, and most importantly, the strategic interaction thesis shows why the Vietnam War wasn't over with quickly, in say, one or two years. As most critics of the US military in Vietnam have observed, the initial strategic interaction was dominated by a conventional attack (US/ARVN) against a GWS (VC). This interaction in fact best characterizes the overall strategic interaction of the war; and as the thesis predicts, one consequence of an opposite-approach interaction is that it makes wars last longer. The failure to achieve quick results with conventional search-and-destroy missions then led US forces to innovate, leading to the CAPs program, Strategic Hamlets (again), and Phoenix. These innovations had the effect of hurting the DRV and VC, but the United States would not advance north of the 17th parallel with ground forces, so the DRV could afford to wait.

If Mack's thesis were sufficient to explain "why big nations lose small wars," political vulnerability would have to *generally* affect the ability of strong actors to defeat weak actors. It doesn't. Political vulnerability operates only when there is an unanticipated delay between the commitment of armed forces and victory.

If Merom's thesis were sufficient to explain "how democracies lose small wars," he would have to support the empirical claim that strategic interactions in small wars are constant, not variable. In other words, he would have to show that, as his case selection implies, all [democratic] strong actors will attack with a conventional attack strategy, and all weak actors will defend with a GWS, terrorism, or nonviolent resistance (i.e., an indirect defense). But we in fact observe variation in strategic interactions in small wars all the time; against all expectations to the contrary, the Taliban did not attempt a GWS against the US-supported Northern Alliance in 2002. They attempted a conventional defense and were soundly defeated. The same was true of the Iraqis a year later. Moreover, the Russian Federation, a nominal democracy, is still prosecuting an *extremely* brutal and yet counterproductive COIN campaign in Chechnya. Even if we accept for the sake of argument that the Russian Federation is not a "real" democracy, clearly the extreme brutality (rape, extortion, looting, murder, torture, indiscriminate shelling) of the Russian campaign is not winning Russia's small war in the Caucasus.

## Conclusion

In Vietnam, the DRV (weak actor) had two entirely distinct militaries ready to oppose US forces: one trained and equipped to fight an indirect war (the VC), the other trained and equipped to fight a direct war (the NVA). This meant that the DRV could be far more nimble than the United States in shifting its strategic approach. As Eliot Cohen, Andrew Krepinevich, Donald Hamilton, and others have argued, with the possible exception of the US Marine Corps – which had considerable operational experience with COIN – the US military could never reconcile itself to the demands of a COIN war (Cohen, 1984: 165; Krepinevich, 1986; Hamilton, 1998: 155). These demands do *not* imply the necessity of creating a force capable of barbarism; as the CAPs demonstrated, it was possible to fight a GWS in the South within the framework of the laws of war. What it was manifestly not possible to do was defeat a people in arms *quickly* by such methods.

Thus the CAP example only underscores the importance of the key causal mechanism of the strategic interaction thesis: when the power relationship implies a quick victory, and the interaction causes a delay, the way is clear for the operation of political vulnerability. That is, even an ideal COIN strategy – one that destroys enemy forces without destroying enemy values – takes time. If such strategies are to become a model for future COIN operations, this implies a counterintuitive policy: when weak actors employ indirect defense strategies, strong actor political and military elites must prepare their publics for long-delayed victories.

In Vietnam, interest asymmetry and regime type helped the DRV inflict costs on the United States and ARVN; and its open alliance with the People's Republic of China (and Soviet Union) made it impossible for the United States to launch a ground invasion in the North. These factors might not have mattered had the DRV escalated to an all-out conventional assault on the South in 1965 (a strategy for which the United States and ARVN were prepared). They also wouldn't have mattered had the United States taken British and French advice and chosen the long and difficult strategy of a law-enforcement rather than a military COIN strategy.[25] To do so would have required three things: first, reform and restructuring of the GVN (the relevant example of success in this regard being Ramon Magsaysay's reforms of the Philippine government during the Hukbalahap insurgency in 1952). Second, the politically difficult – in the US domestic political context – step of persuading the US public of the need for a long struggle. Third, the even more difficult job of convincing the US military to build and deploy sufficient special operations forces to work in close conjunction with well-trained and competently led GVN law enforcement forces. Either same-approach interaction could, without resort to barbarism, have secured US political objectives in Southeast Asia. Although this strategy would suffer from the defect of taking a long time to show results, that cost would be offset by, first, a consistent political effort to keep expectations of a quick victory low, and more importantly, by reducing friendly casualties and the DRV propaganda advantage of frequent and widely publicized incidents of injury to noncombatants.

But, in the event, the United States encouraged the view that the fight to save the GVN was a military matter and that it could be won quickly.[26] The United States attempted to coerce the DRV with

---

[25] See Shaw (2001). Adopting this strategy would count as switching from a war-winning to a war-termination strategy.

[26] This encouragement culminated in the infamous prediction by US commander William Westmoreland – just prior to Tet – that "the enemy's hopes are bankrupt" (see Karnow, 1983: 539). Westmoreland's proclamation mirrors that of French General Henri Navarre's on the eve of the battle of Dien Bien Phu, "Now we can see it clearly, the light at the end of the tunnel" (Karnow, 1983: 189).

firepower (Herring, 1986: 226), and the DRV/VC defended their interests by means of an indirect strategy and at a tremendous cost in lives lost. Stymied, US forces innovated new strategies in order to defeat the DRV/VC, but the reverses they achieved on the battlefield took too long (Karnow, 1983: 464, 480; Herring, 1986: 200). By 1968 the US public had already begun to grasp what the Johnson and Nixon administrations – and the military leadership – could not; by the time US Marines landed at Da Nang in 1965 it was already too late. The war in Vietnam had become what Michael Walzer would later term an anti-social war:

> The war cannot be won, and it should not be won. It cannot be won, because the only available strategy involves a war against civilians; and it should not be won, because the degree of civilian support that rules out alternative strategies also makes the guerrillas the legitimate rulers of the country. The struggle against them is an unjust struggle as well as one that can only be carried on unjustly. Fought by foreigners, it is a war of aggression; if by a local regime alone, it is an act of tyranny. The position of the anti-guerrilla forces has become doubly untenable. (Walzer, 2000: 195–196)

Just as it had to the French public after General Massu's defeat of the FLN in Algeria, the thought of winning such a war soon became intolerable to most Americans. Better to risk a communist takeover of Southeast Asia than to contain communism by means of winning an anti-social war.

# The USSR in Afghanistan: the Afghan Civil War, 1979–1989

The Afghan society may now be regarded a murderous society... We have become soulless and dry, no longer beings of care and love, but brutal and fierce animals. It is not right to name a society murderous, but the Afghan society may be called so... The state is a state of killing, not only in the battlefield but also in the lanes and streets of cities where there is no state of war. No one feels secure, and because of this many families have fled abroad.  Hassan Kakar (1995)

In Afghanistan I served at Ghazni... Life in the unit was fairly calm, unless we were involved in operations, when everything was different... We didn't see any friendly Afghans anywhere – only enemies. Even the Afghan army was unfriendly... Everyone around us was an enemy. I remember an intense feeling of anger toward the rebels because so many of our guys were getting killed. I wanted revenge.

Then I began to doubt the goals and methods of international aid. I had a difficult time deciding what I really believed. I just knew what I had to say during the political instruction meeting: that we were fighting "American aggression" and "Pakis." Why had we mined all the approaches to the regiment? I asked myself. Why were we aiming our machine guns at every Afghan? Why were we killing the people we came here to help?

Whenever a peasant was blown up by a mine, no one took him to the medical unit. Everyone just stood around, enjoying the sight of his death. "This is an enemy," the officer said. "Let him suffer."

Mickola Movchan (a Russian deserter in Afghanistan)

The war between the Soviet Union and resistance forces of Afghanistan began on 27 December 1979, and ended with the withdrawal of Soviet armed forces on 15 February 1989.[1]

---

[1] The fighting did not stop, but for our purposes the asymmetric conflict between the USSR and the various Afghan resistance groups ended when the Soviet troops evacuated Afghan territory.

## The Afghanistan theater

The territory of Afghanistan encompasses a mountainous region of 245,000 square miles, or roughly the size of New Mexico and Arizona together. It is essentially the hub of a wheel which includes the former Soviet Union to the north, Iran to the west, Pakistan to the south and east, and China to the east. As such, it lies along a number of ancient trade routes connecting the east to the west, and its geographic position has been the most important determinant of its foreign policy for centuries.

In terms of ethnicity, religion, and language, the majority ethnic group of Afghanistan are Sunni Muslim Pushtuns (often called "Pathans" in nineteenth-century British writings). Pushtuns make up about 40 percent of the population, followed by Tajiks (20 percent). The next three largest groups – roughly equal in size – are Hazaras (Shi'a Muslims with a distinct racial appearance), Uzbeks, and Aimaq (Magnus & Naby, 1998: 10). The main languages of each group are distinct from each (e.g., Pushtu for Pushtuns), but an inter-ethnic language, Dari, is also available (Magnus & Naby, 1998: 15). Finally, 90 percent of Afghans are Sunni Muslims, while most of the remainder follow variations of Shi'a Islam. When religious identities are most salient, this makes most Afghans natural allies of Pakistan and Saudi Arabia, and creates friction with Iran, which is predominately Shi'a Muslim.

The Pushtun identity is important for two reasons. First, this group has dominated Afghan politics and society for hundreds of years (providing all its rulers, and several for Iran and India as well). Second, the Pushtun identity is important because the Afghan–Pakistani border – established as the so-called Durand Line of 1893 – divides ethnic Pushtuns almost in half (Magnus and Naby, 1998: 36). In fact, what the Pakistanis call the North-West Frontier Province, the Afghans refer to as Pushtunistan.

The internal political struggles which led to a Soviet decision to intervene militarily in Afghanistan are far more nuanced and complex than can be presented here. However its main features are as follows.

After World War II Britain allowed India to become independent in 1947, and after Muslim Pakistan split from Hindu India, the Eisenhower administration calculated that Afghanistan was beyond its sphere of strategic interests (Kakar, 1995: 9; Magnus & Naby, 1998: 59). As such, then President Sardar Muhammad Da'ud Khan was forced to look elsewhere for development aid, which his country needed to build roads, irrigation and power facilities, and a modern military. The USSR stepped into the vacuum, offering billions of rubles to the Da'ud regime, showcasing its assistance as friendly "no strings attached" development aid. But, in 1963, Afghanistan's king, Zahir Shah, dismissed Da'ud as prime minister. During the next fifteen years, Da'ud's successors liberalized Afghan domestic politics while continuing to develop Afghanistan's infrastructure.

In 1965, political liberalization resulted in the formation of the People's Democratic Party of Afghanistan (PDPA) under the leadership of Muhammad Taraki and Babrak Karmal. In 1967, the PDPA split into separate factions: Parcham, headed by Karmal, and the more radical Khalq, headed by Taraki. The liberalization of Afghan politics resulted in accelerating factionalization and a growing opposition to the constitutional monarchy.

In 1973 Da'ud staged a bloodless coup with Soviet and Parchami support and declared Afghanistan a republic. But Da'ud immediately set about slowing the pace of Afghan political reform. He arrested prominent Islamists and Marxists, and began to purge Parchamis from government posts while at the same time reducing Afghanistan's technical and economic dependence on the USSR (he signed development pacts with Iran and Saudi Arabia which together would have dwarfed the entire Soviet aid program of the previous two decades). Alarmed, the Soviets requested an interview with Da'ud in Moscow in April of 1977, and Brezhnev bluntly ordered Da'ud to stop hiring foreign technical specialists on the grounds that many of these were NATO spies. Da'ud retorted angrily that Moscow had no say in Afghanistan's internal politics, and the Soviets decided to replace him (Magnus & Naby, 1998: 118–119, 121).

In July, the Soviets forced the reunification of the two feuding factions of the PDPA, and a year later (April 1978), the PDPA staged a Soviet-engineered coup in which Da'ud and his family were murdered.[2] Taraki and his protégé Hafizullah Amin took over, and began purging the new government of Parchamis (Karmal fled to Moscow). Chaos ensued as the inexperienced Marxists attempted to re-engineer Afghan society overnight. Uprisings soon broke out in major Afghan cities, such as Herat, and were brutally suppressed. Amin eventually

---

[2] Lloyd Rudolph argues that the April 1978 coup caught the Soviets by surprise (Rudolph, 1985: 4).

ousted Taraki, who fled the country. As uprisings continued and DRA desertions increased, Amin's regime threatened to fly apart. Moscow decided that the only way to salvage the situation was to depose Amin and replace him with the more moderate Taraki.[3] But their plans were discovered by Amin, who had Taraki arrested and later murdered after Taraki's return to Kabul. In September 1979 the deeply angered Soviets began elaborate plans to invade Afghanistan and install Babrak Karmal as leader.

## The eve of war: Soviet interests

There is much debate concerning Soviet interests in Afghanistan, but the proximate causes of Soviet intervention appear to reduce to three concerns: (1) the defense of a friendly Marxist regime in a territory bordering the USSR (the Brezhnev Doctrine[4]); (2) the chance to establish a geopolitical bridgehead in the Persian Gulf; and (3) sunk costs.[5]

These three rationales for intervention hardly exhaust the possibilities, but with the advantage of hindsight we can make a better guess as to Soviet interest priorities based on the mission, quality, and quantity of armed forces they committed there.[6] Whatever the disagreements

---

[3] Rudolph suggests that Amin was too much of a Pushtun nationalist for the Soviets, and that they decided to replace him because, among other things, his expansionist nationalism threatened both Zia's Pakistan and Khomeini's Iran (Rudolph, 1985: 39). Urban suggests yet a different rationale for the Soviet decision to oust Amin: he maintained links with the CIA and was secretly in the West's pocket (Urban, 1988: 40).

[4] As with the United States in Vietnam, and Britain in South Africa, part of the subtext of the Brezhnev Doctrine is simple prestige (a social component, avoiding humiliation) and domino logic (a geopolitical component, gaining power or security). In this case, the logic is of the form "if a Marxist regime is defeated here, Marxist regimes everywhere will be weakened" (See Magnus and Naby, 1998: 63).

[5] Magnus and Naby argue that in fact the Soviets were most affected by the sunk costs argument, and by the opportunity to threaten vital US interests in the Persian Gulf: "The Soviets, in fact, cared nothing for the revolutionary transformation of Afghanistan, but they cared a great deal about the control of Afghanistan, which could provide them a secure base (and valuable, well-armed allies) for further advances into more promising areas of the Middle East and South Asia. They wished above all not to lose what they had gained through decades of patient effort and considerable expenditure" (Magnus and Naby, 1998: 122). As we will see below, the Brezhnev Doctrine and sunk costs arguments are probably the strongest. We encountered a variant of the "sunk costs" argument in Chapter 6, when Mussolini invoked it in order to justify his "solution" to the Ethiopian "problem" following the failure of his *fait accompli* strategy.

[6] Analysis of the interests based on Soviet forces alone would be risky because these forces – four motorized rifle divisions composed almost entirely of third-echelon Central Asian reservists – might represent little more than Soviet arrogance or underestimation of Afghan resistance (see a similar analysis of British interests in South Africa in Chapter 4).

about the USSR's long-term objectives in Afghanistan, their immediate objectives were clear from the beginning: (1) replace Amin with Karmal; (2) occupy and stabilize major Afghan cities (Kabul, Herat, Kandahar, Jalalabad); and (3) secure lines of communication between cities (especially the Salang highway, linking Kabul with Termez to the north and Jalalabad to the east). In short, the Soviet mission was strictly limited. Their goal in Afghanistan was to stabilize the new regime under Karmal's leadership, so that Karmal could set about the difficult *political* task of putting the Afghan Humpty-Dumpty back together again (Litwak, 1992: 79). The limited mission, poor quality and small quantity of forces supports the Brezhnev Doctrine[7] and sunk costs arguments better than the geopolitical bridgehead argument (Litwak, 1992: 79–80). The bridgehead argument is further weakened by the fact that the alleged advantages of outright conquest (in terms of air bases and so on) would have been available to the Soviets by treaty anyway.

But why intervene with regular armed forces in the first place? The answer is that Amin had succeeded too well in purging opposition from, and securing control of, the armed forces and secret police. In essence, Amin's efficiency and brutality forestalled the possibility of his being replaced in the old-fashioned way, by a well-organized coup (his discovery of the plot by the Soviets and Taraki to remove him is proof of this). Thus the only means left to the Soviets was direct military intervention with their own armed forces.

In sum, Soviet interests in Afghanistan were defensive from the beginning. Their limited objective was to secure the regime, major urban areas, and communications links so that Afghanistan's new political leadership could consolidate the revolution and pacify the state by political, rather than military means.

## The eve of war: mujahideen interests

As has been persuasively argued by an Afghan historian who lived through these events, the Afghan state as such ceased to exist after the

---

[7] This interpretation is also supported by Litwak. Litwak adds that, in effect, the Soviets were concerned about precedent-setting effects (Duffy Toft, 2003) should an Islamic regime come to power in Afghanistan, because Afghanistan borders Soviet Central Asian Republics (Turkmenistan, Uzbekistan, Tajikistan) which were themselves formerly Islamic states. In other words, the concern was that an Islamic Afghanistan would destabilize Soviet Central Asia (Urban, 1988: 206; Litwak, 1992: 78). In hindsight, this concern (whether it motivated Soviet intervention or not) has proven to be a valid one (Magnus and Naby, 1998: 68).

April 1978 coup which toppled the Da'ud regime (Kakar, 1995: 125). What remained in Afghanistan were two highly factionalized camps gathering around two opposite poles.

On the one side were the various factions of the PDPA, which sought to "reform" Afghan society while enriching themselves and eliminating their rivals. Kakar argues that there were two problems with these reform attempts. First, the PDPA leadership had no cadre of experienced ministers who could oversee the implementation of their radical decrees. Second, they relied on a Soviet or Marxist interpretation of history in order to understand Afghan problems and to prescribe proper solutions:

> each [of the men who replaced Da'ud] was convinced that the PDPA blueprint was the guideline for reorganizing both society and the state. Thus, they relied on Soviet, not Afghan, experience, and thus, too, they broke with the Afghan past. This may explain why, after they rose to power, they became ever more alienated from their own people and ever more disunited among themselves. (Kakar, 1995: 15)

On the other side were a number of mainly rural-based groups with different ideologies, ethnicities, and agendas. Some were Sunni Muslim and others were Shi'a. Of the Shi'a, some were Twelvers and some were Seveners.[8] Among the Sunni Muslims, some were ethnic Pushtuns while others were Tajiks, Turkmen, or Uzbeks. Cordesman and Wagner identify twelve separate resistance groups (Cordesman & Wagner, 1990: 17–19). All the major resistance groups maintained a similar organization: political leadership was located in Peshawar in the North-West Frontier Province of Pakistan, while most field commands were located in home provinces in Afghanistan.[9]

But however many groups or agendas there were, a key feature of the decade-long conflict in the Afghan war was this: so long as Soviet troops were involved in operations, resistance groups were united:

> The invasion turned the civil war into a war of liberation. It gave that war a new meaning, summed up in the word *jehad*, an expression particularly moving to Muslim Afghans in such times ... The Russians were godless communists, and their ruthless suppression

---

[8] Seveners and Twelvers constitute variants of Shi'a Islam. For a concise discussion, see Magnus and Naby, (1998, pp. 84–87).

[9] Kakar argues that Pakistan, fearful of another "Palestinian" situation in the North-West Frontier Province, deliberately fostered the rivalries and factionalization of the resistance groups (Kakar, 1995: 93).

of the Muslims of Central Asia had been related to the Afghans by the thousands of the Muslims of Bukhara who had taken refuge in Afghanistan. (Kakar, 1995: 111)

Furthermore, because Karmal had "arrived on the back of Soviet tanks" the resistance fighters did not distinguish between DRA and Soviet troops. To the mujahideen, they were all "the Russians" (Magnus & Naby, 1998: 139).[10]

In sum, among the constellation of interests and identities that composed the Afghan resistance, a single dominant theme emerged: get the Soviets out (Urban, 1988: 53, 72). Beyond this simple goal there was no consensus, and the lack of a broader consensus made the task of ejecting the Soviets that much more difficult.

## The Afghan Civil War

The Afghan Civil War contained two main strategic interactions. In the first or enclave interaction, the Soviets limited themselves to establishing and protecting key strategic areas, including logistical, urban and industrial sites, and the roads linking them. But this proved difficult, so in order to safeguard key areas, the Soviets launched a series of conventional attacks against suspected mujahideen redoubts throughout Afghanistan. This conventional attack strategy lasted from 1980 until 1982. The mujahideen followed a GWS strategy during this time and throughout the war. In 1982 the Soviets switched to a "scorched earth" strategy. This barbarism strategy sharply escalated civilian deaths and increased the flow of refugees to Pakistan and Iran. More importantly, it began to severely damage mujahideen infrastructure and it took a serious toll on their fighting capacity.

## Interaction one: conventional attack *vs.* GWS

The Afghan war itself began with the invasion of Soviet troops on 27 December 1979. Initial Soviet invasion forces, the 40th Army, consisted

---

[10] There appears to be some problem with this argument however. The departure of the Soviets from Afghanistan in 1989 had two consequences whose effects are difficult to disaggregate: (1) such mujahideen unity as there was quickly diminished after the last Soviet combat units crossed the Amu Darya (Oxus) River, and (2) foreign logistical support for the mujahideen dried up. Both consequences led to a diminished mujahideen fighting capacity, but the first consequence implies that many mujahideen did in fact distinguish between the white Russians and their DRA puppets.

of five divisions – four motorized rifle (MRD) and one air assault division – supported by an additional two air assault regiments (the 103rd and 104th). The plan was for the 66th and 357th MRDs to advance from Kushka in Soviet Turkmenistan to Herat, Farah, and then Kandahar, while the 360th and 201st MRDs moved south from Termez in Soviet Uzbekistan through Mazar-e-Shariff to Kabul. The 105th Guards air assault division and its two attached regiments were already in place at Bagram and along the Salang highway passes, and began the operation to capture Kabul at 7:15 p.m. By 8:45 p.m., the Soviets had announced via a radio station in Termez claiming to be Radio Kabul, that Karmal had taken over the government and requested Soviet assistance. The ground forces now began crossing the Oxus River on pontoon bridges.

The only serious fighting on that first day was between Soviet airborne and special forces troops and Amin's personal guards at the Darulaman Palace on the outskirts of Kabul. The Soviets had done as much as possible to facilitate a quick takeover, including poisoning Amin, emptying fuel from armored vehicles of the two divisions loyal to Amin, and exchanging live rounds for blanks (for "exercises") in the weapons of those same divisions (Kakar, 1995: 23). All that stood between Amin and death were therefore 1800 personal guards who occupied defensive positions in the palace. When the attack on the palace by Soviet special forces units began, Jahandad, the guard commander, came to Amin to ask for instructions. Due to Amin's condition (Kakar claims he was poisoned by the Soviets), however, Jahandad had to make up his own mind. He decided to resist, and the attackers were thrown back several times:

> The confrontation was intense and prolonged. Both sides sustained losses until the Afghans were finally overcome by some kind of nerve gas... The invaders feared that if the Afghans were not soon overcome, forces from the nearby military divisions of Rishkhor and Qargha might join them. (Kakar, 1995: 25)

This passage not only references a violation of the laws of war,[11] but cites its most common rationale: it was "necessary" in order to increase military effectiveness.

---

[11] Kakar notes that none of the 1800 palace defense force survived the attack, which tends to support the argument that something unusual was used to overcome the defenders.

In January 1980, Karmal announced a package of reforms and compromises designed to reestablish government and end resistance and violence. Most Afghans ignored him:

> The Karmal package was a comprehensive one, but it was ignored by a large number of Afghans. To them the pledges of freedom, the release of prisoners and the new trades unions were all irrelevant. What was relevant was that Karmal clearly depended on the army of a foreign power – a power that was perceived as godless and anti-Islamic.
>
> (Urban, 1988: 53)

Most Afghans were outraged by the Soviet invasion. Many quit their jobs and joined the mujahideen. Worse still, entire DRA units defected to the mujahideen. The defection of whole units was a particular problem because it meant the transfer of arms – sometimes sophisticated arms – to the resistance. Karmal's well-intentioned attempt to reach compromises within his government caused still more problems. Amin's Khalqis were still in key positions in the army and secret police, and because Karmal refused to purge them, they remained capable of obstructing his policy initiatives.

By mid-January DRA desertions had become such a problem that Marshal Sokolov, in overall command of Soviet operations in the DRA, mobilized his reserve-echelon forces. In order to seal the Iranian border, Sokolov sent the 5th MRD to Farah and the 54th MRD to Herat. A third MRD, the 16th, was deployed to Mazar-e-Shariff. He also sent the 201st MRD east from Kabul to Jalalabad in order to stabilize the situation there.[12]

Meanwhile, in order to relieve the pressure on the DRA 9th Division at Jalalabad, the Soviets planned to take the offensive in the Kunar valley. The Kunar valley perfectly illustrates the conflict topography of Afghanistan: a long fertile valley flanked by steep mountains containing numerous smaller side canyons. The valleys themselves usually feature a river, which flows down to join other rivers from similar valleys all through the Hindu Kush mountain range. Such roads as there were in Afghanistan usually follow the rivers, and the intersection of rivers thus becomes the site of urban centers and major highway junctions. In short, Afghanistan's valleys open onto strategic values.

---

[12] The DRA 9th division was garrisoned at Jalalabad on the key highway connecting Pakistan to Kabul. Urban estimates that so many of its units defected that by the summer of 1980 its effective strength was down to no more than 1000 (Urban, 1988: 55).

What the Soviets quickly discovered is that they could not achieve their minimal objective of protecting these strategic values because there weren't enough forces among the DRA and the Soviet army combined to protect more than a fraction of them.[13] Convoys of fuel, ammunition, food, and replacement soldiers and parts had to travel the full length of highways which were flanked in many places by these valley openings. Thus, the Soviets found themselves having to mount COIN operations outside of their garrisons simply in order to relieve pressure on them and secure their lines of communication. The Kunar valley operation in March of 1980 was their first major effort, and it proved completely ineffective.

The offensive began with a sustained aerial bombardment, which warned the mujahideen, killed civilians and livestock, destroyed fields, houses and irrigation facilities, and initiated the depopulation of the valley. Next, armored regiments lumbered up the valley floor, suffering numerous ambushes. The column succeeded in relieving the garrison at Asadabad and reestablishing government authority in Asmar, after which it returned to base. Days later the mujahideen returned from the mountain caves where they had hidden as the Soviets "pacified" the valley, and the strategic situation returned to what it had been before the offensive.

In June and July fighting intensified, especially in the three key frontier provinces of Kunar, Nangrahar, and Paktia.[14] The Soviet offensive in Paktia proved to be a major disaster for the Soviets. There were three problems. First, the troops themselves were poorly trained reservists, and the system of enlisted seniority in the Soviet military essentially destroyed the effectiveness of NCOs.[15] Second, the equipment of the Soviet Southern Front Military District was old and obsolete.

---

[13] By way of comparison, at the height of the US commitment in Vietnam, US troops maintained a coverage density of 7.3 soldiers per square mile, while at no time during the decade-long occupation of Afghanistan did Soviet soldiers achieve a coverage density of greater than 0.7 soldiers per square mile (Cordesman and Wagner, 1990: 96). Even restricting Soviet troops to highways, supply depots, and cities was never enough to secure them adequately (Urban, 1988: 119–120).

[14] These were key provinces because they bordered Pakistan, which throughout the war remained the primary conduit of mujahideen logistical support (arms, ammunition, and so on).

[15] Terms of service typically run for two years, and soldiers serving their second year, the "old soldiers," have license to harass and abuse new arrivals, NCO stripes or not (see Urban, 1988: 127–128). This gap in small unit leadership meant that junior officers often had to take on the responsibilities normally fulfilled by NCOs. This seriously degraded the combat effectiveness of these units, especially given their COIN missions.

Armored personnel carriers (APCs) were 10–15 years old, and tanks were often 20-year-old T-55s. Neither vehicle had anti-personnel weapons which could depress or elevate sufficiently to engage targets in steep mountain terrain. Third, the tactics used were ineffective for COIN operations, which require infantry-heavy small units trained to act independently, and supported by helicopters. In the summer of 1980, there were still only an estimated 45–60 helicopters in the whole theater. In the Paktia offensive an entire motorized rifle battalion was wiped out in a single ambush. The first vehicle in the formation was immobilized by a mine or grenade, and the rest of the convoy halted. Once shooting started, the inexperienced troops began firing blindly, and continued firing from within their vehicles until their ammunition ran out. They were then overwhelmed. The defeat at Paktia, along with many other setbacks that summer, prompted a massive Soviet reorganization: "From June 1980 to mid-1981, the 40th Army was restructured from a force of seven [MRDs] to one of three [MRDs], two independent motor rifle regiments and two motor rifle brigades" (Urban, 1988: 67). Tanks were sent out of Afghanistan and helicopters were sent in. From about 60 total helicopters in 1980, by mid-1981, Afghanistan had three complete helicopter regiments of 40–50 machines each. Finally, the vulnerability of fuel convoys prompted the construction of a fuel pipeline from Termez to Pol-e-Khumri in Baghlan province (north of Kabul along the Salang Highway). This pipeline was complete by August of 1980 (Urban, 1988: 68).

Offensive operations continued during the reorganization and, in September, the Soviets launched the first of what would become the focal point of the contest between the Soviet army and mujahideen: the nine Panjsher pacification offensives. The Panjsher valley opened onto a key area of the Salang highway south of the famous tunnel linking north and south Afghanistan through the Hindu Kush mountain range. The lower end of the Panjsher valley thus opened on the main supply route from the USSR to Kabul. Mujahideen under the expert command of Ahmad Shah Massud had been wreaking havoc along this route for months. In September, the Soviets prepared to teach Massud a lesson.

It didn't work. Although the Soviet offensive included a heliborne landing by Soviet air assault troops, the results were the same as at Kunar, except that this time the Soviets lost several helicopters.[16] A second offensive in Panjsher in September (Panjsher II) took a similar

---

[16] The mujahideen claimed to have shot down ten (Urban, 1988: 70).

form and had similar results. Meanwhile, the Soviets moved against several mujahideen strongholds in the Logar valley, which opened on the vital stretch of highway from Kabul south to Jalalabad. Here the Soviets deployed heliborne troops in a new "cordon and search" tactic.[17] These new tactics, along with the deployment of much improved APCs, led to the most successful COIN operations of the year (Urban, 1988: 72). Still, the overall results were quite meager, and the mujahideen still controlled most of the countryside.

In 1981 the USSR reduced its sweep operations and relied more heavily on air power. Most of the few ground offensives which were launched were of the Kunar and Panjsher pattern: they resulted in sporadic desertions, lost equipment, and minor Soviet casualties, while killing noncombatants and destroying Afghan infrastructure.[18] The mujahideen were left largely unscathed.

In 1982 the Soviets returned to large-scale pacification sweeps, and achieved moderate success. In April and May they launched Panjsher V, and in September, Panjsher VI. Neither proved decisive, though again, Soviet tactical (especially air-mobile) and technological innovation made them somewhat more effective than previous Panjsher campaigns. Still, Massud's mujahideen were left with their fighting strength intact, while the Soviets were forced to retreat to their garrisons. Urban gives the relative casualty figures for Panjsher VI as 2000 Soviet, 1200 DRA, 180 mujahideen, and 1200 civilians dead or wounded (Urban, 1988: 109). In other areas, however, the Soviets were roundly defeated. In April an independent DRA division attempted to clear the road from Jalalabad to the Pakistan border and was almost annihilated.

What marked the Panjsher VI campaign off from previous campaigns however, was the shift in Soviet strategy from direct attacks against

---

[17] The tactic worked this way. A village suspected of containing mujahideen was selected for attack. After a preliminary mortar or air strike, an air assault battalion "stop group" is airlifted to a position between the village and the most likely route of retreat. Mines are dropped to seal off others as a motorized rifle regiment slowly moves into and through the village, closely supported by combat helicopters (Isby, 1989: 50).

[18] Note that the Soviet strategy here is not yet barbarism, although it clearly had this effect. Instead, the Soviets were attempting to "delouse" Afghanistan (in both ideological and racial terms, the Soviets viewed the mujahideen as subhuman parasites). But delousing requires tweezers and what the Soviets had was a tommy gun. The results of their "punitive offensives" (a term used by Urban to describe both the motivations and effects of Soviet operations – see Urban, 1988: 88) were akin to attempting to delouse their DRA ally with a tommy gun. For the remainder of the conflict the Soviets could never innovate a way to remove the parasite without also killing its host. After 1982 they simply gave up trying.

mujahideen bases, to the deliberate and systematic destruction of buildings, irrigation systems, crops and orchards (Rais, 1994: 102–103), as well as the deliberate targeting of noncombatants to sow terror and "cleanse" disputed valleys:

> Since they could not differentiate the mujahideen from the locals and since they could not engage the mujahideen in battles, the invaders tried to detach them from their own people. Intending to destroy the rebels' support among the civilian population, they also turned against the non-combatants, destroying their villages, their crops, and their irrigation systems and even killing them. Indiscriminate destruction of property and human life, civilian as well as military, thus became a feature of Soviet military expeditions. This was particularly so when the mujahideen killed Russian soldiers. In such cases the invaders massacred civilians by the droves. By the force of circumstances the invaders found themselves in a situation in which they killed hundreds and thousands of those for whose protection they had purportedly come. (Kakar, 1995: 129)

If Kakar and Rais are right, the Soviets were pursuing the very textbook definition of a barbarism strategy: a systematic targeting of noncombatants in pursuit of a military or political objective. Urban himself notes that the Panjsher VI operation had a devastating effect on Massud's forces:

> For [Massud] this was the more serious long-term cost of Panjsher 6. By October he was forced to appeal for food for his men. Although Massud himself remained alive and much of his army was intact, Panjsher 6 did cause lasting damage to guerrilla infrastructure in the valley, undoing years of work by the mujahideen. Visitors estimated that the population of the valley dwindled from 80,000 prewar to 45,000. (Urban, 1988: 109)

In short, Soviet barbarism appeared to be militarily effective. But was the Soviet strategy a barbarism strategy or was it, as Urban argues, a particularly blunt direct attack strategy which resulted in high collateral damage?

## Interaction two: barbarism *vs.* GWS

There is evidence to support both collateral damage and barbarism interpretations, but the weight of evidence supports the barbarism thesis.

The collateral damage argument is difficult to sustain for three reasons. First, as noted above, by 1987 an Afghan population of roughly

15 million had been reduced by almost 10 percent (Sliwinski, 1989: 39). This means that as a percentage of their population the Afghans suffered more deaths than did the Soviet Union during World War II. Moreover, the war prompted probably the largest mass emigration in history: almost half the civilian population – 6,000,000 Afghans – fled to Iran and Pakistan during the war (Cordesman and Wagner, 1990: 10). These figures by themselves cannot support the barbarism claim because there could be other causes for the high casualties and refugees (such as the complete lack of organized medical facilities, disease or age, or a naturally fearful population), but they are still suggestive of an unusually high devastation rate among noncombatants.

Second, there is widespread agreement on the deliberate destruction of Afghan infrastructure – especially buildings, orchards, and irrigation systems – which cannot be attributed to collateral damage, because such destruction *followed* the conclusion of offensive operations:

> Soviet/Afghan forces stayed in the [Panjsher] valley until 10 September, when they withdrew to Rokka once more. Before they did so, they set about destroying houses, irrigation systems and burning crops. A major refugee flow was triggered. (Urban, 1988: 109)

It is therefore difficult to consider this collateral damage, since the term is invariably used to refer to damage (a) not intended by the aggressor, and (b) *incidental* to an attack against a legitimate target (allowing that the definition of "legitimate" sometimes varies during the course of a conflict).

Third, there are questions concerning the use of mines, chemical weapons, and the treatment of prisoners. As noted above, the Soviets deployed a wide variety of mines as part of their cordon-and-search tactic. The most common (and infamous) such mine is a tiny anti-personnel mine designated PFM-1, which Western sources referred to as a "butterfly" mine. But such mines were not only used to support direct operations, they were also dropped across wide areas along suspected guerrilla supply transit routes, including also fields and pastures. Not surprisingly, the majority of victims were noncombatants. As to the use of chemical weapons, there is strong evidence that the Soviets experimented with a variety of chemical agents in Afghanistan (Isby, 1989: 76; Cordesman and Wagner, 1990: 214–218; Kakar, 1995: 215). Yet while the issue was and remains a highly politicized one, and though no hard evidence was obtained to confirm the use of chemical agents (Urban, 1988: 219; Rais, 1994: 106–108), the balance of evidence suggests they were used as a counterforce weapon against isolated mujahideen strong points.[19] Finally, Soviet troops rarely if ever took prisoners (Kakar, 1995: 246).

In sum, although many of the atrocities cited by witnesses, journalists, and historians were those normally incidental to war, the weight of evidence suggests that the main causes of Afghanistan's high noncombatant casualty and refugee rates were due to the *systematic* and *deliberate* targeting of noncombatants and their food, water, and shelter. These attacks were intended to weaken the mujahideen by disrupting their logistical and intelligence base among the broader civilian population.

The year 1983 marked a lull in the fighting in Afghanistan. Massud signed an armistice with the Soviets in January, and each side paused to lick its wounds. The Soviets undertook very few sweep operations that year, and instead increased their use of air power (again, the disproportionate impact fell on civilians, not mujahideen). They also rotated, retrained, and resupplied their troops with better weapons; including the lighter AK-74 assault rifle, flak jackets, cluster bombs (RBK-250), a new 30 mm automatic grenade-launcher (AGS-17), an improved infantry fighting vehicle (the BMP-2, whose 30 mm cannon could elevate 50°), and RPG-18 rockets.

After the Massud cease-fire expired in 1984, the Soviets launched Panjsher VII in April and May. Warned of the attack, Massud launched a pre-emptive strike on support convoys traveling the Salang highway. His mujahideen destroyed many vehicles, but Soviet response time caught them by surprise and many were surrounded and killed by heliborne air assault troops. Massud launched another pre-emptive raid on April 20, but that same day the Soviets began high-altitude carpet bombing of the valley and mountains. Unnerved, Massud ordered his remaining forces to withdraw to side canyons and avoid

---

[19] Kakar's account contains a number of similarities to those of Coffey and others concerning the Italian use of mustard gas during its conquest of Ethiopia in 1935 (see Chapter 5): "The Soviets used chemical agents in inaccessible areas so that others might not know about it. For this reason, the Soviets and the regime wreaked havoc by helicopter gunships on areas where the presence of foreigners was suspected. Apart from other considerations, the Soviets feared the foreigners would inform the world about their use of chemical agents in Afghanistan. They bombed the few health centers set up in certain areas by French and other physicians. The symbol of the International Committee of the Red Cross was anathema to the Soviets" (Kakar, 1995: 246). If true, the Soviet use of chemical weapons would share the same rationale. Their method of covering it up – the intimidation of foreign aid workers – would also be identical. Only the scale of chemical weapons use would differ.

contact with the mechanized forces advancing along the valley floor. But this time the Soviet operational plan included coordinated attacks up the canyons. These blocking forces had been specially deployed from opposite sides of these canyons so as to trap the mujahideen between two heavily armed and air-supported forces. This plan, and the new Soviet combined-arms tactics were taking a much heavier toll than usual (Urban, 1988: 147). After the battle, both sides claimed victory, although the Soviets clearly had the better claim: they had captured an important mujahideen leader and established a new series of fortified posts throughout key areas of the valley. They killed many more mujahideen than in any previous punitive offensive, and were later able to claim that civilians in the area were able to resume "a normal life" (Urban, 1988: 148). On the other hand, the mujahideen could claim victory because (a) they had managed to evacuate non-combatants before the bombing; (b) they had not been destroyed as a fighting force and they had shot down many Soviet helicopters which had been attempting to support side-canyon clearing operations; and (c) the Soviet decision to build fortified posts meant their job would soon be even easier with more attractive targets close to home.

This last point proved especially important, because although the Soviets viewed these fortified posts as a clear threat to the mujahideen, they soon proved otherwise.[20] Once built, such forts had to be manned and constantly supplied with replacements, food, fuel, and ammunition. This meant a much smaller distance for the guerrillas to travel in order to impose costs on the Soviets by ambushing supply convoys.[21]

---

[20] Had the Soviets read their history books they'd have understood why. The French tried the same tactic in Algeria in the 1830s against Abd-el-Kader (Asprey, 1994: 97), and later in Vietnam in the 1950s. It was a disaster both times. The British were only able to make it work during the South African War because they could use the entire black African population of South Africa as a strategic resource. There are no other examples of the successful use of a fortified line or blockhouse strategy.

[21] In *Seven Pillars of Wisdom*, T.E. Lawrence describes the advantages of keeping the Turks in Medina, and the terminus of a long and vulnerable line of communications: "One afternoon I woke from a hot sleep, running with sweat and pricking with flies, and wondered what on earth was the good of Medina to us? Its harmfulness had been patent when we were at Yenbo and the Turks in it were going to Mecca: but we had changed all that by our march to Wejh. Today we were blockading the railway, and they only defending it. The garrison of Medina, reduced to an inoffensive size, were sitting in trenches destroying their own power of movement by eating the transport they could no longer feed. We had taken away their power to harm us, and yet wanted to take away their town ... What on earth did we want it for?" (Lawrence, 1926: 189). In a sense, what the Soviets had unwittingly done was agree to build small "Medinas" all along the Panjsher valley floor.

The personnel inside these posts could not exert anything other than a negative influence on such civilians as remained in the valley:

> The militia posts were also unable to influence the districts where they were stationed. Their presence in the midst of the hostile rural people was merely an odious symbol of the regime. When the mujahideen attacked that symbol, the militiamen played havoc with their guns on the villages... [Villagers] begged the mujahideen to leave their villages or not to fire at the posts. A rift was thus created between the villagers and the mujahideen. This was a victory for the regime. A network of military posts throughout the country would have enabled the regime to pacify the land, but the government was, of course, unable to create such a system. (Kakar, 1995: 174)

Note that such a network was precisely what the British *had* been able to create, maintain, and expand in South Africa. But the Soviets simply did not have the mission (or the resources proportional to it) to build such a network. Again, T. E. Lawrence's thinking on the subject is illustrative. Here he calculates what it would take for the Turks to control the 100,000 square miles of territory ranging from the Hejaz to Syria:

> Then I figured out how many men they would need to sit on all this ground, to save it from our attack-in-depth, sedition putting up her head in every unoccupied one of those hundred thousand square miles. I knew the Turkish Army exactly, and even allowing for their recent extension of faculty by aeroplanes and guns and armoured trains ... still it seemed they would have need of a fortified post every four square miles, and a post could not be less than twenty men. If so, they would need six hundred thousand men to meet the ill wills of all the Arab peoples, combined with the active hostility of a few zealots. (Lawrence, 1926: 192–193)

This then establishes the limited mission of the limited contingent as a major explanatory factor in the strategy the Soviets pursued.[22] The territory of Afghanistan is 245,000 square miles; and even acknowledging that the Soviets only needed to control some lesser portion of that, they never had sufficient troops with which to do it (Urban, 1988: 119–120). In fact, the Soviets were so thinly spread in Afghanistan that Massud could use threats to these posts to manipulate the pace of operations in other provinces.

---

[22] Kakar goes so far as to suggest a direct connection between the barbarism strategy and the limited number of Soviet troops assigned to the theater (see below).

Little would change from 1985 until the Soviet withdrawal in 1989. In 1985, Mikhail Gorbachev came to power and in May, Babrak Karmal was replaced by Mohammed Najibullah, who had been head of the DRA secret police (KhAD) under Karmal. Although Gorbachev clearly did not share the views of his predecessors regarding the costs and benefits of the Afghan adventure, he gave his newly appointed Southern Front commander, Mikhail Zaitsev, one year to engineer a military solution to the Afghan problem. The operations of 1985 accelerated the Soviets' barbarism strategy:

> Soviet artillery and rocket-launchers supplemented aircraft to achieve de-population through firepower, an approach mandated by the continued weakness of Kabul regime forces... The destruction of rural agriculture was the goal of offensives in Laghman and in the Helmand Valley. (Isby, 1989: 34)

But, after three years, the Soviets had clearly begun to hit the flat of the curve in terms of the military effectiveness of their depopulation strategy. Zaitsev intensified the use of air power and especially heliborne-supported operations, but the mujahideen refused to unravel. Why?

In 1986, Soviet operations focused more on interdiction of mujahideen supplies. Having destroyed almost entirely the mujahideen supply infrastructure in Afghanistan through the cumulative effects of four years of barbarism, the mujahideen had by this time become almost entirely dependent on logistical support from Iran, Saudi Arabia, and the United States (Rais, 1994: 112–113). This support arrived mainly at Karachi, and flowed from there north through Peshawar and Quetta to mujahideen forces throughout Afghanistan. In 1985 the SA-7 (shoulder-fired surface-to-air missiles, or SAMs) used by the mujahideen with moderate effect were supplemented by British-made Blowpipe SAMs. In 1986, the mujahideen began to receive the much more effective US-made Stinger SAMs. This prompted the Soviets to increase their pressure on Pakistan. They did this by means of a limited number of minor raids on mujahideen bases in Pakistan, and by attempting to bribe non-Pushtun tribes along the Pakistani side of the border to interdict mujahideen convoys into Afghanistan. The effort proved an expensive failure.

But the biggest problem of 1986 proved to be the Stingers. In a major offensive in the Nangrahar province, "three out of four Soviet helicopters in a formation were destroyed in quick succession by US-made heat-seeking man-portable Stinger [SAMs]" (Isby, 1989: 38). The increase in attrition of Soviet helicopters had a disproportionate impact on its military effectiveness, because for the prior six years the entire force structure and organization of the Soviets in Afghanistan had come to rely almost entirely on air-mobile tactics and weapons.[23] In 1987 things only got worse:

> [The Stinger] was the most effective [weapon] which the mujahideen received ... It became "a turning point of the campaign." From then on Stingers partly neutralized Soviet aerial offensives. According to the estimates of Pakistan's Intelligence Service (ISI), "During the summer of 1987 the mujahideen hit an average of 1.5 aircraft of varied description every day." By the end of 1987 the military situation had deteriorated to the extent that even Najibullah admitted that "80 percent of the countryside and 40 percent of towns were outside the control of his government." (Kakar, 1995: 260)

Zaitsev, in other words, had inherited a heliborne-dependent force in 1985, and the arrival of Stingers in quantity in 1986 and especially 1987 made it difficult for him – given the constraint in overall forces and one-year time deadline – to engineer a military victory using that now highly specialized force. Gorbachev called a halt, and the Soviets began the sequential withdrawal of their forces, which ended as the last Soviet unit crossed the Oxus River into the USSR on February 15, 1989.

## Outcome: mujahideen win

Although Urban's book was published prior to the end of the war, he proposes some useful victory conditions:

> Victory in the war in Afghanistan will be defined as the circumstances under which the Soviet army (or the bulk of it at least) leaves. If the PDPA regime survives and continues a slow expansion of support, then the Soviets will have won. If the regime collapses, even within a year or two of the withdrawal, the USSR will be judged to have experienced a humiliation on the scale of Vietnam.
>
> (Urban, 1988: 221)

---

[23] This is not the same thing as saying that technology won the war for the mujahideen. What it did do was make it impossible for Zaitsev to meet his one-year deadline. Had he been given more time, it's possible the Soviets could have developed and deployed effective countermeasures without escalating.

The regime collapsed within three years of the Soviet departure, so by Urban's criteria the Soviet intervention may be judged either a success, or a humiliation somewhat less severe than the scale of Vietnam.

In March of 1989, the mujahideen began a series of offensives between the Pakistani border and Jalalabad, which came under siege. In April, the mujahideen began to form regular army units in preparation for drives on Kabul. They spent most of 1990 consolidating and reorganizing. In March of 1991 they captured Khost, taking 2200 prisoners. In July, the Wakhan corridor fell, opening the road transport of supplies from Pakistan to Badakhshan. In September, the United States agreed to halt all military aid by the end of the year and, in November, the Soviets begin withdrawing 300 SCUD missile operators from Afghanistan. On December 8, the Soviet Union ceased to exist, and Soviet assistance to the Najibullah regime terminated. In April of 1992, Najibullah appealed to the United States for help in stopping the spread of fundamentalist Islam in Central Asia, and on April 12 the Salang highway fell to the mujahideen. Two days later, Massud and his allies captured the airbase at Bagram. On April 18, Herat, Kunduz, and Shindand air base fell. Two days later, Najibullah was stopped at Kabul airport as he attempted to board a plane to join his family in Delhi. He took refuge in the UN compound.[24] The mujahideen continued to close in on Kabul, which they occupied on April 27, 1992, the 14th anniversary of the coup which had toppled Da'ud.

The costs to each side in terms of casualties are not entirely clear. Cordesman and Wagner estimate (Cordesman and Wagner, 1990: 10; see also Isby, 1988: 62) that the Soviets lost no more that 15,000 men killed and about three times that many wounded.[25] DRA losses are cited as 34,000–42,000 killed or wounded, and 52,000–60,000 desertions. The mujahideen lost about 140,000–200,000 killed or wounded. Fully half the civilian population of Afghanistan was either killed or made refugees (about 1,500,000 and 6,000,000 respectively).

The Soviets did not achieve their political objectives in Afghanistan. They were not able to secure the DRA from attacks even in Kabul; and the DRA itself could never gain enough legitimacy among the Afghan people to mount a political challenge to the authority of the

[24] Najibullah remained at the UN compound until the Taliban – a group of conservative Sunni Islamists trained and supplied by Pakistan – captured Kabul in September of 1996, when he was taken from the compound and hanged.
[25] Borovik reports that this is a gross underestimate: according to his research, there were already 20,000 Soviet casualties by 1981 alone (Borovik, 1990: 281).

mujahideen. Even more importantly, within a year, the Taliban – a group of Islamic extremists and the very type of regime which the Soviets most feared would come to power in Afghanistan – became the *de facto* government of all but a tiny fraction of territory held by the Northern Alliance.

## Analysis: competing explanations of the Afghan Civil War's outcome

### Actor interests

In the Afghan Civil War the USSR's interests were not explained by its material preponderance relative to that of the mujahideen. The USSR invaded Afghanistan with the minimal objective of establishing and securing a friendly Marxist regime in Kabul. They anticipated that once stabilized, the Karmal regime would be able to successively broaden support (by jailing extremists and initiating reforms and development projects) until the Soviet military presence was no longer necessary. But their presence galvanized opposition and instantly delegitimized the Karmal regime beyond any hope of salvation. Why did they stay after it became apparent that their original assumptions were wrong? More importantly, why didn't they escalate, as the United States had done in Vietnam?

They stayed because they overestimated their own military capabilities. They also overestimated the degree to which the DRA could operate independently of Soviet support, and the degree to which the Afghan people would consider the DRA to be independent. They also stayed because they not only feared to suffer the humiliation of the defeat of a friendly Marxist regime on their borders,[26] but because they feared its replacement by an Islamic fundamentalist regime in Kabul.[27]

The Soviets did not escalate because they believed they could innovate – strategically, tactically, technologically, and politically – new ways of increasing their military effectiveness without increasing their costs in terms of blood and time. Their depopulation strategy,

---

[26] A question of negative precedent setting: if the USSR could not defend a friendly and *proximate* Marxist regime from a shaggy, fundamentalist rabble, how could other, more distant allies count on it?

[27] Events subsequent to their departure appear to bear this concern out: two days after the collapse of the Najibullah regime in Kabul, civil war erupted in the former Soviet Republic of Tajikistan.

heliborne-assisted cordon-and-search tactics, new equipment, and reorganization, training and supply of DRA units are all evidence of this.

Their decision to stay implies that Soviet interests in Afghanistan were higher than those suggested by the interest asymmetry argument, yet their refusal to escalate suggests that their interests in Afghanistan were in fact limited – a term that applies equally to their forces and their objectives in Afghanistan. Which is it?

There is no definitive way to answer this question, but the best evidence supports the argument that whatever their initial objectives the fact of the war and mujahideen resistance increased the importance of the outcome for the Soviets far beyond that predicted by the interest asymmetry argument. The Soviets did not leave until after they had killed or displaced half of Afghanistan's civilian population, and gained the promise of a dramatic reduction of foreign support for the mujahideen. Meanwhile, they continued to pour billions of rubles in development and military aid into Afghanistan, and Najibullah's regime was able to survive until the collapse of the Soviet Union itself in 1991. Put more bluntly, the real reason the Soviets did not escalate is because they believed they had achieved their limited objectives in Afghanistan.

The mujahideen fought as though their very survival was at stake, and the extreme brutality of Soviet and DRA operations in Afghanistan make it clear that they were correct. Once the Soviets withdrew, however, the mujahideen began to fight among themselves. This only accelerated once the government which had been imposed on the Afghan people by the Soviet Union collapsed in 1992.

### Regime types, strategy, and vulnerability

In 1979 the Soviet Union was an authoritarian regime under the leadership of Leonid Brezhnev. Even after the accession to power of Mikhail Gorbachev in 1985, his policy of *glasnost* was not applied to the war in Afghanistan:

> Much of what we try so desperately to conceal, the Americans know better than the Soviets. If I try to publish some information that we consider top secret, but that appeared in the American press a long time ago, the censor will still cross it out. An obvious question presents itself: once the American people know something about the Soviet Army, why don't the Soviet people have the right to know it, too?
>
> (Borovik, 1990: 127)

Its press was tightly controlled, its soldiers' letters were censored, and its people had no say in its foreign policy.[28] Its initial conventional attack strategy in Afghanistan was based on its mission, its force structure, and its assumptions about the quantity and quality of the resistance it expected to encounter. The third-echelon mechanized forces which swept into Afghanistan on December 27, 1979 did not expect resistance, and they encountered very little until after they had settled into garrison. Their initial punitive offensives into major Afghan valley systems were little more than a show of force intended to cow the "backward reactionary peasants" who opposed the efforts of the PDPA to advance the standard of socialism.

But the Afghans were not cowed, they were outraged.

The conventional attack strategy initially thought sufficient to intimidate the Afghans soon changed to a COIN campaign which is best understood in Soviet historical context:

> In the case of Afghanistan, one may not rule out a centrally-organized strategy aimed at what Louis Dupree described as "migratory genocide." The transfer of population was a part of the Soviet counter-insurgency doctrine which had been practiced before in its wars in Central Asia. An effective counter-insurgency war could not be fought against guerrillas swimming in a sea of a supportive population. The Kabul regime, having failed to win the hearts and minds of the Afghans, collaborated with the Soviet forces in depopulating areas of tough resistance. (Rais, 1994: 102–103)

This is another way of saying that barbarism is a traditional COIN strategy in Soviet military doctrine. Since the Soviet Union's regime type did not change from 1917 until its collapse in 1991, it is difficult to evaluate the impact of regime type on the decision to switch to a barbarism strategy in the Soviet case.

Difficult, but not impossible; there are two ways to understand the relationship of regime type to strategy in the Afghan Civil War. First, the interstate dimension was clearly a concern even for Brezhnev. Satellite and signals intelligence data would quickly make both the build-up and deployment of troops in Afghanistan evident to the world. But Brezhnev calculated that just as it had in Hungary in 1956 and in Czechoslovakia in 1968, international public opinion would soon "blow over":

---

[28] Soldiers' letters were mostly *self*-censored: soldiers knew their families would be worried, and most often wrote "encouraging" letters home so as not to worry their parents (Tamarov, 1992).

> This Soviet expectation eroded gradually as it became necessary to increase the numbers of their "limited contingent" and to play the leading role in fighting as the effectiveness of the Afghan military declined precipitously as a result of increased desertions and internal conflict between the overwhelmingly Khalqi military and the new Parchami regime. Simultaneously, the transformation of the war from a civil conflict to an international one aroused the Afghan people to increased resistance, which gained more effective international support. The reality of war, symbolized to the world by the dramatic increase in refugees, made it impossible for the Soviets to practice political "damage control." (Magnus & Naby, 1998: 129)

Brezhnev was wrong, and he left his successors to pay the price. Admittedly, this price was not prohibitive at first. The United States led a boycott of the 1980 Olympic Games in Moscow, and the Carter administration embargoed wheat to the USSR. But with the accession to power of Mikhail Gorbachev, the closest thing to a regime change in the USSR since Khrushchev's denunciation of Stalin soon made the Afghan adventure prohibitively expensive.

True, the Soviet people still did not have a direct say in foreign affairs, and they were never told the real casualty figures in Afghanistan, but for a new leadership attempting to bring the Soviet Union into the twenty-first century intact, Afghanistan had become an albatross:

> The war in Afghanistan . . . did not fit into Gorbachev's overall policy of *glasnost* and *perestroika*. He felt that it had turned into a debacle for the Soviet Union and was too closely associated with the policies of the Brezhnev era and the renewed Cold War. *Glasnost* meant that it was no longer possible to keep the price of the war a secret . . .
>
> (Magnus and Naby, 1998: 132)

Gorbachev was attempting to harmonize what his predecessors had always considered to be mutually exclusive aims: nationalism, liberalism, and socialism. Like Afghanistan's Mahmud Beg Tarzi, Gorbachev had become his own country's "greatest modern liberal thinker." Unlike Tarzi, however, Gorbachev was in charge.

In sum, the long history of authoritarian regime-types in the Soviet Union had made it possible to prosecute a barbarism strategy without sustaining domestic political costs.[29] Barbarism had become its

---

[29] Interstate military intervention such as that of NATO in Kosovo in 1999 was then, as now, out of the question: Russia is still a big country and one still armed with thermonuclear missiles besides.

standard COIN strategy. But communications and military intelligence technology and the accession to power of a reform-minded general secretary changed this. The Soviet barbarism strategy began to impose international political costs almost from its outset. Domestic costs were experienced within the USSR because many Soviet boys returned home in zinc coffins, while many others returned shattered by mines or by the experience of combat. These costs were not experienced by the Soviet people as a whole until after 1986, when *glasnost* made it possible to share more stories about the Afghan campaign and its costs.[30]

As to regime type and political vulnerability, the Soviet regime was at no time vulnerable to the sorts of political costs anticipated by the interest asymmetry argument. If the trade-offs mechanism anticipated by Mack's argument were operating, we'd expect to see major battle-field defeats result in either pressure to withdraw or escalation. Yet Soviet commitment in terms of men and materiel remained constant over time. Moreover, even *glasnost* and *perestroika* combined did not create conditions which made possible a public outcry on the war – at least not one of a scale sufficient to force the regime to reconsider its foreign policy.

### Arms diffusion

In this case the arms diffusion argument gets its strongest support. The mujahideen gained increasing advantages from arms they received through Iran and Pakistan, and these increased the costs of conquest and occupation to the Soviet Union and its DRA client. What is most important to recognize, however, is that in no theater of war has the crucial relationship between technology, tactics, climate, and terrain been made clearer than in Afghanistan.

Soviet motorized infantry and armored columns were very often disabled with technology as simple as pushing boulders onto roads

---

[30] In fairness, however, the immense pride (in many cases deserved) and propaganda surrounding the Soviet victory in World War II (what the Soviets called "The Great Patriotic War"), and the officially released casualty figures from the war, made it difficult for many average Soviet citizens to appreciate the sacrifices of their Afghan veterans. Vladislav Tamarov, a Russian survivor of the Afghan war, notes that "In the United States there are 186 psychological rehabilitation centers open to help Vietnam veterans. But where are we in the Soviet Union to go for help? We don't even have one such center. And so we look for that kind of help from people. That is when we run up against misunderstandings. From these misunderstandings comes the high divorce rate among Afghan vets, from these misunderstandings comes the turning inward, into oneself" (Tamarov, 1992: 7).

and then tossing Molotov cocktails onto the engine compartments of immobilized vehicles. Then simple machine-gun fire – a technology dating in its most serious use from World War I – would finish the job of the convoy's complete destruction. Essentially, the mujahideen used simple technology to exploit weaknesses in Soviet tactics and strategy.

This was especially the case after 1986, when the arrival of US-made Stinger SAMs dramatically shifted the balance of power in Afghanistan. As observed above, it was not so much the Stingers themselves that mattered, but rather the context: the Soviets had used heliborne infantry and helicopter gunships to exploit a weakness in mujahideen tactics, only to find the tables turned once their helicopters fell prey to the Stingers. There is no question that had the USSR been ruled by a Stalin or even a Brezhnev, the Soviets in Afghanistan would have innovated around this weakness. But Gorbachev called a halt to the war, wisely reckoning that to win it would gain the USSR little, and might require the invasion of Pakistan.

### Strategic interaction

The Afghan Civil War had two strategic interactions, and during the first the Soviet pursued a particularly blunt conventional attack strategy against a mujahideen GWS. Neither side had adequate leadership, training, or equipment, but Soviet forces were so thoroughly unsuited to a COIN mission that their failures must be attributed almost entirely to strategic interaction. They swung a blunt club, and the mujahideen ducked and stabbed them in the foot with a sharp stick. The strategic interaction was opposite-approach and the Soviets were forced to reorganize and switch strategies.

But the second interaction of the war turned far more deadly for the mujahideen. The Soviets consciously and deliberately targeted non-combatants and their support infrastructure as a COIN strategy. According to the strategic interaction thesis, barbarism should have been the ideal counter-GWS strategy, quickly destroying the mujahideen as a fighting force. It did not do this, but the reason it did not does not refute the strategic interaction thesis. Instead, it highlights a specific condition under which the dynamic does not apply.

The very real destruction of Afghan infrastructure and the mass killing and forced emigration of peasants did hurt the mujahideen, but most, like Massud's Panjsher fighters, managed to reorganize themselves and their resources to compensate. After 1983 they began to rely more for intelligence on sympathizers within the DRA, and more on logistical support from foreign sympathizers.[31] They were still able to mount offensive operations, and Massud was able to do so farther and farther from his home bases of support (a sign that they mattered less as the war dragged on). But this made them proportionately more dependent on outside support. The degree of mujahideen dependence on outside support is revealed in the sharp decline of their fighting capacity after the Soviet evacuation in 1989 (Cordesman and Wagner, 1990: 97; Magnus and Naby, 1998: 134, 159): Not only had they fallen increasingly to fighting among themselves, but the flow of arms quickly dried up.

In sum, the Afghan Civil War makes it clear that the more independent guerrillas are of their popular support base due to outside support, the more insulated they will be from the devastating effects of barbarism, *assuming they are able to gain good intelligence*. However, outside aid poses its own risks. First, it may provoke guerrillas to attempt to defeat the strong actor in decisive engagements (such as the Tet Offensive of 1968, which proved a military disaster). Second, if the contest is fought on nationalistic terms, as it was in Afghanistan, foreign assistance – especially military advisors – can be used to paint its recipients as the lackeys of the foreign powers supplying the arms and other support. The Karmal (and later Najibullah) regimes attempted and failed to tar the Islamic mujahideen with the foreign lackey brush. They failed because the United States did not send military advisors to Afghanistan in quantity. But the mujahideen had no difficulty convincing Afghan and international audiences alike that the PDPA regime was the mere puppet of Soviet interests.

Even so, the operational impact of the Soviet barbarism strategy should not be underestimated. These depredations *hurt* the mujahideen, and while the most successful commanders adapted themselves to the changes, others could not, and their forces were either killed, captured, or dispersed.

## Conclusion

The Afghan Civil War was an asymmetric conflict between the DRA and its Soviet masters (strong actor), and the Afghan mujahideen (weak actor).

The Soviets had a number of interests in Afghanistan, and the two most important were negative: (1) defending a friendly Marxist regime,

---

[31] They were also able to rely on the military intelligence of the ISI, Pakistan's highly-rated intelligence service.

and (2) thereby preventing the accession of a radical Islamic republic on its southern border. To these seemingly limited objectives it was willing to commit a force of four MRDs, one-and-a-half Air Assault divisions, and lavish economic aid. It did not act as if its survival was at stake, but neither can its level of interest in Afghanistan be explained by its relative power, as implied by the interest asymmetry argument.

Mujahideen interests were in ejecting the Soviets from Afghanistan, where the PDPA regime which controlled Kabul was not distinguished from the Soviets. To this end they fought as if their survival was at stake.

In sum, hypothesis 8 – relative material power explains relative interests in the outcome of an asymmetric conflict – receives moderate support. It cannot be rejected, but neither can it be accepted as an explanation of Soviet interests. Did relative power and regime type explain political vulnerability?

According to the interest asymmetry thesis, a major military setback should have caused the Soviets to reevaluate their occupation regardless of their regime type. This didn't happen. Every year brought a mix of successes and failures, with the successes short lived and the failures at times catastrophic. Yet there is no evidence that the failures ever provoked the sort of trade-offs anticipated by the interest asymmetry argument. Even commanding generals were not cashiered after such failures. Instead of withdrawing, the Soviets attempted gamely to learn from their failures and innovate around them. They often succeeded, but never in a way which could compensate for their relatively low numbers. In short, relative power asymmetry did not cause political vulnerability. Instead, the Soviet Union's authoritarian regime type insulated it from such vulnerabilities.

Regime type also made it possible for the Soviets to avoid the three most common defects of a barbarism strategy. Authoritarian regimes are first of all free to construct the enemy as they see fit. Second, and more importantly, the lack of public access to accurate information about the costs of a conflict short-circuits domestic unrest and, hence, political vulnerability. Third and finally, authoritarian regimes do not by definition contain a mechanism by which popular will can be translated into foreign policy. These are, of course, ideal-type descriptions but, in the Soviet case during the Afghan Civil War, this is the way things worked. Thus, the decision to switch from a direct attack to a barbarism strategy was a doctrinaire response to a recognition that the Soviet mission had changed to COIN.

The mujahideen did not have a regime type, and cannot be considered as even a remotely unified actor. On the contrary, some commentators argue that this lack of unity actually proved to be an asset, because it gave the Soviets no way to decapitate resistance leadership:

> Among significant features of Pushtun life are the practice of Islam, mainly in its Sunni aspect among nearly all Pushtuns, the nonhierarchical structure of tribal groups, and the Pushtun code known as the Pushtunwali. All three features have come to contribute significantly to the persistence of the Afghan resistance to the Soviet army at first, and then to the stubborn inability of the Pushtuns either to agree among themselves on how a new government should be formed or to work with like-minded ideological groups to end the civil war.
> (Magnus and Naby, 1998: 14)

Others emphasize the problems of lack of unity and hierarchy:

> Some analysts have said that this disorganization is a strength, because it means that the resistance cannot be decapitated. It is nothing of the sort: without unity and organisation they cannot take the initiative. If they cannot take the initiative, victory is impossible.
> (Urban, 1988: 216–217)

In the context of GWS, Urban is simply wrong. The mujahideen could win by simply not losing, and having no hierarchical structure only made it more difficult for the Soviets to defeat them.[32]

Arms diffusion also receives some support in this case. But a close examination of how arms technology interacted with tactics and strategy makes it clear that the logic of the arms diffusion argument, hypothesis 6 (the better armed a weak actor is, the more likely it is that a strong actor will lose an asymmetric conflict), is only weakly supported here.

Strategic interaction explains why the Soviets lost the first interaction of the war, but it doesn't explain the second. From 1980 to 1982, the Soviet pursued a conventional attack strategy against a mujahideen GWS (opposite-approach). It failed on every count. Yet after the switch to a barbarism strategy in 1983 (same-approach), the USSR did not win, and in 1989 it withdrew from Afghanistan completely. Why?

Barbarism should have been an ideal COIN strategy because the Soviets were not vulnerable to domestic or interstate political costs

---

[32] Contrast this with the Algerian resistance against France from 1958 to 1962. The FLN did have a hierarchical structure and the French were able to exploit this by means of, among other things, torture.

associated with its prosecution.[33] Moreover, it should have devastated the intelligence and logistical capacity of the mujahideen. Instead, it only provided the mujahideen with defectors and recruits. Barbarism wasn't decisive in Afghanistan because the mujahideen were able to rely on intelligence and logistical support from foreign powers from the sanctuary of Pakistan and Iran. The mujahideen had in fact become so dependent on this aid that when it ceased in 1989 and 1990 it shattered their ability to topple the illegitimate government of Najibullah. Not until the logistical supply tap was turned back on – this time for the Taliban – did that change. Afghanistan therefore highlights one condition under which barbarism is less effective as a COIN strategy: when the guerrillas have access to a significant source of intelligence and logistical support (and sanctuary) beyond the reach of the strong actor, and beyond its capacity to interdict.[34]

In sum, strategic interaction best explains the outcome of Soviet intervention in the Afghan Civil War. Once it became clear that the fight in Afghanistan was a COIN struggle, the Soviets had three strategic choices. First, continue with the present strategy, perhaps sending more troops and equipment to the theater. Second, withdraw in some way which could save face yet end the war. Third, switch to a barbarism strategy. The Soviets chose the third option and their strategy succeeded in hurting the mujahideen and killing or making refugees of nearly half of Afghanistan's pre-war civilian population. The mujahideen faced an even starker choice after the Soviets switched strategies: either give up or continue with a strategy which would force them to rely more and more on outside powers for support.

---

[33] This contrasts with the Italian case in Chapter 5, because Italy was a minor power and even the slightest real sanction by Britain (such as closing the Suez Canal to Italian transport) or France would have been sufficient to force Italy to withdraw.
[34] The same proved true of US experience in Vietnam, with Laos and Cambodia playing unwilling host to DRV supply transits. Unlike the USSR, the United States was initially less circumspect about violating the neutrality of Laos and Cambodia in its efforts to interdict supplies flowing from the DRV to the VC in the South. But then neither Laos nor Cambodia were nuclear powers or strong allies of the United States, whereas from 1979 to 1989 Pakistan was both. The KLA in Kosovo in 1999 also serves as an example of this problem. Serb barbarism rapidly depopulated Kosovo of ethnic Albanians, and eviscerated what had been a relatively incompetent (though impassioned) KLA resistance. But, unless willing to invade Albania, the Serbs could never eradicate the KLA, and in the event Serb barbarism only served to prompt NATO intervention and keep NATO united in its efforts to punish Milosevic. On the relationship between Serb and Serb-supported barbarism in Kosovo and NATO intervention, see, e.g., Daalder and O'Hanlon (2000).

In the end, no one really won the war. The Soviets left in 1989 and the DRA fell in 1992. The mujahideen were almost entirely overcome by the Taliban – a group of extremely conservative Islamists supported by both Pakistan and Saudi Arabia. Afghanistan itself has been devastated on a scale not witnessed since the destruction of Germany and the Soviet Union in World War II.

## 8  Conclusion

The vast majority of wars do not come into the heavyweight range, but are distinguished more by their duration and bitterness than their weaponry. In a way they become more amenable to Western intervention when they do develop into straightforward clashes between regular forces. Civil wars, involving irregular fighters and skirmishes in the streets, with political confusion rife and good intelligence at a premium, present an appalling prospect to outsiders. Decisive victories are few and far between. Even success can mean a long-term commitment of troops to sustain an uneasy peace.

Freedman

This book began with a puzzle. How do the weak win wars? Through a combination of statistical tests and the tracing of causal logic through historical case studies, I have shown that weak actors – in this case mainly states – win wars against much stronger adversaries when they are able to adopt and maintain an ideal counterstrategy. Strategy, in other words, can multiply or divide applied power.

Strong actors come to a fight with a complex combination of interests, forces, doctrine, military technology, and political objectives, but because armed forces are thought to be versatile in their employment, and because strong actors are only relatively, not absolutely, strong, strong actors do have choices in the strategies they use. Similarly, weak actors often face constraints in their choice of strategies, but strategy is never endogenous.

### The dynamics of asymmetric conflict

International relations theory leads us to expect few asymmetric conflicts because large gaps in relative power imply unambiguous conflict outcomes. The stronger you are, the less likely I am to challenge you.[1] The weaker you are, the more likely I am to provoke you, knowing you wouldn't dare object. More importantly, the greater the disparity in power, the more *quickly* we expect the strong to subdue the weak if it comes to blows.

In this book I examined three arguments that had the potential to explain why strong actors lose to weak actors; using the puzzle of increasing strong actor failures over time as a kind of test of the arguments' soundness and generality. The first and strongest of these alternative explanations was Andrew Mack's interest asymmetry thesis, but nature-of-actor (including Merom's "democratic social squeamishness" argument), and arms diffusion arguments were also introduced and tested.

## Competing explanations of asymmetric conflict outcomes

The best alternative general explanation of asymmetric conflict outcomes over time is Andrew Mack's interest asymmetry thesis. Mack's explanation reduces to a simple explanatory model. He argues that structure explains actor interests, which in turn determine relative political vulnerabilities, which explain outcomes. A strong actor's survival will not be at stake, so its interests – understood here to mean willingness to sustain costs – will be relatively low. This vulnerability makes it much more likely that a strong actor will be forced by domestic political opposition or elite rivalry to withdraw from a conflict if it suffers unanticipated costs or a military setback. This explains why "big nations lose small wars."

A second argument was that perhaps strong actors with democratic regime types lost asymmetric conflicts because they were weak willed, or too casualty sensitive, or too vulnerable to domestic criticism; whereas authoritarian strong actors were more likely to win because they could field more ruthless or efficient militaries, and were insulated from domestic criticism, making it possible, in Merom's words, to

---

[1] It is not only the force applied that causes this effect, it is more importantly the force *available* to be applied that matters most. This is why it makes sense to argue that the dynamics of asymmetric conflict apply even though so-called strong actors are often not overwhelmingly strong within a given conflict theater. Strong actors have choices about their other commitments and the relative priorities of their interests. Weak actors understand this, and can never rely on the existence of other commitments as a guarantee against future strong-actor escalation. On this point see Schelling (1966: 2–6).

"escalate the level of violence and brutality necessary" in order to win (Merom, 2003: 15).

A third argument was that the diffusion of relatively advanced small arms and other military technology to the developing world in and of itself made conquest and occupation of weak actors more difficult; essentially, because like strategy, technology can also be a force multiplier, weak actors were not really as weak as anticipated.

## Strategy and strategic interaction

Mack was right about the problem of vulnerability, but his argument overemphasizes the link between relative power and interests, and fails to identify the key permissive condition under which such vulnerability operates: a significant and unanticipated delay between the commitment of armed forces and the attainment of pre-war military or political objectives. If the conflict is over quickly – which is what we expect in very asymmetric conflicts – then how can political vulnerability operate?[2]

This leads to the question of why some asymmetric conflicts – such as the USSR's invasion of Hungary in 1956, or the US-led Gulf Coalition in Iraq in 1991 – are quick and decisive, while others – such as the US intervention in Vietnam in 1965, or the USSR's in Afghanistan in 1979 – drag on? This book has shown that the interaction of the strategies actors employ predicts the duration of the conflict, and provides the missing condition necessary for the operation of political vulnerability.

The importance of strategy as the key variable intervening between a given actor's material resources and outcomes requires us to consider both the range of strategies available to actors and the interaction of those choices in the conflicts themselves.

---

[2] Mack and Merom each focus on cases featuring opposite-approach interactions, in which a strong actor (advanced industrial country) using a conventional attack strategy attacks a weak actor (economically backward nation in arms) using GWS or terrorism. The strategic interaction thesis explains why strong-actor failure in these cases is overdetermined. Mack offers the best general explanation of the two, erring only in overestimating the degree to which actor motivation and regime type affects outcomes, and by omission of the key variable (strategic interaction) that determines how long an asymmetric conflict will last. Merom offers a more detailed account of how democratic strong actors lose, but errs in his overestimation of the utility of brutality in winning small wars in the post-World War II period. Democracies, for example, have won two small wars in the last half-century *without* recourse to barbarism. Britain succeeded in the Malayan Emergency of 1948, and under the leadership of Ramon Magsaysay, the Philippines (with US support) succeeded against the Hukbalahap in 1952.

## Strategy

For purposes of this analysis I reduced a wide array of specific attacker and defender strategies to four: two for attackers and two for defenders. Attacker (strong actor) strategies are conventional attack and barbarism. Defender (weak actor) strategies are conventional defense and GWS.[3]

I then simplified each actor's range of strategic options further into two analytically distinct strategic *approaches*: direct and indirect. Direct approaches – conventional attack and defense – target an adversary's armed forces with the aim of destroying or capturing that adversary's *capacity* to fight. Indirect approaches – barbarism and GWS – aim at destroying an adversary's *will* to fight.

These simplifications – and they are that – highlight what is most important about the role of strategy in mediating between raw power resources and asymmetric conflict outcomes: strategic interaction.

## Strategic interaction

Once a strategy is chosen, is it the best strategy under the circumstances? In this context "circumstances" means *given the other actor's strategy*. Each strategy has an ideal counterstrategy. Actors can dramatically increase the effectiveness of their own strategy (essentially multiplying their forces) by guessing correctly about their adversary's strategy and then selecting and executing that ideal counterstrategy.[4]

Specifically, similar approaches (indirect–indirect, or direct–direct) imply defeat for the weak actor and victory for the strong. These wars will be over quickly, making political vulnerability (whether caused

---

[3] These strategies are detailed in Chapter 2 . They are ideal-type constructions and by no means exhaustive representatives of their approach categories (e.g., "conciliation" is another indirect-approach strategy available to strong actors). Each of these four strategies (save perhaps barbarism) is represented by an extensive literature which need not be reviewed here. I have instead simplified and fixed the meanings of the most relevant strategic options, which actors may pursue independently, sequentially, or simultaneously.

[4] This said, executing an ideal strategy may be difficult for at least two reasons. First, a given actor's forces may have been trained, armed, and prepared for a different strategy against a different enemy. Switching strategies – especially in the middle of a fight – can therefore be risky. All other things being equal, it will be easier to switch to a different strategy in the same approach (say, from terrorism to nonviolent resistance or GWS) than to a different strategy in an opposite approach (say, from conventional defense to GWS). Second, some of the strategies themselves cannot be quickly implemented; when guerrilla warfare as a *tactic* is not supported by a previous period of social organization it tends to fail. This was the experience of, e.g., Che Guevara in Bolivia.

by asymmetric interests, as argued by Mack, or by regime type, as argued by Merom) irrelevant. By contrast, opposite approaches (direct–indirect, indirect–direct) favor weak actors at the expense of strong actors. They will drag on, forcing strong actors – especially democratic strong actors – to make tough and costly decisions in order to continue with any prospect of success.

### My argument

Relative power, regime type, and political vulnerability are necessary but not sufficient to explain variation in asymmetric conflict outcomes. The strategies actors use are important (as are the constraints actors face when evaluating competing offensive and defensive strategies), but what is more important is how opposing strategies interact. I hypothesized that same-approach strategic interactions would favor attackers in proportion to their advantage in material resources. Opposite-approach strategic interactions would favor defenders, regardless of the attackers' material preponderance.

Assuming the strong actor is in each case the attacker and the weak actor the defender, the expected relationship of strategic interaction to conflict outcomes can be seen in Figure 3 in Chapter 2. In same-approach interactions the strong actor wins because there is nothing to deflect or mediate the use of its material advantages in resources, including soldiers and wealth. In opposite-approach interactions, the strong actor's resources are deflected (weak actors attempt to avoid open confrontation contact with a strong actors' armed forces) or directed at values which don't necessarily affect the capacity of the weak adversary to continue to impose costs on the strong actor (e.g., capturing cities and towns).

## Statistical evidence

The core claim of strategic interaction theory – hypothesis 5: strong actors are more likely to win same-approach interactions and lose opposite approach interactions – received strong statistical support. For this relationship see Figure 4 in Chapter 2: Clearly, weak actors do better when strategies are opposite than when they are similar. A strong actor using a direct approach (say, a blitzkrieg or standard offensive campaign employing infantry, artillery, armor, and motorized infantry) is likely to lose against a weak actor employing a GWS, but likely to win quickly against a weak actor employing a standard defense (such as

Taliban forces in Afghanistan in 2001). Weak actors were nearly three times as likely to win opposite-approach interactions (63.6 percent) as same-approach interactions (23.2 percent). Three other important propositions were tested. First, I tested whether and to what degree external noncombat support for weak actors might make their victory more or less likely. Although a lack of available data made it impossible to evaluate the positive value of this relationship, I was able to determine that even when weak actors received no external support, they were still more than twice as likely to win when strategies were opposite than when they were similar. Second, I argued that the main reason opposite-approach interactions favored weak actors is because time is an important cost for strong actors,[5] and opposite-approach interactions take longer to resolve themselves. A statistical review of all asymmetric conflicts since 1816 strongly confirmed this proposition: opposite-approach interactions take longer than same-approach interactions. Finally, I explained the trend toward increasing strong actor failures over time by recourse to a state socialization argument: actors – whether states, boxers, terrorists, or firms – imitate the successful practices of other actors.[6] At a minimum then, the number of opposite-approach asymmetric conflicts should increase over time in proportion to the number of wars in which the weak won. They do. Thus, this book's statistical tests of the strategic interaction thesis strongly support its logic.

## Evidence from cases

The causal logic of competing arguments was tested in five historical case studies. The aim was to establish the relative impact of each actor's interests, regime type, weaponry, and strategy on the outcome.

## The Murid War, 1830–59

The Murid War pitted the Russian Empire (strong actor) against a coalition of Caucasian tribes under the banner of Muridism (weak actor). Russia's interests focused on protecting its communications with Georgia. Murid interests were in establishing their political and religious independence from Russia.

---

[5] It is an important cost for both actors, but because their power advantage leads to the expectation of *quick* victory, the cost of delays is effectively multiplied for strong actors.
[6] Waltz has already been cited on this point. But see also, Porch (1996: xvii).

In terms of regime type and vulnerability, Russia simply was not politically vulnerable. The lack of a serious security threat from the Caucasus should have made even authoritarian Russia sensitive to resource trade-offs, and politically vulnerable in this sense. Yet during the Murid War, Russia faced two potentially serious interstate conflicts, and neither caused political vulnerability. Regime type did affect the strategies employed by each side. Russian strategy changed to suit each new tsar's preferences: sometimes scrupulously avoiding barbarism, for example, and other times targeting noncombatants with vigor. Shamil was just as autocratic about strategy. He was able to go against his own soldiers' training and inclinations in ordering a switch to a conventional offensive in Kabardia.

The arms diffusion argument was not supported in the Murid War. The Murids did not receive weapons or ammunition from abroad, and the effectiveness of each side's arms technology depended on the system of its use, which in turn depended on variations in terrain and climate. Heavy artillery proved vital to the Russian effort to conquer the Murids, but was effective only under circumstances where Russian forces were willing to ignore the staggering toll in casualties required to maneuver the guns into position. The brief capture of artillery by the Murids proved to be – contrary to expectation – a military disaster.

In terms of strategy, the war played itself out in three strategic interactions. The Russians won the first interaction: barbarism against a Murid GWS (same-approach).[7] They lost the second interaction: a Russian conventional attack strategy against a Murid GWS (opposite-approach). The final interaction was again same-approach: a Russian conciliation strategy opposed by a Murid GWS. The Russians won, and Shamil went into exile.

The outcome of the Murid War was determined by Russia's extreme – almost historically unique – cost insensitivity.[8] This insensitivity was

---

[7] Since their aim was conquest and subjugation, rather than annihilation, the victory would prove elusive. In theory, Russia's willingness and ability to resort to barbarism should have deterred subsequent Murid resistance. It did not. Instead, it only stimulated and intensified resistance. If democracies lose small wars because they can't escalate to the level of brutality necessary to win, then Merom's thesis will have a tough time explaining why authoritarian regimes don't win small wars more often than they do.

[8] Recall, however, that Alexander did not approve of barbarism as a Russian military strategy, however effective. This is worrisome for Merom's model, which holds that in general authoritarian regimes will be able to win small wars because they will escalate the level of violence to barbarism. The Murid War shows that even in an autocratic regime, "normative difference" between state and society can exist and affect strategy (and, by extension, costs and outcomes).

due to its regime type and to the fact that Russia's public was almost entirely illiterate. But the costs – half a million casualties and twenty-nine years – are best explained by the strategic interaction thesis.

## The South African War, 1899–1902

The South African War pitted Great Britain – then the world's preeminent great power – against two of the world's smallest states – Orange Free State and Transvaal (the weak actor).

British political elites calculated that control of Orange Free State and Transvaal was vital for three reasons. First, they believed control of Cape Town was key to maintaining sea communications with India and their other colonial possessions. Second, allowing the Boer republics to "dictate" to the British might encourage the majority population of Cape Colony – Afrikaners – to seize control of the Cape. Third and finally, it might also make Britain appear weak-willed in relation to its European great-power rivals, thus encouraging interference or intervention from those rivals.[9] Employing a domino-like logic throughout, the British therefore calculated that the subjugation of Orange Free State and Transvaal were vital interests. The Boer were interested in maintaining their independence and their way of life (in particular, the institution of slavery).

Two factors explain British political vulnerability in the South African War: regime type and time to objective. As leaders of a democratic state, British policymakers could not make policy without taking public reaction and judgments into account. In the South African War there were two loci of vulnerability for Britain: *jus ad bellum* – the justness of Britain's resort to force in South Africa – and *jus in bello* – the justness of its conduct in that war. Kruger's ultimatum spared British elites from difficulties over *jus ad bellum*: the British public recognized the legitimacy of self defense as a justification for the resort to arms. But what of the moral conduct of the war itself? The concentration camp controversy very nearly forced Britain's withdrawal from the war short of achieving its political objectives.[10] But had the war been

[9] It might also set a bad precedent *vis-à-vis* other empire colonials, who might then think of rising up to challenge British colonial rule.
[10] The South African War must count as a problem for Merom's thesis, because Britain was a democracy, and yet had no difficulty escalating to the level of brutality (not to mention its own costs in terms of blood and treasure) necessary to win the war. Merom's own account of the nature and consequences of British COIN strategy (especially under

over by Christmas or soon after – as widely anticipated by British elites and the British public – neither concern would have mattered. It therefore makes sense to ask: what caused the delay in a war in which Great Britain out-powered the Boer by a ratio of more than 5:1?

The delay was caused in part by the fact that the Boer possessed modern rifles, and were skilled in their use. The British had never fought a major engagement against an enemy so equipped, and it took time for them to adapt, tactically, to the new situation. But the real reason the war was not over by Christmas was because (1) the British dramatically underestimated the Boer; (2) the Boer were much more mobile; and (3) the Boer had better intelligence. But the battles fought through 1900 made it clear that not even the possession of superb infantry rifles, superior artillery, and highly mobile forces could compensate for the overwhelming number of Britain's forces in South Africa. British forces simply steamrolled the Boer, moving in an almost straight line from Cape Colony to Pretoria. The arms diffusion argument therefore counts as a partial explanation of the South African War's outcome.

The real cause of the delay was a shift to a GWS by the Boer in March of 1900. The British won the first interaction of the war (same-approach) after overcoming their initial shock and after deploying sufficient troops in theater. By February of 1900 the conventional war was over and the Boer had lost. But after the fall of Bloemfontein the Boer leadership chose to switch to a GWS. Strategic interaction is the best explanation of the South African War's outcome. Once it became clear that the capture of the Boer capitals would not force the Boer to surrender, Britain had three strategic options. First, continue with the present strategy, perhaps sending more troops, equipment, and horses to the theater. Second, offer the Boers terms: something which could save face yet end the war. Third, switch to a barbarism strategy: take the gloves off and go after Boer noncombatants, either by holding them hostage or by killing them outright in reprisal for continued resistance. The British chose the third option, and the war ended soon after.

---

Kitchener) are misleading in this regard. He suggests that Kitchener's barbarism was restrained by Whitehall, but no one taking the history of the war seriously could support such a claim, except perhaps the weakest form of argument that, barbaric as Kitchener's farm burnings and concentration policies were, "they could have been worse" (see Merom, 2003, pp. 61–62).

## The Italo-Ethiopian War, 1935–1940

The Italo-Ethiopian War pitted fascist Italy (strong actor) against imperial Ethiopia (weak actor). Italian interests reduced to revenge for the defeat at Adowa in 1896, responsibility for civilizing a barbarous black African state in the Horn of Africa, and resources with which to ameliorate its poverty and population problems. Italy's interests in conquest were higher than expected by the interest asymmetry thesis, and because a large portion of fascism's legitimacy lay in its alleged masculine military superiority, any defeat in Ethiopia would have to be regarded as a threat to the regime's survival. Ethiopia's interests (survival) were high also; but Ethiopians had a more subtle and more dangerous interest as well: reenacting the glory of the defeat of an arrogant Italian invader.

Italy's regime type affected its strategic choices. Italy's resort to barbarism (first mustard gas and later murder and mass murder) presupposed the management and control of information on the conduct of the campaign.[11] In terms of political vulnerability then, Mussolini's government remained remarkably safe throughout the conflict. On the Ethiopian side, Haile Selassie – though nominally Ethiopia's emperor – had far less control over his princes and generals. Ethiopia's feudal regime type made it impossible for the emperor to impose his preferred defensive strategy and the impact proved devastating.[12] Regime type mattered much more than suggested by the interest asymmetry thesis.

Arms diffusion played no significant role in the Italo-Ethiopian War. Because no weapon on the Ethiopian side acted to increase the costs of conquest or occupation by the Italians, the arms diffusion hypothesis was not tested.

With one exception, each strategic interaction of the war favored an Italian military victory. The first interaction featured a conventional attack against a conventional defense (same-approach), and Italy appeared poised to lose this fight due to bad generalship. The stalling

[11] Cf. fascist legitimacy observation above (p. 116). Even if the Italian people had no mechanism to turn discontent into a shift in Italian foreign or military policy, the regime still maintained a vital interest in controlling the public's perceptions of the war.

[12] The case highlights the limits of the notion of strategic *choice* in war; in theory, a threat to survival should override petty organizational, cultural, or other prejudices in a choice of strategy. Yet as this case illustrates, Ethiopians preferred to risk defeat rather than adopt the "inglorious" defense strategy of striking the enemy where weak and then "running away."

of the Italian advance, combined with the surprisingly (to the Italians) effective Ethiopian counterattacks, led to a shift in Italian strategy. Italy supplemented a conventional attack strategy with a super-weapon[13] against an Ethiopian conventional defense. Ethiopia's organized resistance collapsed within a few months. But Italian barbarism sparked renewed resistance. The Italians would have won this third interaction of the conflict (same-approach: barbarism *vs.* GWS), but before it could register a military impact Mussolini cancelled it. The fourth interaction of the war reverted to a conventional attack against any organized resistance (opposite-approach). Only where Ethiopian forces sought to engage the Italians directly, as at Gojjam, did the Italians win. In the remainder of the country, the Italian conventional attacks were countered by a GWS, and the Italians lost. The costs to the Italians of such operations were staggering, and the combination of those costs and the perceived need to become security self-sufficient in the event of war in Europe, led to yet another shift in Italian strategy.

This fifth interaction of the war introduced a conciliation strategy for Italy, opposed by an Ethiopian GWS (same-approach). Conciliation proved the most effective of all the strategies the Italians had attempted since marching into Addis Ababa in May of 1936. Only one rebel leader held out, and it seemed likely that but for the outbreak of World War II, even Abebe Aregai would have been forced to flee Ethiopia or submit. The Italians would have almost certainly won the war.

But World War II changed all of this. The contest in Ethiopia ceased to be between occupying Italians and an Ethiopian resistance, and shifted to become a fight between the British and Italians fought across Ethiopia, Sudan, British Somaliland, and Kenya (it also ceased to be an asymmetric conflict as defined here). Within a few months, British forces invading from the south soundly defeated the Italians and entered Addis Ababa.

### Leadership

In the Italo-Ethiopian War, the problem of poor Italian leadership is an important explanation of the war's outcome. In the first interaction Italian timidity threatened the entire invasion, which for political and

---

[13] Again, the effectiveness of a given military technology can vary a great deal depending on context. In Europe during World War I, the use of chemical weapons had not given either side a strategic advantage. In Ethiopia, however, the use of such weapons could be (and was) decisive during the conventional phase of the war.

ideological reasons demanded a swift and decisive victory. It was this timidity that allowed the Ethiopians to seize the initiative, and it was further incompetence that resulted in a series of Italian defeats which threatened to throw them back into Eritrea. Poor Italian leadership thus became the proximate cause of Italy's resort to mustard gas attacks.

In sum, the outcome of the Italo-Ethiopian War is best explained by strategic interaction and poor Italian military leadership. Once it became clear that the capture of Addis Ababa would not force the Ethiopians to surrender, the Italians had three strategic choices. First, continue with the present strategy, perhaps sending more troops and equipment to the theater. Second, offer the Ethiopians terms: something which could save face yet end the war. Third, switch to a barbarism strategy: take the gloves off and go after Ethiopian "rebels" and their families. The AOI generally chose the third option, though it shifted strategies and innovated a number of times, slowly and painstakingly improving its advantage until World War II came to Africa and swept them away.

Italy would have won the war in Ethiopia had World War II not intervened. But after a few years, at most, Italy would have lost Ethiopia even without the intervention of the British in North Africa because its ideal COIN strategy – conciliation – was one it was economically incapable of sustaining. Italy's earlier resort to barbarism – both the use of mustard gas and mass murder – had raised the costs of a policy of bribery beyond what it could afford to pay.

## The United States in Vietnam, 1965–1973

US intervention in the Vietnamese civil war pitted the United States and GVN (strong actor) against the DRV and VC (weak actor). US interests were in defending the GVN from a communist takeover, furthering its strategy of Soviet containment. DRV and VC interests reduced to survival, but survival expanded to include the ejection of all foreigners and foreign "influences" from Vietnam.

The DRV and GVN both had authoritarian regime types while the United States had a democratic regime type. But, in Vietnam, political vulnerability depended less on regime type and more on location. The real fight in Vietnam was over which of the two *local* governments could most credibly claim to represent Vietnamese *national* aspirations. The DRV had a head start due to its organization, and its courage and sacrifice against the Japanese in World War II and against the French after 1945. The GVN began with a credible nationalist, but Diem – the very definition of an autocrat – could not see an interest in Vietnam separate from his own. He restructured the GVN and its military to serve one purpose at the expense of all others: to keep him in power. Diem's assassination and the later introduction of US combat troops foreclosed any possibility of the GVN winning the fight for nationalist legitimacy. This put the democratic United States – vulnerable due to its regime type – in the position of having to support an illegitimate (and corrupt) GVN.

Arms diffusion did play a role in Vietnam, but the increase in costs to the United States and GVN of Soviet and Chinese (not to mention inadvertent GVN) support were not what drove the United States out of Vietnam. Most US casualties during the war were not caused by direct enemy action, either in terms of air defense or guerrilla attacks. Most were inflicted by relatively primitive explosive devices and booby traps – some improvised from common materials.

Strategic interaction best explains the costs of the conflict for each side, especially in terms of time. The US military has rarely won the first battles of any war in which it participated. Instead, its strengths have always lain in its ability to learn quickly and adapt to a wide variety of combat conditions. Vietnam proved a case in point. The US military began by underestimating its adversary's will and capacity to fight. It ignored the considerable COIN experience of France and, to a lesser extent, Great Britain. But it ended by innovating a number of strategies capable of neutralizing the VC and eviscerating the NVA. By 1969 the military contest was over and the United States had won. But the political contest ended in a US defeat, and the strategic interaction explains why.

No war in the twentieth century was more complex than the Vietnam War. It featured at least five adversaries (the DRV, VC, China, and USSR against the GVN and United States) and four over-lapping strategic interactions. The United States lost ROLLING THUNDER, which featured US barbarism against an NVA conventional defense (opposite-approach). But the United States won the main force units war: an NVA conventional attack against a US conventional defense (same-approach). The United States lost the main guerrilla war in the south, which featured a US conventional attack against a VC GWS (opposite-approach), but won the "other" guerrilla war when it initiated the Phoenix Program (barbarism) against a VC GWS (same-approach). Most importantly, the US Marine Corps – the

US military institution with the most historical experience of fighting small wars – innovated a strategy capable of defeating the VC *without* a resort to barbarism. The CAP program's only liability proved to be its costliness in terms of time.

In sum, in most wars military victory leads to political victory, and the duration and quality of that political victory bear some meaningful relationship to the means used to overcome a resisting military. If barbarism is employed to achieve military victory, any peace that follows will be fragile and costly at best. The United States and GVN did use barbarism and did overcome the DRV and VC militarily. Strategic interaction explains why the war took as long as it did, how the United States was able to defeat the DRV and VC, and why, after doing so *it was nevertheless forced to abandon the GVN*. But, in the Vietnamese civil war, military supremacy proved meaningless. The political contest for Vietnam was what mattered and it was already lost before the US marines came ashore at Da Nang. Even had the United States adopted an ideal counterstrategy against each of the two militaries it faced – no easy task – it still could not have won the war politically (i.e., coerced the DRV into accepting a divided Vietnam). At best, the United States would have driven its enemies into Laos, Cambodia, and China, and then been forced to spend decades attempting – under constant duress and with little hope of success – to engineer a viable nationalist alternative to the DRV.

## The Afghan Civil War, 1979–89

The Afghan Civil War pitted the DRA and its Soviet allies (strong actor) against the Afghan mujahideen (weak actor). Soviet interests in the outcome of the Afghan Civil War did not rise to the level of survival, but were far more intense than expected by the interest asymmetry argument. They reduced to (1) defending a friendly Marxist regime, and (2) thereby preventing the accession of a radical Islamic republic on its southern border. Mujahideen interests were in ejecting the Soviets from Afghanistan, where the PDPA regime which controlled Kabul was not distinguished from the Soviets. To this end they fought as if their survival was at stake.

According to the interest asymmetry thesis, a major military setback should have caused the Soviets to re-evaluate their occupation regardless of their regime type. This didn't happen. Instead of considering a withdrawal, the Soviets attempted gamely to learn from their failures and innovate around them. They often succeeded, but never in a way which could compensate for their relatively low numbers.[14] In short, the Soviet Union's authoritarian regime type insulated it from political vulnerability.

Regime type also made it possible for the Soviets to manage the domestic political opposition.[15] Authoritarian regimes are first of all free to construct the enemy as they see fit (democratic regimes do the same thing but with much less freedom). In previous wars the Soviets had shown a remarkable capacity to control the public's access to reliable information about the domestic costs of war, especially casualties. In this war, however, Soviet efforts to control this information failed: the combination of letters home and an unprecedented network of soldiers' mothers combined to make it increasingly clear that Soviet soldiers were getting killed in numbers far larger than claimed by the government. However, there remained no mechanism by which rising alarm and discontent could be translated into a shift in Soviet policy or strategy.[16]

In no other case does the arms diffusion argument receive stronger support than in the Afghan Civil War. From 1979 until 1986, the Soviet Union's troops and its DRA allies had better weapons than the mujahideen but, with the exception of the combat helicopter, most of that better technology was of dubious utility in the rugged mountains of Afghanistan. As Soviet and DRA forces innovated better COIN tactics they came to rely more and more heavily on combat helicopters. By 1986 their tactics – including the use of heliborne special operations troops as blocking forces during canyon sweeps – made them both disproportionately powerful and vulnerable. That vulnerability was

---

[14] Numbers are not a reliable indicator of interests. As in the case of US intervention in Vietnam, the Soviets had higher-than-expected interests (including the problem of "credibility"), but were constrained to observe limits in the number of troops deployed for fear of escalating the conflict to another world war.

[15] Domestic political opposition is one of two risks of adopting a barbarism strategy post-World War II; the other is foreign military intervention. Here regime type plays no role whatsoever. As in its later forays into Chechnya (1994 and 1999), Russia's nuclear status precluded foreign military intervention. Milosevic's Serbia, the Taliban in Afghanistan, and Saddam Hussein in Iraq were not as well protected and were therefore subject to invasions justified in large measure by accurate reports of barbarism.

[16] The Soviet intervention in Afghanistan strongly supports Merom's model of an authoritarian regime's advantages in small wars, but presents the problem that the Soviets and DRA together employed a strategy of *exceeding* brutality yet still *lost the war*. Brutality or barbarism may not therefore be as effective and efficient as Merom's model suggests (see Merom, 2003: pp. 42–46).

made salient by a US-supplied shoulder-launched anti-aircraft missile called the Stinger. Almost overnight what had been an unopposed tactical advantage turned into an unmitigated tactical liability. In 1985, the accession of Mikhail Gorbachev resulted in new calculations of Afghanistan's political importance. Gorbachev placed a time limit on Soviet support of the DRA. The mujahideen use of Stingers meant that in order to maintain combat effectiveness, the Soviets would have to innovate or dramatically increase their numbers. Gorbachev's accession meant that there would be no time to innovate and no increase in troops. The arms diffusion argument therefore receives strong support in the Afghan Civil War. Combined with the shift in Soviet leadership, it raised the costs of occupation beyond what the Soviets could afford. They therefore left.

Strategic interaction explains why the Soviets lost the first interaction of the war, but it doesn't explain the second. From 1980 to 1982, the Soviets pursued a conventional attack strategy against a mujahideen GWS (opposite-approach). It failed on every count. Yet after a switch to barbarism in 1983 (same-approach), the Soviets did not win, and in 1989 they withdrew from Afghanistan completely. Why?

### *External support for weak actors: sanctuary*

According to the strategic interaction thesis the Soviets should have won. Barbarism should have been an ideal COIN strategy because the Soviets were not vulnerable to domestic or interstate political costs associated with its prosecution. Moreover, it should have devastated the intelligence and logistical capacity of the mujahideen and to a large extent it did.[17] Its primary impact, however, was to provide the mujahideen with defectors. Barbarism didn't work in Afghanistan because the mujahideen were able to rely on foreign intelligence and logistical support and operate from sanctuaries in Pakistan and Iran. The mujahideen became so dependent on this aid that when it ceased in 1989 and 1990, it shattered their ability to topple the illegitimate government of Najibullah. Afghanistan therefore highlights one condition under which barbarism is ineffective as a counterinsurgency strategy: when

---

[17] Mujahideen intelligence was much diminished as a result of Soviet barbarism. But *relative* to the DRA and the Soviets, each of whom maintained an urban-bound and mechanized force, it remained superior and benefited from US technical intelligence support.

the guerrillas have access to a significant source of sanctuary,[18] intelligence, and logistical support outside the control of the strong actor.

In sum, if we wish to explain why the USSR failed in Afghanistan, what mattered most was strategic interaction. Once it became clear that the fight in Afghanistan was a counterinsurgency struggle, Soviet doctrine led them to go after mujahideen noncombatants. The strategy hurt the mujahideen logistical and intelligence infrastructure, but sealing the border with Pakistan proved impossible. The Soviets succeeded in killing or making refugees of roughly half of Afghanistan's pre-war civilian population. The mujahideen faced an even starker choice after the Soviets switched to barbarism: either give up or continue with a strategy which would rely more and more on outside powers for support.

In the end, no one won the war. The Soviets left in 1989 and the DRA fell in 1992. The mujahideen were subsequently almost entirely overcome by the Taliban – a group of extremely conservative Islamists raised in and funded by Pakistan, as well as by Saudi Arabia. Afghanistan itself was devastated on a scale not witnessed since the destruction of Germany in World War II.

## How the weak win wars

### *Key findings*

The combination of a large-*n* statistical analysis and a structured, focused comparison of historical case studies strongly supports the strategic interaction thesis over the explanations offered by its rivals. The book's large-*n* analysis confirmed that strategic interaction is highly correlated with asymmetric conflict outcomes. This relationship was statistically significant, and supports my claim that same-approach interactions favor strong actors, while opposite-approach interactions favor weak actors. Besides testing the logic of competing explanations of asymmetric conflict outcomes, the five historical case studies provided sixteen separate tests of the strategic interaction thesis.[19] The results of these tough tests strongly support the logic of the strategic interaction thesis, *even though in the Murid, Italo-Ethiopian, and Afghan*

---

[18] Pakistan played host to the best of the mujahideen resistance and Pakistan was both a nuclear power and an ally of the United States.

[19] As noted in Chapter 2 (fn. 47), these cases are in this sense anomalous: 77.5 percent of asymmetric conflicts feature a single strategic interaction from beginning to end.

*Civil Wars, the actual outcome of the conflict was strongly affected by extreme cost insensitivity, incompetent leadership, and external support for the weak actor respectively.*

The expected and actual outcomes of the strategic interactions in the five historical case studies are summarized in Table 3.[20]

### Alternative hypotheses

Hypotheses 5, 6, and 8 were evaluated in the individual case studies. Hypothesis 5 – strong actors are more likely to win same-approach interactions and lose opposite-approach interactions – was supported in all five cases. In each case, same-approach interactions made it possible for the strong actor to apply the full weight of its advantages in material power to the fight, and this imposed severe costs on weak actors (sometimes they switched strategies, sometimes they gave up). Opposite-approach interactions made it possible for weak actors to avoid defeat and thus made conflicts drag on. As a result, weak actors did better in opposite-approach interactions, avoiding costs while at the same time inflicting them on their stronger adversaries. Hypothesis 6 – the better armed a weak actor is, the more likely it is that a strong actor will lose an asymmetric conflict – was not supported. In each case, including even the Afghan Civil War, the impact of technology depended on strategy and tactics in the context of climate and terrain. When weak actors had better technology but the wrong strategy, as in the first year of the South African War – they lost quickly and decisively. Hypothesis 8 – relative material power explains relative interests in the outcome of an asymmetric conflict – was refuted. In no case was an actor's interest in the outcome of a fight explained by its relative power.

Hypotheses 7, 7a, and 9 can only be evaluated across cases. Hypothesis 7 – authoritarian strong actors fight asymmetric wars better than do democratic strong actors – was not supported. In fact, it may be the case that authoritarian and democratic actors fight asymmetric wars the same way; both Britain and the USSR began with direct strategies and resorted to barbarism when the going got rough. On the other hand, hypothesis 7a – authoritarian strong actors fight asymmetric wars in which the weak actor uses an indirect strategy better than do democratic strong actors – was supported here. Public reaction to

---

[20] Table 3 features summaries of thirteen strategic interactions. I count eleven because although an indirect strategy (targeting an adversary's will rather than capacity to fight) "conciliation" is a war-termination strategy rather than a war-winning strategy.

Table 3. Strategic interactions and conflict outcomes in five historical cases

| Phase | Strong actor strategy | Weak actor strategy | Strategic interaction | Winner |
|---|---|---|---|---|
| The Murid War, 1830–59 | | | | |
| 1 | barbarism | GWS | same-approach | Russia |
| 2 | conventional attack | GWS | opposite-approach | Murids |
| 3 | [conciliation] | GWS | [same-approach] | Russia |
| The South African War, 1899–1902 | | | | |
| 1 | conventional attack | conventional defense | same-approach | Britain |
| 2 | conventional attack | GWS | opposite-approach | Boer |
| 3 | barbarism | GWS | same-approach | Britain |
| The Italo-Ethiopian War, 1935–40 | | | | |
| 1 | conventional attack | conventional defense | same-approach | *Ethiopia* |
| 2 | conventional attack/barbarism | conventional defense | same-approach | Italy |
| 3 | barbarism | GWS | same-approach | Italy |
| 4 | conventional attack | GWS | opposite-approach | Ethiopia |
| 5 | [conciliation] | GWS | [same-approach] | Italy |
| The United States in Vietnam, 1965–73 | | | | |
| 1 | barbarism | conventional defense | opposite approach | DRV |
| 2 | conventional attack | conventional defense | same-approach | United States |
| 3 | conventional attack | GWS | opposite-approach | VC |
| 4 | barbarism | GWS | same-approach | United States |
| The Afghan Civil War, 1979–89 | | | | |
| 1 | conventional attack | GWS | opposite-approach | mujahideen |
| 2 | barbarism | GWS | same-approach | *mujahideen* |

Italic denotes outcome not entirely explained by strategic interaction theory.

Britain's resort to barbarism nearly forced it from the war, but at no time did the USSR's resort to barbarism threaten to do so. Thus, to the extent that an authoritarian regime type insulates an actor from the costs and risks of initiating a barbarism strategy, and to the extent that barbarism is a *militarily effective* COIN strategy, this support for hypothesis 7a should come as no surprise. Finally, hypothesis 9 – authoritarian and democratic strong actors share roughly equal political vulnerability in a prolonged asymmetric conflict – was decisively rebutted here. Britain was at considerable risk of being forced from the war after Emily Hobhouse brought the concentration camp controversy to light. But the Russian Empire, the Italian Fascists, and USSR were never at risk of similar problems. Italy ran a risk in 1935 that its fellow European states would demand its withdrawal from Ethiopia or halt the use of mustard gas, but in the event the weakness of Europe's great powers allowed him to get away with the brutal attack and profound immiseration of a League member.

### Explaining strong actor failure

Strong actors lose small wars under a number of conditions. First, when strong actors are also great powers they have strong adversaries. They devote considerable resources to building forces to secure their interests against threats from those adversaries. Not only are forces built and equipped for use against other great powers, but they are trained to fight and react in a certain way. Doctrine, equipment, and training are all tightly intermeshed, and building new forces with different skills and doctrines is costly.[21]

In the Murid War, the first Russian forces to come up against the Murids were trained and equipped to fight European-style adversaries on hilly, sparsely forested, or open terrain. Their officers had been trained on the maxims of Suvorov, and other famous Russian generals who had engineered the total defeat of Napoleon's *Grande Armée*. Their first clash with the agile Murids in the steep mountain defiles of the Caucasus came as a jarring shock, and it required nearly thirty years of

---

[21] Even more seriously, officers and men trained in one context are often not useful in another. Britain's military ineffectiveness in World War I was often said to be due to the fact that much of its officers' combat experience was "colonial." The reverse also holds true: commanders who excel at conventional operations rarely do as well in COIN operations. On the differences in leadership in conventional and unconventional settings, see, e.g., Bowden (2000: 172–174), and Marquis (1997: 4, 8).

struggle, innovation, retraining, and new technology in order to defeat the Murids.

The British came to South Africa buoyed by years of success in small wars against the tribes and kingdoms which peppered their vast empire. They came piecemeal, ill-equipped, and ill-trained to fight the mounted Boer on the hot and mountainous veld. Time and again the British lined up against the Boer for their Aldershot exercises: artillery preparation of the enemy line, infantry advance in close order, fix bayonets for the charge, and cavalry to annihilate the routed foe. But what they found was counter-battery fire, and a wall of lead from well-aimed fast repeating invisible rifles which devastated their closely packed infantry advances. Then, after suffering this withering fire, they charged the enemy positions only to find a few dead Boer and the rest of the commando trotting off on their horses, kicking up dust in the distance. The British needed a new army, new training, new equipment, many more horses, and many more men in order to bring the Boer to bay.

The Italians came to Ethiopia with precisely the quantity and quality of troops they required in order to conquer Ethiopian tribes united under Haile Selassie. By all accounts, with the exception of the Black Shirt divisions, Italy's soldiers fought well. But Italy's military leadership was so poor as to almost cause Italy's defeat against the mostly barefoot, poorly armed and outnumbered Ethiopian warriors.

The United States arrived in Vietnam with the conviction that its unmatched technology and long history of military victory would prove decisive. True, US forces had suffered a near rout in the early months of the Korean Conflict, but US General Matthew Ridgeway's reapplication of basic soldiering discipline had restored US forces to combat effectiveness, turning the tide and pushing the North Koreans back. As a result, in Vietnam many US generals believed that talk of "new" or "unconventional" warfare was a smokescreen for a lack of good discipline and aggressiveness. They were wrong. As in all such conflicts lower and mid-level officers (lieutenants through lieutenant colonels) did most of the rapid learning and adaptation; while senior officers attempted to apply the weight of their own, often marginally-relevant, experience to the difficult problems facing US forces in Vietnam.[22] The US military had the right forces and doctrine to defeat the NVA, but in the years following World War II it had systematically

---

[22] The best account of this is Sheehan (1988). See also Krepinevich (1986).

gutted its COIN capabilities (Marquis, 1997: Ch. 2). What it needed in Vietnam was *two* armies,[23] and what it had was one army desperately trying to adapt to two different military universes.

The Soviets entered Afghanistan in 1979 with four motorized rifle divisions at two-thirds strength. These reservists had outdated equipment, and they had been trained to use that equipment in large-scale operations on open terrain. They were unsuited in every imaginable way to prosecute a COIN war in mountainous terrain. During their decade-long struggle to defeat the mujahideen, the Soviets innovated an almost entirely new army: new doctrine, new technology, new training, and different troops.

All of this demonstrates that strong actors – especially great powers – who have not recently fought small wars will tend to enter them unprepared to fight them in terms of either doctrine or equipment. Even those who have recently fought such wars may find their experiences in one theater against one adversary do not transfer well to different theaters and different adversaries. This doesn't imply that strong actors must lose asymmetric conflicts, but rather that their initial costs will be higher than anticipated by conventional IR theory, and by the political elites charged with committing armed forces to combat.

After combat is joined, strong actors can lose if they adopt the wrong strategy given their adversary's strategy. If weak actors choose a conventional defense strategy, strong actors can lose if they attempt to use strategic air power (indirect-approach) to win. The costs in terms of time and the collateral damage which inevitably follows such attacks provoke outrage internationally, and often domestically as well. Either sort of outrage can create pressure to cease hostilities short of achieving a strong actor's political objectives. If weak actors choose an indirect defense strategy, strong actors can lose if they attempt to use a conventional attack strategy (direct-approach) to win. GWS is specifically designed to trade time for territory, so unless strong actors are willing to commit millions of troops for decades, they are unlikely to win against an adversary that avoids contact and strikes when and where least expected.

Strong actors can use barbarism to defeat weak actors using a GWS or nonviolent resistance *militarily*. But whether authoritarian or

---

[23] See Cohen (1984: 180) on the desirability of creating two distinct forces to fight two distinct types of war.

221

democratic the costs for strong actors of achieving such victories – even in narrow military terms – appear to have risen steadily since the end of World War II. More importantly, strong actors can no longer win a subsequent peace against weak actors they've overcome by barbarous means.[24] And strong actors can also lose if they attempt to use a risky barbarism strategy to overcome recalcitrant defenders employing a GWS. Increasingly, barbarism appears to be stimulating military resistance rather than deterring it. The risks of barbarism are greater for democratic regimes than for authoritarian regimes, but both may face the problem of international sanction. For strong actors who are great powers or superpowers, the costs of international sanction may be negligible, but for strong actors who are minor powers – such as Italy in 1935, or Serbia in 1999, the risk of international sanctions can be prohibitive.[25] Democratic strong actors also face domestic risks when prosecuting a barbarism strategy: the effects of Britain's concentration camp policy in the South African War, for example, would almost certainly have forced its withdrawal from the war had there not been such a long delay between the effects and their political impact in Britain. In the digital age, such delays have shrunk dramatically, and barbarism is much more difficult to conceal than at the turn of the century.

In sum, the problem for strong actors is weak actors who pursue an indirect defense strategy, such as a GWS or terrorism. This presents strong actors with three unpalatable choices: an attrition war lasting perhaps decades; costly bribes or political concessions, perhaps forcing political and economic reforms on repressive allies as well as adversaries; or the deliberate harm of noncombatants in a risky attempt to win a military contest quickly and decisively.

## Limitations of the strategic interaction theory

At this point in the analysis the strategic interaction thesis can be established as a full theory of asymmetric conflict outcomes. It has survived two different and tough tests, and been shown to subsume competing explanations, such as interest asymmetry, nature-of-actor,

---

[24] Even in cases where the political *aim* of attacking forces is genocide, the technical requirements for achieving genocide are, fortunately, beyond reach even for the most advanced states. There will always be survivors and witnesses, and this creates the likelihood of revenge attacks of varying degrees of severity following the perpetration of barbarism.

[25] Italy did not suffer from these sanctions because Britain and France turned a blind eye.

and arms diffusion arguments; strategic interaction theory brackets the conditions under which each of these important factors operates. Finally, strategic interaction theory explains the fact of strong actor failure in a way consistent with the observed trend toward increasing strong actor failures over time.

As a general theory, it will be relatively less satisfying as a complete explanation of any particular asymmetric conflict outcome, but relatively more satisfying as an explanation of all asymmetric conflict outcomes, and in particular as a guide to strategy and policy. It has application, for example, to counterterrorism as well as COIN strategy (Arreguín-Toft, 2002), both of which will prove vital subjects for US policymakers in the coming decades.

But as with any general theory it is not without its limitations. First, although strategic interaction theory highlights the limitations of narrow or material definitions of "power," it does not comprehensively resolve those limitations. Consider strategic interaction in the Russo-Japanese War of 1905, for example. The Russian Empire was the strong actor and Japan the weak one. The strategic interaction was same-approach but Russia lost. Why? Although the statistical analysis in Chapter 2 reports the conflict this way, it is clear that another necessary nuance of power must be a maritime/continental power distinction. Russia was a continental power, Japan a maritime power. Japan won because the key battles were fought at sea (even the bloody battle for Port Arthur was determined by the superior ability of the Japanese to deploy ground forces and reinforcements by sea).[26] In demonstrating that military effectiveness depends both on raw resources and the interaction of plans for the employment of those resources, this analysis has established beyond question that power is more nuanced than realist international relations theory has to date allowed,[27] yet a true general definition of power remains beyond its scope.

Second, nothing in this analysis has made it possible to disaggregate the effects of anti-colonialism and nationalism from those of strategic interaction – at least not in the trend aspect of the argument. Clearly, the

---

[26] Other examples include Britain's successful resistance to Napoleon's France in the nineteenth century and to Hitler's Third Reich in 1941.

[27] This is not the same thing as allowing that the realist IR theory definition of power is a "straw man" in terms of argumentation. This too-simple definition of power is neither my own nor is it a straw man. It is not a straw man because *it is still relied upon by policymakers in the real world to make calculations of the likelihood of success and failure in asymmetric conflicts.*

success of Mao's resistance to Japan and the Kuomintang was due to strategic interaction. But could Mao have knit together the mass movement he did without Chinese nationalism? No. In fact, nationalism – religious or ethnic – may count as a permissive condition of a GWS *with the capacity to evolve into a conventional sustained offensive.* The Avars of Daghestan could not have managed a coordinated *offensive* against the Russian Empire alone. Something – an idea and a charismatic leader – had to knit together the patchwork of feuding tribes into a cohesive movement before skilful offensive operations became possible. On the other hand, nationalism represented in a same-approach strategic interaction will have no impact on conflict outcomes, asymmetric or otherwise. The Belgians were nationalistic and lost quickly to the Germans in 1914. The French were nationalistic yet lost handily to the Germans in 1940. The Arabs are nationalistic and far more numerous than the Israelis, yet their zeal has never been translated into military victory. In sum, the best terrorist, guerrilla, and nonviolent resistance movements will be nationalistic, but not all nationalists will oppose strong actors by means of terrorism, GWS, or nonviolent resistance.

### Theoretical and policy implications

Material power is useful for theory building because it is quantifiable and measurable in a way that courage, leadership, and dumb luck are not. This study has demonstrated empirically that relative material power is more than simply a methodologically useful concept; taken alone, it explains a majority of conflict outcomes since 1800. The strategic interaction thesis makes clear, however, the limitations of relative material power by highlighting the conditions under which it matters more or less.

This analysis suggests key policy implications for both weak and strong actors. For weak actors, successful defense against a strong actor depends on an indirect strategy. Because indirect strategies such as GWS and nonviolent resistance depend on strong social support, weak actors must either work tirelessly to gain and maintain the support (sympathy or acquiescence) of a majority of the population in question, or risk becoming dependent on a foreign donor of logistical support and arms.[28] Given the risks involved with either aiding or taking part in a guerrilla resistance, gaining strong social support is

---

[28] The latter option may keep the insurgency alive, but it cannot substitute for a genuine and locally based network of social support.

itself no mean feat. Additionally, weak actors must have or gain access to the physical or political sanctuary necessary to make an indirect strategy a viable choice. For strong actors, the strategic interaction theory suggests that weak adversaries employing an indirect defense will be difficult to defeat. Of course, not all or even most asymmetric conflicts need follow this pattern but, when they do, and when a resort to arms seems the only viable option, how should a strong actor such as the United States react?

One response might be a resort to barbarism, which appears to be an effective military strategy for defeating an indirect defense.[29] But even a cursory review of postwar conflicts reveals that at best barbarism can be effective *only* as a military strategy: if the desired objective is long-term political control – e.g., nation-building, "peace" keeping, or other stability or transition missions – barbarism invariably backfires. The French, for example, used torture to quickly defeat Algerian insurgents in the Battle of Algiers in 1957. But when French military brutality became public knowledge it catalyzed domestic political opposition to the war in France, and stimulated renewed and intensified resistance by the non-French population of Algeria (Mack, 1975: 180; Asprey, 1994: 669–671). Within four years, France had abandoned its claims in Algeria even though it had "won" the war. Barbarism thus sacrifices victory in peace for victory in war – a poor policy at best (Liddell Hart, 1967: 370). The same must be said of counterterrorist barbarism: assassination, torture, and random reprisal. These counterterrorist strategies have been doggedly and expertly pursued for more than forty years by the Israelis in Palestine, but they have brought the Israelis no closer to peace.

An ideal US strategic response therefore demands three key elements: (1) preparation of public expectations for long wars despite US

---

[29] This is the essence of Merom's argument: democracies lose small wars because they're *generally* too reluctant to suffer the casualties and brutality necessary to win. Beyond the cases he analyzes, however, are many that don't fit this pattern. Authoritarian strong actors with no limits on their willingness to use barbarism or suffer casualties have lost small wars, and democratic actors have won small wars even while refusing to resort to barbarism (e.g., Britain in the Malayan Emergency of 1948). The same logic – that barbarism pays – appears at first to be true of counterterrorism and terrorism as well. Laura K. Donohue analyzes the impact of British counterterrorist legislation in Northern Ireland and concludes that Britain's numerous "temporary" and "emergency" measures – which were never temporary, and which violated civil liberties and due process – proved highly effective in the short term. Her analysis suggests, however, that insurgents always found a way around such measures, eventually prompting yet another round of "emergency" restrictions (see Donohue, 2001: 322–323).

technological and material advantages; (2) the development and deployment of armed forces specifically equipped and trained for COIN operations;[30] and (3) an awareness of and preparation for the political consequences of military victory. Without a national consensus and realistic expectations, the United States would be politically vulnerable in an asymmetric conflict. Without more special operations forces – the self-reliant and discriminate armed forces necessary to implement an ideal COIN strategy – what begins as military operations against isolated violent minorities will tend to escalate into wars against an entire society (Walzer, 2000: 187). It is crucial to add that in order to be effective these forces will need to be supported by a human intelligence network that may take a state such as the United States years to build.[31] Without a well thought-out postwar plan emphasizing economic recovery under a competent and uncorrupt administration, even rapid military victories can degenerate into desultory insurgency.

As Eliot Cohen argued twenty years ago, the United States must be prepared to fight and win both conventional and asymmetric wars. Strategic interaction theory shows why the two missions demand two kinds of armed forces: one to defend US interests in conventional wars, and one to defend them in small wars or against terrorists. It also highlights the importance of politics and diplomacy in combating insurgencies and terrorists. Determined insurgents and terrorists are difficult to defeat. But where strong actors have succeeded, they have done so most dramatically by preceding *discriminate* military attacks with meaningful political and economic reforms – reforms that effectively isolated guerrillas or terrorists from their the base of social support.[32] This was the pattern of British success in Malaya in 1948, and of US and Philippine government success in the Philippines in 1952. By contrast, military and economic support for repressive, corrupt, and incompetent regimes led to superpower defeats in Vietnam and Afghanistan.

Thus, strategic interaction theory explains not only how the weak win wars, but how the strong lose the peace. Contrary to Merom's

---

[30] See, for example, May, in Hoffmann *et al.* (1981: 8, 9); Hoffmann (*ibid.*: 10); Cohen (1984: 166–167); and Johnson (2001: 181–182).

[31] Conventional US forces are already well supplied with the kinds of technical intelligence – satellite and electronic spectrum intelligence – necessary to achieve overwhelming victory.

[32] This will not stop all terrorism but it will make such terrorism as survives (a) less deadly, and (b) less likely to be viewed by target audiences as much more than criminal or irrational behavior.

thesis, following World War II the unrestrained application of brute force *rarely* wins wars and can never win the peace. This is true for two reasons. First, it has proven technically impossible to entirely destroy a people or to destroy them sufficiently to foreclose the possibility of a future backlash (the Hutus murdered Tutsis in Rwanda even more efficiently than the Germans had murdered Jews in World War II, but the Tutsis are in control in Rwanda today and the Jews have their own state). Second, the principle of national self-determination has made it increasingly rational for people to sacrifice their lives for the cause; the implications of murder against a disparate group of unrelated people differ dramatically from the implications of murder against a *national*. In this nationalist context it is much more difficult to coerce a person who would prefer to die than accede; and barbarism-provoked fear is as likely to lead to violent resistance as to cowed compliance.

If the United States wants to win wars it must build two different militaries. If it wants to win the peace – a far more ambitious and useful goal – it must support its resort to arms by eliminating foreign policy double standards and by increasing its capacity and willingness to use methods other than violence to resolve or deter conflicts around the world. So long as the United States continues to support corrupt and repressive regimes in Latin America, Africa, the Middle East, and Asia, terrorists and insurgents will continue to frustrate US interests in global peace and prosperity. The current US government has confused military power with state power, and by over-applying the former has actually undermined its interests. If this policy continues and follows the historical pattern of *every previous attempt to accomplish the same ends* (peace) *by the same means* (the overwhelming application of military force unsupported by political, economic, and administrative resources), the result will be costly quagmires such as Vietnam, Afghanistan (1979 and 2002–), and Iraq (2003–), and a future attack on the United States or its allies that makes the terror attacks of September 11, 2001 pale by comparison.

# Appendix

## Strategic interactions and outcomes, 1816–2003

Table App. 1 A list of cases and key variables

| WARNAME | START | END | OUTCOME (strong actor) | STRATINT |
|---|---|---|---|---|
| Spain–Peru | 1809 | 1816 | wins | same-approach |
| Russo-Georgian | 1816 | 1825 | wins | same-approach |
| Pindari War | 1817 | 1818 | wins | same-approach |
| Kandyan Rebellion | 1817 | 1818 | wins | same-approach |
| Greek War of Independence | 1821 | 1828 | loses/tie | opposite-approach |
| First Anglo-Burmese | 1823 | 1826 | wins | same-approach |
| First Ashanti | 1824 | 1826 | wins | same-approach |
| Javanese | 1825 | 1830 | wins | same-approach |
| Bharatpuran | 1825 | 1826 | wins | same-approach |
| Russo-Circassian | 1829 | 1840 | wins | same-approach |
| Albanian | 1830 | 1831 | wins | same-approach |
| Belgian Independence | 1830 | 1831 | wins | same-approach |
| Murid War | 1830 | 1859 | wins | same-approach |
| First Polish | 1831 | 1831 | wins | same-approach |
| First Syrian | 1831 | 1832 | loses/tie | same-approach |
| Texan | 1835 | 1836 | loses/tie | same-approach |
| Second Seminole War | 1835 | 1842 | wins | same-approach |
| First Zulu | 1838 | 1840 | wins | same-approach |
| First British–Afghan | 1838 | 1842 | loses/tie | opposite-approach |
| Franco-Algerian | 1839 | 1847 | wins | same-approach |
| Bosnian–Turkish | 1841 | 1841 | wins | same-approach |
| Baluchi–British | 1843 | 1843 | wins | same-approach |
| First Maori | 1843 | 1848 | wins | same-approach |
| Franco-Moroccan | 1844 | 1844 | wins | same-approach |
| First British–Sikh | 1845 | 1846 | wins | same-approach |
| First Kaffir War | 1846 | 1847 | wins | same-approach |

Table App. 1 (cont.)

| | | | OUTCOME | |
| WARNAME | START | END | (strong actor) | STRATINT |
| --- | --- | --- | --- | --- |
| Cracow Revolt | 1846 | 1846 | wins | same-approach |
| Austro-Sardinian | 1848 | 1849 | wins | same-approach |
| First Schleswig-Holstein | 1848 | 1849 | wins | same-approach |
| Hungarian | 1848 | 1849 | wins | same-approach |
| Second British–Sikh | 1848 | 1849 | wins | same-approach |
| Roman Republic | 1849 | 1849 | wins | same-approach |
| Second Kaffir | 1850 | 1853 | wins | same-approach |
| La Plata | 1851 | 1852 | wins | same-approach |
| Second Anglo-Burmese | 1852 | 1853 | wins | same-approach |
| First Turko-Montenegran | 1852 | 1853 | loses/tie | same-approach |
| Third Seminole War | 1855 | 1858 | wins | same-approach |
| Yakima War | 1855 | 1858 | loses/tie | opposite-approach |
| Anglo-Persian | 1856 | 1857 | wins | same-approach |
| Second Opium War | 1856 | 1860 | loses/tie | same-approach |
| Kabylia Uprising | 1856 | 1857 | wins | |
| Tukulor–French War | 1857 | 1857 | wins | same-approach |
| French–Indochinese | 1858 | 1863 | wins | same-approach |
| Second Turko-Montenegran | 1858 | 1859 | loses/tie | same-approach |
| Spanish–Moroccan | 1859 | 1860 | wins | same-approach |
| Italo-Roman | 1860 | 1860 | wins | same-approach |
| Second Maori | 1860 | 1870 | wins | same-approach |
| Apache and Navaho War | 1860 | 1865 | wins | same-approach |
| Taiping Rebellion | 1860 | 1864 | wins | same-approach |
| Nien Rebellion | 1860 | 1868 | wins | same-approach |
| Franco-Mexican | 1862 | 1867 | loses/tie | same-approach |
| First Sioux War | 1862 | 1864 | wins | same-approach |
| Second Polish | 1863 | 1864 | wins | same-approach |
| Spanish–Santo Dominican | 1863 | 1865 | loses/tie | |
| Second Schleswig-Holstein | 1864 | 1864 | wins | same-approach |
| Lopez War | 1864 | 1870 | wins | opposite-approach |
| Spanish–Chilean | 1865 | 1866 | wins | same-approach |
| British–Bhutanese | 1865 | 1865 | wins | same-approach |
| Second Sioux War | 1865 | 1868 | loses/tie | opposite-approach |
| First Cretan | 1866 | 1867 | wins | opposite-approach |
| Ten Years War | 1868 | 1878 | wins | same-approach |
| Algerian | 1871 | 1872 | wins | |
| Second Apache War | 1871 | 1873 | wins | same-approach |
| Second Ashanti | 1873 | 1874 | wins | same-approach |
| Tonkin | 1873 | 1885 | wins | same-approach |
| Dutch–Achinese | 1873 | 1878 | wins | same-approach |
| Red River Indian War | 1874 | 1875 | wins | same-approach |
| Balkan | 1875 | 1877 | wins | opposite-approach |
| Third Apache War | 1876 | 1886 | wins | opposite-approach |
| Third Sioux War | 1876 | 1877 | wins | same-approach |
| Ninth Kaffir | 1877 | 1878 | wins | same-approach |

Table App. 1 (cont.)

| WARNAME | START | END | OUTCOME (strong actor) | STRATINT |
|---------|-------|-----|------------------------|----------|
| Russo-Turkoman | 1878 | 1881 | wins | same-approach |
| Second British–Afghan | 1878 | 1880 | wins | same-approach |
| British–Zulu | 1879 | 1879 | wins | same-approach |
| Gun War | 1880 | 1881 | wins | same-approach |
| First Boer War | 1880 | 1880 | loses/tie | same-approach |
| Tunisian | 1881 | 1882 | wins | |
| Franco-Indochinese | 1882 | 1884 | wins | same-approach |
| Mahdist | 1882 | 1885 | loses/tie | same-approach |
| First Franco-Madagascan | 1883 | 1885 | wins | same-approach |
| Sino-French | 1884 | 1885 | loses/tie | same-approach |
| Russo-Afghan | 1885 | 1885 | wins | same-approach |
| Third Anglo-Burmese | 1885 | 1886 | wins | same-approach |
| First Mandigo-French War | 1885 | 1885 | wins | same-approach |
| First Italo-Ethiopian | 1887 | 1887 | loses/tie | same-approach |
| Second Cretan | 1888 | 1889 | wins | |
| Dahomey | 1889 | 1892 | wins | same-approach |
| Second Senegalese | 1890 | 1891 | wins | same-approach |
| Messiah War | 1890 | 1891 | wins | same-approach |
| Congo Arabs | 1892 | 1892 | wins | |
| Franco-Thai | 1893 | 1893 | wins | |
| Third Ashanti | 1893 | 1894 | wins | same-approach |
| Matabele–British War | 1893 | 1893 | wins | same-approach |
| Sino-Japanese | 1894 | 1895 | loses/tie | same-approach |
| Franco-Madagascan | 1894 | 1895 | wins | same-approach |
| Balian | 1894 | 1894 | wins | |
| Cuban | 1895 | 1898 | wins | same-approach |
| Italo-Ethiopian | 1895 | 1896 | loses/tie | same-approach |
| Fourth Ashanti | 1895 | 1896 | wins | same-approach |
| Third Cretan | 1896 | 1897 | loses/tie | same-approach |
| Druze–Turkish | 1896 | 1896 | wins | |
| First Philippine | 1896 | 1898 | loses/tie | opposite-approach |
| Sudanese War | 1896 | 1899 | wins | same-approach |
| Greco-Turkish | 1897 | 1897 | wins | same-approach |
| Indian Muslim | 1897 | 1898 | wins | same-approach |
| Nigerian | 1897 | 1897 | wins | same-approach |
| Hut Tax | 1898 | 1898 | wins | same-approach |
| Second Philippine | 1899 | 1902 | wins | same-approach |
| Second Boer War | 1899 | 1902 | wins | same-approach |
| Somali Rebellion | 1899 | 1905 | wins | same-approach |
| Russo-Manchurian | 1900 | 1900 | loses/tie | same-approach |
| Ilinden | 1903 | 1903 | wins | same-approach |
| Russo-Japanese War | 1904 | 1905 | loses/tie | same-approach |
| South West African Revolt | 1904 | 1905 | wins | opposite-approach |
| Maji–Maji Revolt | 1905 | 1906 | wins | opposite-approach |
| Second Zulu War | 1906 | 1906 | wins | same-approach |

Table App. 1 (cont.)

| WARNAME | START | END | OUTCOME (strong actor) | STRATINT |
|---|---|---|---|---|
| Spanish–Moroccan | 1909 | 1910 | wins | same-approach |
| First Moroccan | 1911 | 1912 | wins | same-approach |
| First Balkan War | 1912 | 1913 | loses/tie | same-approach |
| Tibetan War of Independence | 1912 | 1913 | loses/tie | same-approach |
| Second Moroccan | 1916 | 1917 | wins | |
| Arab Revolt | 1916 | 1918 | loses/tie | opposite-approach |
| Irish Troubles | 1916 | 1921 | loses/tie | opposite-approach |
| Yunnan | 1917 | 1918 | wins | |
| First Sino-Tibetan | 1918 | 1918 | loses/tie | |
| Russo-Polish | 1919 | 1920 | loses/tie | same-approach |
| Lithuanian–Polish | 1919 | 1920 | wins | same-approach |
| Hungarian–Allies | 1919 | 1919 | wins | same-approach |
| Franco-Turkish | 1919 | 1922 | loses/tie | same-approach |
| Third Afghan | 1919 | 1919 | wins | same-approach |
| Franco-Syrian | 1920 | 1920 | wins | |
| Iraqi–British | 1920 | 1921 | wins | |
| Sanusi | 1920 | 1932 | wins | same-approach |
| Riffian | 1921 | 1926 | wins | |
| Druze Rebellion | 1925 | 1927 | wins | same-approach |
| US–Nicaraguan | 1927 | 1933 | wins | opposite-approach |
| Chinese Muslims | 1928 | 1928 | wins | |
| Chinese Civil War | 1930 | 1935 | wins | same-approach |
| Manchurian | 1931 | 1933 | loses/tie | |
| Soviet–Turkestani | 1931 | 1934 | wins | |
| Italo-Ethiopian | 1935 | 1936 | wins | same-approach |
| Sino-Japanese | 1937 | 1941 | wins | same-approach |
| Chankufeng | 1938 | 1938 | loses/tie | same-approach |
| Winter War | 1939 | 1940 | wins | same-approach |
| Franco-Thai | 1940 | 1941 | loses/tie | |
| Indonesian Independence | 1945 | 1946 | loses/tie | same-approach |
| Indochinese | 1945 | 1954 | loses/tie | same-approach |
| Madagascan | 1947 | 1948 | wins | |
| First Kashmir | 1947 | 1949 | wins | same-approach |
| Palestine | 1948 | 1949 | loses/tie | same-approach |
| Malayan Rebellion | 1948 | 1957 | wins | same-approach |
| Hyderabad | 1948 | 1948 | wins | |
| Korean Conflict | 1950 | 1953 | loses/tie | same-approach |
| Sino-Tibetan | 1950 | 1951 | wins | same-approach |
| Philippines | 1950 | 1952 | wins | same-approach |
| Kenya | 1952 | 1956 | wins | same-approach |
| Tunisian Independence | 1952 | 1954 | loses/tie | |
| Moroccan Independence | 1953 | 1956 | loses/tie | |
| Algerian | 1954 | 1962 | loses/tie | same-approach |
| British–Cypriot | 1954 | 1959 | loses/tie | same-approach |
| Cameroon | 1955 | 1960 | loses/tie | |

Table App. 1 (cont.)

| WARNAME | START | END | OUTCOME (strong actor) | STRATINT |
|---|---|---|---|---|
| Russo-Hungarian | 1956 | 1956 | wins | same-approach |
| Sinai | 1956 | 1956 | wins | same-approach |
| Tibetan | 1956 | 1959 | wins | opposite-approach |
| Cuba | 1958 | 1959 | loses/tie | opposite-approach |
| South Vietnam | 1960 | 1965 | loses/tie | opposite-approach |
| Congo | 1960 | 1965 | wins | same-approach |
| Kurdish | 1961 | 1963 | wins | |
| Angola–Portugal | 1961 | 1975 | loses/tie | |
| Sino-Indian | 1962 | 1962 | wins | same-approach |
| Guinea Bissau | 1962 | 1974 | loses/tie | opposite-approach |
| Mozambique | 1964 | 1975 | loses/tie | opposite-approach |
| Vietnam | 1965 | 1975 | loses/tie | opposite-approach |
| Second Kashmir | 1965 | 1965 | loses/tie | same-approach |
| Six Day War | 1967 | 1967 | loses/tie | same-approach |
| Israeli–Egyptian | 1969 | 1970 | loses/tie | same-approach |
| Bangladesh | 1971 | 1971 | wins | same-approach |
| Philippine–Moro | 1972 | 1980 | wins | same-approach |
| Yom Kippur War | 1973 | 1973 | loses/tie | same-approach |
| Turko-Cypriot | 1974 | 1974 | wins | same-approach |
| Eritrean | 1974 | 1991 | loses/tie | same-approach |
| Kurdish Autonomy | 1974 | 1975 | wins | same-approach |
| East Timor | 1974 | 1975 | loses/tie | opposite-approach |
| Vietnamese–Cambodian | 1975 | 1979 | wins | same-approach |
| Western Sahara | 1975 | 1983 | wins | |
| Chadian Civil War | 1975 | 1988 | wins | same-approach |
| Ethiopia–Somalia | 1977 | 1978 | wins | same-approach |
| Afghanistan | 1978 | 1989 | loses/tie | same-approach |
| Sino-Vietnamese | 1979 | 1979 | wins | same-approach |
| Peruvian Civil War | 1982 | 1992 | wins | same-approach |
| Tamil Rebellion | 1983 | 1990 | loses/tie | opposite-approach |
| Sino-Vietnamese | 1985 | 1987 | loses/tie | same-approach |
| Gulf War | 1990 | 1991 | wins | same-approach |
| Iraq–Kuwait | 1990 | 1990 | wins | same-approach |
| Kurdish Rebellion | 1991 | 1999 | wins | same-approach |
| Serbian Rebellion | 1991 | 1996 | loses/tie | opposite-approach |
| Russo-Chechen | 1994 | 1996 | loses/tie | same-approach |
| Kosovo I | 1998 | 1999 | wins | same-approach |
| Kosovo II | 1999 | 1999 | wins | same-approach |
| Russo-Chechen II | 1999 | | | same-approach |
| Anti-Taliban | 2002 | 2002 | wins | same-approach |
| Gulf War II | 2003 | 2003 | wins | same-approach |

Number of cases = 202

## Associated statistics for wins and losses over time

Table App. 2 Correlation Coefficients of Strategic Interaction (STRATINT) and External Support for Weak Actors (WASUPP)

|  | OUT2 | OUT3 |
|---|---|---|
| STRATINT | −0.28 | −0.29 |
| WASUPP | −0.30 | −0.28 |

$p < 0.01$

## Associated statistics for correlation between strategic interaction and conflict duration, 1800–2003

Table App. 3 Strategic Interaction (STRATINT) by collapsed duration of war (WARDUR2)

| STRATINT | WARDUR2 | | | | |
|---|---|---|---|---|---|
|  | 1 (0–1 years) | 2 (2–5 years) | 3 (6–9 years) | 4 (10–14 years) | 5 (15–50 years) |
| Same-strategic | 93 | 38 | 14 | 4 | 2 |
| expected count | 84.7 | 41.9 | 17.5 | 5.2 | 1.7 |
| row percent | 61.6 | 25.2 | 9.3 | 2.6 | 1.3 |
| Opposite-strategic | 4 | 10 | 6 | 2 | 0 |
| expected count | 12.3 | 6.1 | 2.5 | .8 | .3 |
| row percent | 18.2 | 45.5 | 27.3 | 9.1 | 0 |
| Column totals | 97 (56.1 percent) | 48 (27.7 percent) | 20 (11.6 percent) | 6 (3.5 percent) | 2 (1.2) |
| Chi-Square | Value | DF | Pearson | | |
| Significance | 17.273 | 4 | 0.002 | | |

## Associated statistics for interaction phase types, 1800–2003

Table App. 4 Interaction Phase Type (INTPTYPE) Distribution, 1800–2003

| Value Label | Value | Frequency | Percent | Valid Percent | Cum Percent |
|---|---|---|---|---|---|
| Single interaction | 0 | 140 | 69.7 | 78.7 | 78.7 |
| Sequential interaction | 1 | 28 | 13.9 | 15.7 | 94.4 |
| Simultaneous interaction | 2 | 10 | 5.0 | 5.6 | 100.0 |
| | | 23 | 11.4 | Missing | |
| | | ----- | ----- | ----- | |
| Total | | 201 | 100.0 | 100.0 | |
| Valid cases: 178 | Missing cases: | 23 | | | |

# References

Anderson, Benedict, 1991. *Imagined Communities: Reflections on the Origin and Spread of Nationalism*. London: Verso.

Andreski, Stanislav, 1968. *Military Organization and Society*. Berkeley: The University of California Press.

Arreguín-Toft, Ivan, 2001. "How the Weak Win Wars: A Theory of Asymmetric Conflict," *International Security*, vol. 26, no. 1: 93–128.

2002. "Tunnel at the End of the Light: A Critique of US Counter-Terrorist Grand Strategy," *Cambridge Review of International Affairs*, vol. 15, no. 3: 549–563.

2003. "The [F]utility of Barbarism: Assessing the Impact of the Systematic Harm of Non-Combatants as a Strategy in War," paper presented at the annual meeting of the American Political Science Association.

Asprey, Robert B., 1994. *War in the Shadows: The Classic History of Guerrilla Warfare from Ancient Persia to the Present*. New York: Little, Brown and Company.

Baddeley, John F., 1908. *The Russian Conquest of the Caucasus*. London: Longmans, Green & Co.

Bartov, Omer, 1992. *Hitler's Army: Soldiers, Nazis, and War in the Third Reich*. New York: Oxford University Press.

Bennett, D. Scott, and Allan C. Stam III, 1998. "The Declining Advantages of Democracy: A Combined Model of War Outcomes and Duration," *Journal of Conflict Resolution*, vol. 42, no. 3: 344–366.

Blainey, Geoffrey, 1988. *The Causes of War*, 3rd ed. New York: The Free Press.

Blanch, Lesley, 1960. *The Sabres of Paradise*. New York: The Viking Press.

Blaufarb, Douglas S., and George K. Tanham, 1989. *Who Will Win? A Key to the Puzzle of Revolutionary War*. New York: Crane Russak.

Borovik, Artyom, 1990. *The Hidden War: A Russian Journalist's Account of the Soviet War in Afghanistan*. New York: The Atlantic Monthly Press.

Boserup, Anders, and Andrew J. R. Mack, 1975. *War Without Weapons: Non-Violence in National Defense*. New York: Schocken Books.

Brown, Frederick Z., 1980. "Comment on Mueller: American Misperceptions," *International Studies Quarterly*, vol. 24, no. 4: 525–529.

Callwell, C.E., 1996. *Small Wars: Their Principles and Practice*, 3rd ed. Lincoln: University of Nebraska Press.

Caputo, Philip, 1996. *A Rumor of War*. New York: Henry Holt and Company.

Chaliand, Gérard, ed., 1982. *Guerrilla Strategies: An Historical Anthology from the Long March to Afghanistan*. Berkeley: University of California Press.

Charnay, J. P., 1994. "Strategy," in André Corvisier and John Childs, eds., Chris Turner, trans., *A Dictionary of Military History and the Art of War*. Cambridge, Mass: Blackwell, pp. 768–774.

Clodfelter, Mark, 1989. *The Limits of Air Power: The American Bombing of North Vietnam*. New York: The Free Press.

Coffey, Thomas M., 1974. *Lion by the Tail: The Story of the Italian–Ethiopian War*. London: Hamish Hamilton.

Cohen, Eliot A., 1984. "Constraints on America's Conduct of Small Wars," *International Security*, vol. 9, no. 2: 151–181.

Connor, Walker, 1969. "Ethnology and the Peace of South Asia," *World Politics*, vol. 22, no. 1: 51–86.

Cordesman, Anthony H., and Abraham R. Wagner, 1990. *The Lessons of Modern War, Volume III: the Afghan and Falklands Conflicts*. Boulder: Westview Press.

Corvisier, André, and John Childs, 1994. "Indirect Warfare," in Corvisier and Childs, *A Dictionary of Military History and the Art of War*. Cambridge, Mass: Blackwell, p. 378.

Corvisier, André, and Barry Paskins, 1994. "Laws of War," in Corvisier and Childs, *A Dictionary of Military History and the Art of War*. Cambridge, Mass: Blackwell, pp. 443–453.

Craft, Cassady, 1999. *Weapons for Peace, Weapons for War: The Effects of Arms Transfers on War Outbreak, Involvement, and Outcomes*. New York: Routledge.

Daalder, Ivo H., and Michael E. O'Hanlon, 2000. *Winning Ugly: NATO's War to Save Kosovo*. Washington, DC: Brookings Institution Press.

Del Boca, Angelo, 1969. *The Ethiopian War, 1935–1941*. Chicago: University of Chicago Press.

De Wet, Christiaan, 1902. *The Three Years' War*. New York: Charles Scribner's Sons.

Debray, Regis, 1968. *Revolution in the Revolution*. New York: Penguin.

Desch, Michael C., 2002. "Democracy and Victory: Why Regime Type Hardly Matters," *International Security*, vol. 27, no. 2: 5–47.

Donohue, Laura, 2001. *Counter-terrorist Law and Emergency Powers in the United Kingdom, 1922–2000*. Portland, Or: Irish Academic Press.

Douhet, Giulio, [1927] 1972. *The Command of the Air*. New York: Arno Press.
   1999. "Command of the Air," in David Jablonsky, ed., *Roots of Strategy: Book Four*. Mechanicsburg, PA: Stackpole Books, pp. 263–408.

Downes, Alexander, 2003. "Targeting Civilians in War: the Starvation Blockades in World War I". Paper Presented at the 105th Annual Meeting of the American Political Science Association, September, Philadelphia, Pennsylvania.

Ellis, John, 1976. *A Short History of Guerrilla Warfare*. New York: St. Martin's Press.

1995. *From the Barrel of a Gun: A History of Guerrilla, Revolutionary and Counter-Insurgency Warfare, from the Romans to the Present.* London: Greenhill Books.

Elman, Miriam Fendius, 1995. "The Foreign Policies of Small States: Challenging Neorealism in its Own Backyard," *British Journal of Political Science,* vol. 25: 171–217.

Fremont-Barnes, Gregory, 2003. *The Boer War: 1899–1902* (Oxford: Osprey Publishing).

Galtung, Johan, 1976. "Two Concepts of Defense," in *Peace, War, and Defense: Essays in Peace Research,* vol. II. Oslo: International Peace Research Institute, pp. 328–340.

Gammer, Moshe, 1994. *Muslim Resistance to the Tsar: Shamil and the Conquest of Chechnia and Daghestan.* London: Frank Cass & Co.

Gast, Leon, 1996. *When we were Kings.* Polygram Film Productions.

George, Alexander L., David K. Hall and William R. Simons, eds., 1971, *The Limits of Coercive Diplomacy: Laos, Cuba, Vietnam.* Boston: Little, Brown and Company.

Guevara, Che, 1961. *Guerrilla Warfare.* New York: Monthly Review Press.

Hamer, W. S., 1970. *The British Army: Civil Military Relations, 1885–1905.* Oxford: Clarendon Press.

Hamilton, Donald W., 1998. *The Art of Insurgency: American Military Policy and the Failure of Strategy in Southeast Asia.* Westport, CT: Praeger.

Hehn, Paul N., 1979. *The German Struggle Against Yugoslav Guerrillas in World War II: German Counter-Insurgency in Yugoslavia, 1941–1943.* Boulder, CO: Eastern European Quarterly.

Herring, George C., 1986. *America's Longest War: The United States and Vietnam, 1950–1975,* 2nd ed. New York: McGraw Hill.

Hobson, J. A., 1900. *The War in South Africa: Its Causes and Effects.* London: James Nisbet & Co.

Hoffmann, Stanley, *et al.,* 1981. "Vietnam Reappraised," *International Security,* vol. 6, no. 1: 3–26.

Howard, Michael, 1961. *The Franco-Prussian War.* New York: Methuen.

Iklé, Fred Charles, 1991. *Every War Must End,* revised. New York: Columbia University Press.

Independent International Commission on Kosovo, 2000. *Kosovo Report: Conflict, International Response, Lessons Learned.* New York: Oxford University Press.

Isby, David C., 1989. *War in a Distant Country, Afghanistan: Invasion and Resistance.* London: Arms and Armour Press.

James, Anthony, 1996. *Guerrilla Warfare: A Historical, Biographical, and Bibliographical Sourcebook.* Westport, CT: Greenwood Press.

Johnson, Chalmers, 1968. "The Third Generation of Guerrilla Warfare," *Asian Survey,* vol. 12: 435–447.

1973. *Autopsy on Peoples War.* Berkeley: University of California Press.

Johnson, Wray R., 2001. *Vietnam and American Doctrine for Small Wars.* Bangkok: White Lotus Press.

Kakar, M. Hassan, 1995. *Afghanistan: The Soviet Invasion and the Afghan Response, 1979–1982.* Berkeley: University of California Press.

Karnow, Stanley, 1983. *Vietnam: A History.* New York: Viking Press.

Katzenbach, E. L., 1962. "Time, Space and Will: The Politico-Military Strategy of Mao Tse-tung," in Ltc. T. N. Greene, ed., *The Guerrilla and How to Fight Him.* New York: Praeger, pp. 11–21.

Katzenbach, Edward L., and Gene Z. Hanrahan, 1955. "The Revolutionary Strategy of Mao Tse-Tung," *Political Science Quarterly,* vol. 70, no. 3: 321–340.

Kohn, George C., 1986. *A Dictionary of Wars.* New York: Facts on File Publications.

Krebs, Paula M., 1992. "'The Last of the Gentlemen's Wars': Women in the Boer War Concentration Camp Controversy," *History Workshop Journal,* vol. 33: 38–56.

Krepinevich, Andrew F. Jr., 1986. *The Army and Vietnam.* Baltimore: Johns Hopkins University Press.

Lake, David A., 1992. "Powerful Pacifists: Democratic States and War," *American Political Science Review,* vol. 86, no. 1: 24–27.

Laqueur, Walter, 1976. *Guerrilla: A Historical and Critical Study.* Boston: Little, Brown and Company.

Lawrence, T. E., 1926. *Seven Pillars of Wisdom: A Triumph.* New York: Doubleday.

Lea, Henry Charles, 1968. *Superstition and Force: Essays on the Wager of Law, the Wager of Battle, the Ordeal, Torture,* 2nd revised ed. New York: Greenwood Press.

Leepson, Mark, ed., with Helen Hannaford, 1999. *Webster's New World Dictionary of the Vietnam War.* New York: Macmillan.

LeMay, Curtis R. with Major General Dale O. Smith, 1968. *America Is in Danger.* New York: Funk & Wagnalls.

Liddell Hart, B. H., 1967. *Strategy,* 2nd revised ed. New York: Praeger Publishers.

Litwak, Robert S., 1992. "The Soviet Union in Afghanistan," in Ariel E. Levite, Bruce W. Jentleson, and Larry Berman, eds., *Foreign Military Intervention: The Dynamics of Protracted Conflict.* New York: Columbia University Press, pp. 65–94.

Mack, Andrew J. R., 1975. "Why Big Nations Lose Small Wars: The Politics of Asymmetric Conflict," *World Politics,* vol. 27, no. 2: 175–200.

Magnus, Ralph H., and Eden Naby, 1998. *Afghanistan: Mullah, Marx, and Mujahid.* Boulder, CO: Westview Press.

Mao, Tse-tung, 1961. *On Guerrilla Warfare,* Samuel B. Griffith, tr. New York: Praeger Publishers.

    1968. "Primer on Guerrilla Warfare," in Donald Robinson, ed., *The Dirty Wars: Guerrilla Actions and Other Forms of Unconventional Warfare.* New York: Delacorte Press.

Marquis, Susan L., 1997. *Unconventional Warfare: Rebuilding US Special Operations Forces.* Washington, DC: Brookings Institution Press.

May, Ernest, 2000. *Strange Victory: Hitler's Conquest of France.* New York: Hill & Wang.

McCarthy, Ronald M., and Gene Sharp, 1997. *Nonviolent Action: A Research Guide.* New York: Garland.

Mearsheimer, John, 1983. *Conventional Deterrence*. Ithaca, NY: Cornell University Press.

2001. *The Tragedy of Great Power Politics*. New York: W.W. Norton & Company.

• Merari, Ariel, 1993. "Terrorism as a Strategy of Insurgency," *Terrorism and Political Violence*, vol. 5, no. 4: 213–251.

Merom, Gil, 2003. *How Democracies Lose Small Wars: State, Society, and the Failures of France in Algeria, Israel in Lebanon, and the United States in Vietnam*. New York: Cambridge University Press.

1921. *Our Air Force, the Keystone of National Defence*. New York: E. P. Dutton & Company. "Winged Defense," in David Jablonsky, ed., *Roots of Strategy: Book Four*. Mechanicsburg, PA: Stackpole Books, pp. 409–516.

Mockler, Anthony, 1984. *Haile Selassie's War: The Italian–Ethiopian Campaign, 1935–1941*. New York: Random House.

Moisie, Edwin, E., 1996. *Tonkin Gulf and the Escalation of the Vietnam War*. Chapel Hill, NC: University of North Carolina Press.

Mueller, John, 1980. "The Search for the "Breaking Point" in Vietnam: The Statistics of a Deadly Quarrel," *International Studies Quarterly*, vol. 24, no. 4: 497–519.

Muraise, Eric, 1964. *Introduction à L'Histoire Militaire*. Paris: Charles-Lavauzelle.

Mussolini, Benito, 1995. "The Vital Need for Empire," in Roger Griffin, ed., *Fascism*. New York: Oxford University Press, pp. 74–75.

Nasson, Bill, 1999. *The South African War, 1899–1902*. New York: Oxford University Press.

Nutter, John Jacob, 1994. "Unpacking Threat: A Conceptual and Formal Analysis," in Norman A. Graham, ed., *Seeking Security and Development: The Impact of Military Spending and Arms Transfers*. Boulder: Lynne Rienner Publishers, pp. 29–49.

Nye, Joseph S., Jr., 2004. *Soft Power: The Means to Success in World Politics*. New York: Public Affairs.

Pakenham, Thomas, 1979. *The Boer War*. New York: Random House.

Pape, Robert Antony, 1990. "Coercive Air Power in the Vietnam War," *International Security*, vol. 15, no. 2: 103–146.

1996. *Bombing to Win*. Ithaca: Cornell University Press.

1997. "Why Economic Sanctions Do Not Work," *International Security*, vol. 22, no. 2: 90–136.

• 2003. "The Strategic Logic of Suicide Terrorism," *American Political Science Review*, vol. 97, no. 3: 343–361.

Paret, Peter, and John Shy, 1962. *Guerrillas in the 1960s*, 2nd ed. New York: Praeger Publishers.

Parker, Christopher S., 1999. "New Weapons for Old Problems: Conventional Proliferation and Military Effectiveness in Developing States," *International Security*, vol. 23, no. 4: 119–147.

Parker, Geoffrey, 1994. "Early Modern Europe," in Michael Howard, George J. Andreopoulos, and Mark R. Shulman, eds., *The Laws of War: Constraints on*

*Warfare in the Western World.* New Haven, CT: Yale University Press, pp. 40–58.

Paul, T.V., 1994. *Asymmetric Conflicts: War Initiation by Weaker Powers.* Cambridge: Cambridge University Press.

Perry, Mark, and Ed Miles, 1999. "Environmental Warfare," in Roy Gutman and David Rieff, *Crimes of War: What the Public Should Know.* New York: W.W. Norton, pp. 132–135.

Pomeroy, William J., 1964. *Guerrilla & Counter-Guerrilla Warfare: Liberation and Suppression in the Present Period.* New York: International Publishers.

Posen, Barry R., 2003. "Command of the Commons: The Military Foundation of US Hegemony," *International Security*, vol. 28, no. 1: 5–46.

Powell, Colin L., 1992. "US Forces: Challenges Ahead," *Foreign Affairs*, vol. 71, no. 5: 32–51.

Press, Daryl, 2001. "The Myth of Air Power in the Persian Gulf War and the Future of Warfare," *International Security*, vol. 26, no. 2: 5–44.

Rais, Rasul Bakhsh, 1994. *War Without Winners: Afghanistan's Uncertain Transition after the Cold War.* Karachi: Oxford University Press.

Ramakrishna, Kumar, 2002. "'Bribing the Reds to Give Up': Rewards Policy in the Malayan Emergency," *War in History*, vol. 9, no. 3: 332–353.

Reiter, Dan, and Allan C. Stam III, 1998. "Democracy and Battlefield Military Effectiveness," *Journal of Conflict Resolution*, vol. 42, no. 3: 259–277.

2002. *Democracies at War.* Princeton, NJ: Princeton University Press.

2003. "Understanding Victory: Why Political Institutions Matter," *International Security*, vol. 28, no. 1: 168–179.

Rhodes, Richard, 2002. *Masters of Death: The SS-Einsatzgruppen and the Invention of the Holocaust.* New York: Alfred A. Knopf.

Roberts, Adam, 1994. "Land Warfare: From Hague to Nuremberg," in Michael Howard, George J. Andreopoulos, and Mark R. Shulman, eds., *The Laws of War: Constraints on Warfare in the Western World.* New Haven, CT: Yale University Press, pp. 116–139.

Rosen, Stephen P., 1982. "Vietnam and the American Theory of Limited War," *International Security*, vol. 7, no. 2: 83–113.

1995. "Military Effectiveness: Why Society Matters," *International Security*, vol. 19, no. 4: 5–31.

Rosen, Steven, 1972. "War Power and the Willingness to Suffer," in Bruce M. Russett, ed., *Peace, War and Numbers.* Beverly Hills: Sage Publications, pp. 167–184.

Rudolph, Lloyd I., 1985. "The Great Game in Asia: Revisited and Revised," *Crossroads*, no. 16: 1–46.

Russett, Bruce M., 1972. *No Clear and Present Danger: A Skeptical View of the US Entry into World War II.* New York: Harper & Row.

Sbacchi, Alberto, 1985. *Ethiopia Under Mussolini: Fascism and the Colonial Experience.* New York: Zed Books.

1997. *Legacy of Bitterness: Ethiopia and Fascist Italy, 1935–1941.* New Jersey: The Red Sea Press.

Schaffer, Ronald, 1985. *Wings of Judgment: American Bombing in World War II.* New York: Oxford University Press.

Schelling, Thomas C., 1966. *Arms and Influence.* New Haven, CT: Yale University Press.

Sharp, Gene, 2003. *There Are Realistic Alternatives.* Boston, MA: The Albert Einstein Institution.

Shaw, Geoffrey D. T., 2000. "Policemen versus Soldiers, the Debate Leading to MAAG Objections and Washington Rejections of the Core of the British Counter-Insurgency Advice," *Small Wars and Insurgencies,* vol. 12, no. 2: 51–58.

Sheehan, Neil, 1989. *A Bright Shining Lie: John Paul Vann and America in Vietnam.* New York: Vintage.

Sliwinski, Marek, 1989. "Afghanistan: the Decimation of a People," *Orbis,* vol. 33, no. 1: 39–56.

Small, Melvin, and J. David Singer, 1983. *Resort to Arms: International and Civil Wars, 1816–1980.* Beverley Hills: Sage Publications.

Smith, Iain R., 1996. *The Origins of the South African War, 1899–1902.* New York: Longman.

Snyder, Glenn H., and Paul Diesing, 1977. *Conflict among Nations: Bargaining, Decision Making, and System Structure in International Crisis.* Princeton: Princeton University Press.

Snyder, Jack, 1991. *Myths of Empire: Domestic Politics and International Ambition.* Ithaca: Cornell University Press.

Sorley, Lewis, 1999. *A Better War: The Unexamined Victories and Final Tragedy of America's Last Years in Vietnam.* New York: Harcourt Brace & Company, 1999.

Stigler, Andrew, 2003. "A Clear Victory for Air Power: NATO's Empty Threat to Invade Kosovo," *International Security,* vol. 27, no. 3: 124–157.

Stubbs, Richard, 1989. *Hearts and Minds in Guerrilla Warfare: The Malayan Emergency 1948–1960.* New York: Oxford University Press.

Summers, Harry G. Jr., 1995. *Historical Atlas of the Vietnam War.* Boston, MA: Houghton Mifflin.

Taber, Robert, 1965. *The War of the Flea: A Study of Guerrilla Warfare Theory and Practice.* New York: Lyle Stuart.

Tamarov, Vladislav, 1992. *Afghanistan: Soviet Vietnam,* Naomi Marcus, Marianne Clarke Trangen, and Vladislav Tamarov, trs. San Francisco: Mercury House.

Thomas, Ward, 2001. *The Ethics of Destruction: Norms and Force in International Relations.* Ithaca, NY: Cornell University Press.

Thompson, James Clay, 1980. *Rolling Thunder: Understanding Policy and Program Failure.* Chapel Hill, NC: University of North Carolina Press.

Thompson, Robert, 1966. *Defeating Communist Insurgency: Experiences from Malaya and Vietnam.* London: Chatto & Windus.

Tin, Bui, 2002. *From Enemy to Friend: A North Vietnamese Perspective on the War.* Annapolis, MD: Naval Institute Press.

## References

Toft, Monica Duffy, 2003. *The Geography of Ethnic Violence: Identity, Interests, and the Indivisibility of Territory*. Princeton, NJ: Princeton University Press.

Turtledove, Harry, 2001. "The Last Article," in Harry Turtledove with Martin H. Greenberg, eds., *The Best Military Science Fiction of the 20th Century*. New York: Del Rey Books, pp. 231–262.

Tzu, Sun, 1988. *The Art of War*, Thomas Cleary, tr. Boston: Shambhala Publications.

Urban, Mark L., 1988. *War in Afghanistan*. New York: St. Martin's Press.

Walt, Stephen S., 1987. *The Origins of Alliances*. Ithaca: Cornell University Press.

2002. "American Primacy: Its Prospects and Pitfalls," *Naval War College Review*, vol. 55, no. 2: 9–28.

Walton, C. Dale, 2002. *The Myth of Inevitable US Defeat in Vietnam*. Portland, OR: Frank Cass.

Waltz, Kenneth N., 1967. *Foreign Policy and Democratic Politics: The American and British Experience*. Boston: Little, Brown & Company.

1979. *Theory of International Politics*. New York: McGraw-Hill.

Walzer, Michael, 2000. *Just and Unjust Wars: A Moral Argument with Historical Illustrations*, 3rd ed. New York: Basic Books.

Watson, Bruce Allen, 1997. *When Soldiers Quit: A Study in Military Disintegration*. Westport, CT: Praeger.

Weigley, Russell Frank, 1997. *The American Way of War: A History of United States Military Strategy and Policy*. Bloomington, IN: Indiana University Press.

Wolf, Eric R., 1973. *Peasant Wars of the 20th Century*. New York: Harper & Row.

# Index

Abrams, Creighton, General 157, 158, 163n
Adowa, battle of (1896) 112, 112n, 116, 117n,
  118, 119
Afghan war (1979–89) 14, 19, 22
  casualties 180, 181–182, 188, 188n, 193n
  ceasefire 183
  (explanations of) outcome 6n, 187,
    188–189, 226
  international response 191–192, 192n
  mujahideen aims/interests 174–175, 190,
    196, 213
  mujahideen (imported) resources 178n,
    186, 193–194, 198, 215n, 215–216
  progress of hostilities 175–181, 183–184,
    202
  Soviet aims/interests 172n, 172–173,
    173n, 189–190, 195–196, 213, 214n
  Soviet resources , 172n, 178–179,
    183, 196
  Soviet strategy/tactics 179, 180n,
    180–183, 184–187, 189–190, 198, 221
  theoretial analysis 189–199, 213–216,
    214n, 217–219
Afghanistan
  ethnography 170
  geography 170, 177, 185
  political history 170–172, 173–174
  post-1989 developments 175n, 188, 190,
    199, 216
  (reductions in) population 182
  US invasion (2001) 19–20, 166, 204–205
air attack 31n, 32n, 40–41, 161
  counter-measures 186–187, 194
  effectiveness 40n, 136–137
Akhulgo, battle of 59
Alexander I, tsar 52
Alexander II, tsar 54, 64, 66, 206n
Alfieri, Dino 133

Algeria *see under* France
Ali, Muhammad 23
Allenby, General 96n
Aloisi, Pompeo, Baron 115, 116n
Amin, Hafizullah 171–172, 176
Andreski, Stanislas 9n
Aosta, Duke of 127n, 127–128, 129–130,
  137, 138
Ap Bac, battle of (1963) 149
*Apocalypse Now* (Coppola, 1979) 160–161
Arab–Israeli conflicts 224
Ardagh, Sir John, Maj.-Gen. 80
Aregai, Abebe 128, 129, 142, 210
arms diffusion theory 10–13, 11n, 42, 202
  applicability to case studies 193–194,
    197, 212, 214–215
  inapplicability/irrelevance to case
    studies 67–68, 70, 101–102, 106,
    136–137, 141, 162–163, 206, 209
artillery, use of 67–68, 70, 101–102
Asian countries, common strategic
  preferences 37
Asquith, H. H., prime minister 87–88
asymmetric conflicts 2–3
  defined 43
  duration 27, 28–29, 35, 46, 164, 202, 205,
    207–208, 213
  frequency 20n, 200–201
  initiation 30n
  theoretical analyses 5, 6n, 20, 24–25
    (*see also* arms diffusion; interest
    asymmetry; strategic interaction)
  unexpected outcomes 21, 157–158
    (*see also* weaker side, victory of)
Athens 2
Auraris, Dejaz 128n
authoritarian regimes
  conduct of hostilities 66–67

*243*

authoritarian regimes (cont.)
  control of information 7, 8–9, 28,
    135–136, 160, 214
  decline in numbers 5, 8
  demands on soldiery 7–8, 9
  local competition 211–212
  military advantages 7–8, 27–28, 42, 68n,
    196, 201–202, 209, 214n, 217–219
  military disadvantages 8–10, 140, 214
  wartime relaxation 8

Baddeley, John F. 52–53, 67
Baden-Powell, Lord 86
Badoglio, General 121, 122–123, 122–123n
bandwagoning 58n
Bao Dai 147
Baratieri, Oreste, General 111–112
barbarism
  aims 34
  counterproductivity 17n, 58, 63, 92, 108,
    126, 127n, 197–198, 221, 225
  defined 31–32, 43
  drawbacks 9–10, 35–36, 41–42n, 213,
    214n, 215–216 (*see also*
    counterproductivity *above*)
  effect on participants 9n
  employment in case studies 53, 70,
    92–94, 107, 143, 153–154, 157, 175,
    180–183
  as end in itself 36n
  international response 222
  military effectiveness 27–28n, 35n, 194–195
  public reactions 100, 217–219 (*see also*
    concentration camps; public opinion)
  reluctance to use 15–16
  use by authoritarian regimes 16, 191, 196
  use by democracies 16
  *see also* air attack; chemical weapons;
    concentration camps; hospitals,
    bombing of; indirect attacking
    strategy; mines; mustard gas
Bariatinsky, Prince 57, 62, 64, 66, 68
Beit, Alfred 76, 79n
Belgium, German invasion (1914) 224
"Black Week" (1899) 86–87
Blanch, Lesley 63
Blaskowitz, Johannes 9–10
blockhouse strategy 96, 184n, 184–185
Blood River, battle of (1838) 73
Boer War *see* South African War
bombing *see* air attack
Botha, Louis 86, 91–92, 93, 105
bravery, role in battle 49
Brezhnev, Leonid 171, 190, 191–192
  Brezhnev Doctrine 172, 172n, 173

Broderick, Lord 91–92n
Bui Tin 161
Buller, Sir Redvers (Lord), General 86,
  89–90
Bullock, Colonel 103n
Bush, George (sr.), President 164

Calley, William, Lt. 9n
Cape Town 72–73, 99
Caputo, Philip 144
Castellano, Professor 124n
Castro, Fidel 58n
casualties 8, 10
Catherine the Great 51, 69
Caucasus
  geography 49–51, 68
  political organization 55 (*see also*
    Muridism)
  population 57
  Russian conquest of *see* Murid Wars
Cavallero, General 128, 128n
cavalry, use of 85n
Chamberlain, Joseph 76, 77, 99–100
Chechnia
  deforestation 50, 50n, 61, 62, 63, 68
  geography 50
  Russian attacks on 53, 58, 166, 214n
chemical weapons 31n, 182–183, 183n, 210n
  *see also* mustard gas
Churchill, Winston 129
Ciano, Galeazzo 129–130
civilians
  casualty figures 162–163n
  execution 31n
  targeting 8, 25
  *see also* barbarism; concentration camps
clemency *see* conciliation
Cohen, Eliot 11, 12, 166, 226
COIN (counterinsurgency) campaigns/
  strategies 31–32, 32n, 41, 102–103, 107,
  155–157, 166–167, 191, 215, 226
Cold War 6–7n, 11–12
collateral damage 181–183
colonialism
  justifications 103n, 116–117, 118n
  struggles against 4n, 37n, 41–42n,
    146–148
commando units, use of 83, 96–97
concentration camps 31n, 32n, 91, 93–94,
  102–103
  conditions 95n
  death rates 94n, 103
  justification 91–92n
  public reaction to 94–96, 106, 222
conciliation 30n, 62–63, 70–71, 138, 210, 211

Conrad, Joseph 72
Constantine, Grand Duke (brother of
    Alexander I) 53–54
conventional attack 34
    conventional responses 38, 102, 137,
        154–155, 203–204
    defined 30–31, 43
    indirect responses 38–39, 64, 102, 138,
        175, 194, 204
    predicted outcomes 38, 39
conventional defense 32, 34, 43, 221
    *see also under* conventional attack;
        indirect attacking strategies
Craft, Cassady 11n
Crimean War 66–67
Cronje, General 88–89
Czechoslovakia
    German invasion 128
    Soviet invasion 191

Daghestan
    geography 50
    leadership 55
    Russian attacks on 53
Da'ud Khan, Sardar Mohammed 170–171,
    188
De Bono, General 119, 120–121, 122, 122–123n
De La Rey, Koos, General 92, 93, 97, 105
De Wet, Christiaan, General 88–89, 90–91,
    92–93, 97, 105
Debra Libanos monastery, massacre at 127
deforestation, as military tactic
    *see* Chechnya
Del Boca, Angelo 110, 114
democracy/ies
    authoritarian measures 8
    military effectiveness 15–18, 28, 166,
        201–202, 217–219, 225n
    strategic choices 99–101, 161–162,
        207–208, 211–212
Diem, Ngo Dinh 148–149, 149–150,
    151, 212
Dien Bien Phu, battle of 144, 167n
divine will (victory as expression of) 26–27
domino theory 82n, 164
Donohue, Laura K. 225n
Douhet, Gulliano 40
Downes, Alexander 35n
Duffy Toft, Monica 78n
Dundonald, Earl, Brig.-Gen. 107

economic sanctions 40, 40n
Eden, Anthony 135
Egypt 130
Eisenhower, Dwight D. 170

Eritrea 111, 113–114, 119n, 119–120, 120n
Ethiopia
    geography 110
    political system 110–111, 118
    *see also* Italo-Ethiopian War
European countries, common strategic
    preferences 37
expanding bullets, prohibition of 103n

*fait accompli,* victory as 26, 116n
Falkland Islands 164
Fawcett, Millicent 95n
Flandin, Pierre-Etienne 135
foreign support (for weaker side) 45–46,
    186, 193
    dependence on 195
    pitfalls 195
France
    German invasion (1940) 224
    involvement in Algeria 42n, 168, 184n,
        197n, 225
    involvement in Vietnam 144, 146n,
        146–148, 148n, 184n
    military strategies 16, 37n
    relations with Italy 112–113, 116–117
franchise, as point of dispute 75n
Franco-Prussian War 39n, 91
Freedman, Lawrence 200
Freitag, General 57, 60, 61

Gammer, Moshe 57n, 61, 67
Gandhi, Mahatma 41n
Geneva Convention *see* laws of war
genocide 222n
geography, influence on combat strategies
    12n, 178
Georgia 69
Gladstone, W. E., prime minister 74–75
gold/gems, discovery of 75, 79n
Goldwater, Barry, Senator 151
Gorbachev, Mikhail 186, 187, 190, 192–193,
    215
Grabbé, General 57
grand strategy, defined 29–30
Graziani, General 122–123, 122–123n,
    126–127, 128, 130–131, 137
Great Trek 73
Grenada 26
Grozny, construction of 53
guerrilla warfare 12n, 14–15n, 16, 25n, 37,
    132–133
    aims 34, 35n
    conditions (un)favorable to 41, 62n, 105,
        197
    defined 32–33, 43

guerrilla warfare (cont.)
  employment in case studies 57, 59–61,
    68, 70–71, 88–89, 90–92, 93, 102,
    106–107, 121–122, 138, 155–156, 175
  evolution into direct strategy 32n
  origins 17n
  rejection 39n, 125, 131, 166
Guevara, Che 58n, 203n
Gugsa, General 120

Hague Convention (1899/1907) 92n, 103n
Haile Selassie, Emperor 109, 109–110, 113n,
    113–114, 118, 119, 120, 121–122,
    125–126, 130, 130n, 131, 132–133,
    209, 220
Halifax, Lord 134–135
Hamilton, Donald 166
Hamzad Beg 55, 64
Hannibal 49
Hely-Hutchinson, Sir Walter 83
Himmler, Heinrich 9–10
Hitler, Adolf 49
Ho Chi Minh 146–147, 149
Hoare, Sir Samuel 116–117n
Hobhouse, Emily 94–95, 95n, 100, 219
Hobson, J.A. 79n
honor, role in military ethos 49, 118
hospitals, bombing of 124, 134
Hungary, Soviet invasion of 191, 202
Hussein, Saddam 50n

incompetence, role in strong-actor setbacks
    68, 70, 131, 137, 138–140, 210–211, 220
India, gaining of independence 170
indirect attacking strategies
  direct responses 39–41, 154, 204
  indirect responses 33–34n, 41, 137,
    203–204
  predicted outcomes 40–41, 42
  by weaker side 40n
  *see also* air attack; barbarism; civilians,
    targeting of; economic sanctions
indirect defensive strategies 27–28,
    221–222, 224
  *see also* conventional attack; guerilla
    warfare; indirect attacking strategies
interest asymmetry, theory of 13–14, 25,
    42–43, 201
  applicability to case studies 66, 69
  inapplicability to case studies 104, 159,
    190, 196, 213–214, 217–219
  weaknesses 14–15
international relations theory
  (conventional approaches) 2, 2n, 4–5,
    23–24, 221, 223, 223n

internment 25
Iraq, conflicts involving 19, 20, 162, 202
  *see also* Kuwait
Israel 225, 227
Italo-Ethiopian Treaty of Amity,
    Conciliation and Arbitration (1928)
    113–114
Italo-Ethiopian War (1935–40) 22, 28, 198n
  casualties 125n
  conclusion 133n
  Ethiopian aims/interests 118, 132–133
  Ethiopian resources 120, 136, 141
  Ethiopian strategy/tactics 121–122, 125
  historical background 111–116
  Italian aims/interests 116–118, 119, 132,
    140
  Italian malpractice (*see* hospitals; laws of
    war; mustard gas)
  Italian strategy/tactics 123–125, 126–129,
    140–141
  progress of hostilities 109–110, 119–129
  theoretical analysis 132–143, 209–211, 219
Italy
  in World War II 129–131
  *see also* Italo-Ethiopian War

Jahandad, Commander 176
Jameson Raid 76, 101
Japan, military initiatives 52, 147, 223–224
  *see also* Russo-Japanese War
Johnson, Lyndon B., president 29n,
    150–152, 153
Joubert, General 85

Kakar, Hassan 169, 174, 176, 181
Karmal, Babrak 171, 172, 173, 176, 177, 186,
    189
Karnow, Stanley 146
Kekevich, General 86
Kennedy, John F., president 150–151
Khazi Muhammad 55, 58, 64
Kimberley, siege of (1899–1900) 86, 88
Kitchener, Lord 86, 88, 89, 93–94, 96–97, 98,
    103n, 207–208n
Kock, General 84–85, 85n
Korean War (1950–3) 11–12, 45n, 220
Kosovo 19, 33–34n, 40n, 41n, 198n
Krepinovich, Andrew 166
Kruger, Paul, president 74–75, 76, 77–78,
    80–81, 84n, 93, 101
Kuwait, Iraqi invasion/expulsion 19, 49, 164

Labouchère, Henry 88n
Ladysmith, siege of (1899–1900) 85n,
    85–86, 88

Lansdowne, H. C. K. Petty-Fitzmaurice,
    marquess of 79
Lawrence, T. E. 23, 130, 185
laws of war, violations of 31n, 103n,
    103–104, 160–161, 176
  alleged 124n
  attempts at concealment/justification
    124, 124n, 127, 133–136
  *see also* chemical weapons; hospitals,
    bombing of; mustard gas
League of Nations 113, 114, 115–116, 118,
    132–133, 134–135
Lloyd George, David, PM 95

Mack, Andrew J. R. 5–7, 13, 14–15n, 16,
    17–18, 24, 25n, 27, 28–29, 161, 165, 201,
    202, 202n
Mafeking, siege of (1899–1900) 86, 88
Magsaysay, Ramon 167
Majuba Hill, battle of (1881) 75
Malayan Emergency (1948) 17, 202n, 226
Manchuria *see* Japan
Mao Tse-tung 12n, 32n, 33, 34, 37, 41n,
    223–224
Massu, General 42n, 168
Massud, Ahmad Shah 179, 180, 181,
    183–184, 185, 188, 194–195
McNamara, Robert S. 29n, 153
Mearsheimer, John 3n
Menelik II, emperor of Ethiopia 111–112, 118
Merom, Gil 15, 16–18, 29, 67, 161–162, 166,
    201–202, 202n, 206n, 207–208n, 225n,
    226–227
Methuen, Lord 86
Meyer, Lucas 83–84
Milner, Alfred 76–77, 77n, 80, 83n, 98,
    99–100
Milosevic, Slobodan 40n
mines, use of 182
Mitchell, William 40
Molotov, Vyacheslav 148
motivation (levels of) 24
Movchan, Mickola 169
mujahideen *see* Afghan war; foreign
    support
Murid War (1820–49) 22
  cost 49
  historical background 51–54
  outcome 64, 206n
  progress of hostilities 57
  Russian aims/interests 65–66
  Russian military strategy 50–51, 53,
    58–59, 63–64
  theoretical analysis 64–71, 205–207, 206n,
    219–220

Muridism 55, 58, 224
  military organization 56, 70
  religious dogma 56
Mussolini, Benito 112n, 113–114, 116n,
    116–118, 117n, 120–121, 122, 125n, 126,
    127, 128, 129, 132, 133, 135–136, 137,
    140–141, 172n
mustard gas, use of 122–125, 122–123n,
    125–126, 131–132, 133–136, 137
  attempts at concealment/justification
    *see under* laws of war, violations of
  effects on victims 123–124
My Lai massacre 9n, 160–161

Najibullah, Mohammed 186, 188, 188n, 190
Napoleonic wars 17n, 49, 52, 60n
nationalism 5, 6–7n, 37n, 62n, 195,
    223–224
NATO, military activities 19, 31n
nature-of-actor theory *see* authoritarian
    regimes; democracies
naval warfare, strategies 50n
Navarre, Henri, General 167n
Nazis, treatment of occupied territories
    9–10, 35–36, 36n
Nguyen Co Thach 157n
Nguyen Khanh, General 150
Nicholas I, Tsar 53–54, 59, 64, 66, 70
noncombatants, targeting of 31–32
  *see also* civilians
Northern Ireland 225n

Orange Free State 73–74, 88n, 98

Pakenham, Thomas 79, 82, 85–86, 87–88, 98
Pakistan 170
  *see also* Afghan War: mujahideen
    resources
Paktia offensive (1980) 178–179
Panjsher offensives (1980–5)179–181,
    183–184
Pape, Robert 40, 40n, 152–153n
Paskyevitch, General 57–58, 59, 63, 68
Patriot Act (US 2002) 8
Paul, T. V. 6n
Paul I, Tsar 51–52
Persia, conflicts with Russia 51–52, 66
Peter the Great 51, 69
Philippines 202n, 226
Phoenix program 156–157, 157n
Poland, German occupation of 9–10
political vulnerability, impact on military
    strategy 13–14, 24, 25, 42–43
  absence of 66, 67, 69–70, 141, 206, 214
  in Soviet Union 193

political vulnerability, impact on military
strategy (cont.)
in UK 100, 105–106, 207–208
in United States 159, 161–162, 165, 213
in Vietnam 211–212
Posen, Barry 12–13
posts, fortified *see* blockhouse strategy
power
defined 2n, 3n, 223, 223n, 224
relationship with conflict outcomes 2–3,
63, 65, 69, 71, 140
*see also* interest asymmetry
precedent, setting of (as factor in
determining strategy) 78–79,
116–117n, 173n, 189n
*see also* domino theory
prisoners of war
inability to hold 97
mistreatment 8
refusal to take 183
public opinion, impact on military strategy
78, 87, 94–96, 99–101, 105–106,
161–162, 209n

racial issues, role in South African war 77n
Ras Imru, General 123, 126
Ras Kassa, General 122
Ras Mulugetta, General 122
Ras Seyum, General 122
Rhodes, Cecil 74, 76, 76n, 79n, 86, 100
Rhodes, Richard 9–10
Ridgeway, Matthew, General 220
Roberts, Lord 86, 88, 88n, 89, 90, 90n, 92–93,
94, 100, 107
Roghe, Bruno 133
Rolling Thunder, Operation (1965–68)
152–153n, 154n, 156–157
Russia
activities post-1992 166
political organization 54–55, 65, 66–67
population 57
*see also* Murid War; Soviet Union
Russo-Japanese War (1905) 223
Rwanda 227

Sbacchi, Alberto 141n
Schwarzkopf, Norman 49
September 11 attacks 227
Shamil (Murid leader) 49–50, 52, 54, 55–56,
58–61, 60n, 64, 70, 206
downfall 62–63, 67, 68
Shepstone, Sir Theophilus 74
Sherman, William, General 91
Smith, Iain R. 79, 81
Smuts, Jan 78, 82, 91, 92, 93, 97, 105

social structure, relationship with military
effectiveness 6–7n
*see also* democracies; public opinion
"socialization" (of strategy) 36–37, 205
Sokolov, Marshal 177
Sorley, Lewis 163n
South African War 20, 22, 43–44n, 44n,
81–82
Boer aims/interests 80n, 80–81, 99, 104
Boer strategy/tactics 33n, 82, 84–85,
90–92, 107n
British aims/interests 76–80, 99, 207
British strategy/tactics 32n, 87–88, 89,
92–94, 184n, 185, 220, 222
casualties 98 (*see also under* concentration
camps)
historical background 72–76
outcome 97–98, 105, 108
pre-war negotiations 80–81
progress of hostilities 82–94, 96–97
theoretical analysis 98–108, 207–208,
207–208n, 217
uniforms 103n
South Vietnam, political regime 148–150
Soviet Union 5, 8
dissolution 188
involvement in Afghanistan (pre-1979)
171–172
military strategies/traditions 37, 38,
178n, 191, 192–193, 193n
political system 190–193
*see also* Afghan War; Cold War
Sparta 2
Stalin, Joseph 8
Steer, George 130–131, 131n
Steyn, Marthinus, President 76, 80–81, 82,
93, 101, 107n
Stinger missiles 186–187, 194
Strategic Hamlets program 156
strategic interaction thesis 6–7, 18, 21,
24–25, 27, 29, 44–45n, 222–223,
224–227
application to case studies 63–64, 65, 68,
70–71, 102–104, 106, 137–143, 163–166,
194–195, 197–199, 206–207, 208,
209–211, 212–213, 215–216
central hypotheses 42, 46–47, 203–204,
217–219
empirical evaluation 43–47, 204, 216–219
exceptions 112n
limitations 223–224
strategy/ies
choice of 29n, 37–38, 200, 203, 203n, 209n,
221–222
counterstrategies 34–35

strategy/ies (cont.)
  defined 29, 29n
  limited aims 32n, 159
  switches 36, 36n, 43–44n, 44n, 70, 102,
    106–107, 212
  types 30, 34–35, 203, 203n
  *see also* conventional attack; conventional
    defense; guerrilla warfare; indirect
    attacking strategies; strategic
    interaction thesis
Suez Canal 99
Sun Tzu 48
survival, as reason for going to war 25,
  164–165
Suvorov, Alexander 60, 219
Sweden, war with Russia 51
Symons, Sir Penn 79, 83–84

tactics, defined 29–30
Tajikistan 189n
Talana Hill, battle of (1899) 83–84
Tamarov, Vladislav 193n
Taraki, Muhammad 171–172
Tarzi, Mahmud Beg 192
technology (military) 4n, 5, 187n
  relationship with combat effectiveness
    11–13, 67–68, 217
  spread of 11, 12n
  *see also* arms diffusion
Tembian, battle of 122
terrorism 32n
  countermeasures 225, 226n
  war on 21, 38
Tet Offensive (1968) 157, 163,
  163n, 195
Thatcher, Margaret, PM 164
Thucydides 2
time, significance to military objectives
  106, 164–165
  *see also* asymmetric conflicts: duration
Tonkin Gulf incident (1964) 151n
Tran Hung Doo 146
Transvaal 73, 74–75, 98
Trezzani, General 138n
Turtledove, Harry 41n

Umberto, King of Italy 111–112
underestimation of opposition
  by Russia/Soviet Union 69n, 191
  by UK 79, 81, 87, 89–90, 100
United Kingdom
  involvement in Ethiopia 119n, 129–131,
    130n, 142, 210
  military history/limitations 37n, 79n,
    85–86, 101–102

parliamentary proceedings 91–92n,
    95–96, 116–117n
  relations with Italy 112–113
    116–117
  *see also* Malayan Emergency; South
    African War
United States
  domestic policy/legislation 8, 25
  foreign policy 19–21, 26, 192
  military effectiveness 12–13
  military history/strategies 37, 38, 212
  military strategy, ideal/future 225–227
  *see also* Afghanistan; Iraq; Korean war;
    Kuwait; Vietnam war; World War II
unpreparedness, role in strong-actor
  setbacks 219n, 219–221
  *see also* United Kingdom: military history
Urban, Mark L. 181, 187, 197

Veliaminov, General 48, 54
Vietnam
  Democratic Republic of (DRV) 147,
    148–149, 150, 157, 158, 159–161
  economy 145
  geography 145
  political history 145–148, 146n
  *see also* France; Vietnam War
Vietnam war (1965–73) 22, 44n, 45n, 178n
  civilian casualties 158n
  (explanations of) outcome 6n, 14, 157,
    158n, 226
  progress of hostilities 152–157, 167–168,
    202
  theoretical analysis 43–44n, 157–168,
    211–213
  US aims/interests 150–152, 151n, 159,
    214n
  US engagement in 14, 144–145,
    151–152
  US strategy/tactics 16, 29n, 40–41n, 50n,
    155–157, 164, 167–168, 189, 198n,
    220–221
  Vietnamese aims/interests 158
  Vietnamese resources 162–163, 166
  Vietnamese strategy/tactics 154–155,
    160–161
Vittorio Emmanuele II of Italy 113
Voronzov, Count 57, 59–61, 60n, 62–63,
  66, 68

Wal Wal, Ethiopia 114–116
Waltz, Kenneth 18, 36–37
Walzer, Michael 168
Watson, Bruce 9n
Watson, C. Dale 17n

weaker side, victory of
  frequency 3–4, 43–45
  historical trends 4n, 4–5, 36, 46, 47n, 205
  reasons 6–7n, 16–17n
Westmoreland, William 167n
White, Sir George, General 83, 84–86
Wilson, Woodrow, President 146–147
Wingate, Orde, Major 142
World War I 210n, 219n
World War II
  aftermath 10–11, 12, 17, 18, 37,
    41–42n
  Allied strategies 25, 32n, 40–41n
  commencement 128

duration 164
impact on war on Ethiopia 129, 131, 142,
  210
motives for engagement 8, 25

Yermolov, Mikhail 50n, 52–54, 63–64, 68
Yevdomikov, General 57
Yohannes IV, emperor of Ethiopia 111
Yugoslavia 36n

Zahir Shah, King 171
Zaitsev, Mikhail 186, 187
Zhou Enlai 148
Zulus, conflicts involving 74

# CAMBRIDGE STUDIES IN INTERNATIONAL RELATIONS

89  *Patrick M. Morgan*
    **Deterrence now**

88  *Susan Sell*
    **Private power, public law**
    The globalization of intellectual property rights

87  *Nina Tannenwald*
    **The nuclear taboo**
    The United States and the non-use of nuclear weapons since 1945

86  *Linda Weiss*
    **States in the global economy**
    Bringing domestic institutions back in

85  *Rodney Bruce Hall and Thomas J. Biersteker (eds.)*
    **The emergence of private authority in global governance**

84  *Heather Rae*
    **State identities and the homogenisation of peoples**

83  *Maja Zehfuss*
    **Constructivism in International Relations**
    The politics of reality

82  *Paul K. Huth and Todd Allee*
    **The democratic peace and territorial conflict in the twentieth century**

81  *Neta C. Crawford*
    **Argument and change in world politics**
    Ethics, decolonization and humanitarian intervention

80  *Douglas Lemke*
    **Regions of war and peace**

79  *Richard Shapcott*
    **Justice, community and dialogue in international relations**

78  *Phil Steinberg*
    **The social construction of the ocean**

77 *Christine Sylvester*
**Feminist International Relations**
An unfinished journey

76 *Kenneth A. Schultz*
**Democracy and coercive diplomacy**

75 *David Houghton*
**US foreign policy and the Iran hostage crisis**

74 *Cecilia Albin*
**Justice and fairness in international negotiation**

73 *Martin Shaw*
**Theory of the global state**
Globality as an unfinished revolution

72 *Frank C. Zagare and D. Marc Kilgour*
**Perfect deterrence**

71 *Robert O'Brien, Anne Marie Goetz, Jan Aart Scholte and Marc Williams*
**Contesting global governance**
Multilateral economic institutions and global social movements

70 *Roland Bleiker*
**Popular dissent, human agency and global politics**

69 *Bill McSweeney*
**Security, identity and interests**
A sociology of international relations

68 *Molly Cochran*
**Normative theory in international relations**
A pragmatic approach

67 *Alexander Wendt*
**Social theory of international politics**

66 *Thomas Risse, Stephen C. Ropp and Kathryn Sikkink (eds.)*
**The power of human rights**
International norms and domestic change

65 *Daniel W. Drezner*
**The sanctions paradox**
Economic statecraft and international relations

64 *Viva Ona Bartkus*
**The dynamic of secession**

63  *John A. Vasquez*
    **The power of power politics**
    From classical realism to neotraditionalism

62  *Emanuel Adler and Michael Barnett (eds.)*
    **Security communities**

61  *Charles Jones*
    **E. H. Carr and international relations**
    A duty to lie

60  *Jeffrey W. Knopf*
    **Domestic society and international cooperation**
    The impact of protest on US arms control policy

59  *Nicholas Greenwood Onuf*
    **The republican legacy in international thought**

58  *Daniel S. Geller and J. David Singer*
    **Nations at war**
    A scientific study of international conflict

57  *Randall D. Germain*
    **The international organization of credit**
    States and global finance in the world economy

56  *N. Piers Ludlow*
    **Dealing with Britain**
    The Six and the first UK application to the EEC

55  *Andreas Hasenclever, Peter Mayer and Volker Rittberger*
    **Theories of international regimes**

54  *Miranda A. Schreurs and Elizabeth C. Economy (eds.)*
    **The internationalization of environmental protection**

53  *James N. Rosenau*
    **Along the domestic– foreign frontier**
    Exploring governance in a turbulent world

52  *John M. Hobson*
    **The wealth of states**
    A comparative sociology of international economic and political change

51  *Kalevi J. Holsti*
    **The state, war, and the state of war**

50  *Christopher Clapham*
    **Africa and the international system**
    The politics of state survival

49 *Susan Strange*
**The retreat of the state**
The diffusion of power in the world economy

48 *William I. Robinson*
**Promoting polyarchy**
Globalization, US intervention, and hegemony

47 *Roger Spegele*
**Political realism in international theory**

46 *Thomas J. Biersteker and Cynthia Weber (eds.)*
**State sovereignty as social construct**

45 *Mervyn Frost*
**Ethics in international relations**
A constitutive theory

44 *Mark W. Zacher with Brent A. Sutton*
**Governing global networks**
International regimes for transportation and communications

43 *Mark Neufeld*
**The restructuring of international relations theory**

42 *Thomas Risse-Kappen (ed.)*
**Bringing transnational relations back in**
Non-state actors, domestic structures and international institutions

41 *Hayward R. Alker*
**Rediscoveries and reformulations**
Humanistic methodologies for international studies

40 *Robert W. Cox with Timothy J. Sinclair*
**Approaches to world order**

39 *Jens Bartelson*
**A genealogy of sovereignty**

38 *Mark Rupert*
**Producing hegemony**
The politics of mass production and American global power

37 *Cynthia Weber*
**Simulating sovereignty**
Intervention, the state and symbolic exchange

36 *Gary Goertz*
**Contexts of international politics**

35  *James L. Richardson*
    **Crisis diplomacy**
    The Great Powers since the mid-nineteenth century

34  *Bradley S. Klein*
    **Strategic studies and world order**
    The global politics of deterrence

33  *T. V. Paul*
    **Asymmetric conflicts: war initiation by weaker powers**

32  *Christine Sylvester*
    **Feminist theory and international relations in a postmodern era**

31  *Peter J. Schraeder*
    **US foreign policy toward Africa**
    Incrementalism, crisis and change

30  *Graham Spinardi*
    **From Polaris to Trident: The development of US Fleet Ballistic Missile technology**

29  *David A. Welch*
    **Justice and the genesis of war**

28  *Russell J. Leng*
    **Interstate crisis behavior, 1816–1980: realism versus reciprocity**

27  *John A. Vasquez*
    **The war puzzle**

26  *Stephen Gill (ed.)*
    **Gramsci, historical materialism and international relations**

25  *Mike Bowker and Robin Brown (eds.)*
    **From Cold War to collapse: theory and world politics in the 1980s**

24  *R. B. J. Walker*
    **Inside/outside: international relations as political theory**

23  *Edward Reiss*
    **The Strategic Defense Initiative**

22  *Keith Krause*
    **Arms and the state: patterns of military production and trade**

21  *Roger Buckley*
    **US-Japan alliance diplomacy 1945–1990**

20  *James N. Rosenau and Ernst-Otto Czempiel (eds.)*
    **Governance without government: order and change in world politics**

19  *Michael Nicholson*
    **Rationality and the analysis of international conflict**

18  *John Stopford and Susan Strange*
    **Rival states, rival firms**
    Competition for world market shares

17  *Terry Nardin and David R. Mapel (eds.)*
    **Traditions of international ethics**

16  *Charles F. Doran*
    **Systems in crisis**
    New imperatives of high politics at century's end

15  *Deon Geldenhuys*
    **Isolated states: a comparative analysis**

14  *Kalevi J. Holsti*
    **Peace and war: armed conflicts and international
    order 1648–1989**

13  *Saki Dockrill*
    **Britain's policy for West German rearmament 1950–1955**

12  *Robert H. Jackson*
    **Quasi-states: sovereignty, international relations and the Third
    World**

11  *James Barber and John Barratt*
    **South Africa's foreign policy**
    The search for status and security 1945–1988

10  *James Mayall*
    **Nationalism and international society**

 9  *William Bloom*
    **Personal identity, national identity and
    international relations**

 8  *Zeev Maoz*
    National choices and international processes

 7  *Ian Clark*
    **The hierarchy of states**
    Reform and resistance in the international order

 6  *Hidemi Suganami*
    **The domestic analogy and world order proposals**

 5  *Stephen Gill*
    **American hegemony and the Trilateral Commission**

4 *Michael C. Pugh*
**The ANZUS crisis, nuclear visiting and deterrence**

3 *Michael Nicholson*
**Formal theories in international relations**

2 *Friedrich V. Kratochwil*
**Rules, norms, and decisions**
On the conditions of practical and legal reasoning in international relations an domestic affairs

1 *Myles L.C. Robertson*
**Soviet policy towards Japan**
An analysis of trends in the 1970s and 1980s